POEMS
AND CH
AFRIC

"Sympathy
The heartbreaking ya Angelou her
memorable book title, "I know why the caged bird
sings," is an unforgettable evocation of the need for
people to be free.

"The Negro Speaks of Rivers" *by Langston Hughes*
One of the greatest poems in American literature, the
powerful rhythm rolls out with a message that goes
deep—a reminder of the antiquity and importance of
the African-American's past.

"Iron Flowers" *by Kalamu ya Salaam*
A portrait of Haiti, this evocative lyric captures the
experience of poverty both material and spiritual.

"Momma Sayings" *by Harryette Mullen*
The delicious nostalgia of this ode by a daughter is
rife with humor, love, and those oft-repeated sayings
that seep into our subconscious and one day unex-
pectedly leap from our own mouths.

"Say Hey Homeboy (for Sterling Plumpp)"
by Charlie R. Braxton
In the words of this contemporary writer, "the music
flows mellow steady," and creates a gem of a poem
whose lines "bring the world a little closer/to the pain/
the anguish & beauty of a native son."

Jerry W. Ward, Jr., is Lawrence Durgin Professor
of Literature at Tougaloo College. He is co-editor of
the anthology *Black Southern Voices*.

Recommended Reading from SIGNET

TROUBLE THE WATER

250 Years of African-American Poetry

Edited and with an Introduction by

JERRY W. WARD, JR.

A MENTOR BOOK

1300 297 - 707

MENTOR
Published by New American Library, a division of
Penguin Putnam Inc., 375 Hudson Street,
New York, New York 10014, U.S.A.
Penguin Books Ltd, 27 Wrights Lane, London W8 5TZ, England
Penguin Books Australia Ltd, Ringwood, Victoria, Australia
Penguin Books Canada Ltd, 10 Alcorn Avenue,
Toronto, Ontario, Canada M4V 3B2
Penguin Books (N.Z.) Ltd, 182–190 Wairau Road,
Auckland 10, New Zealand

Penguin Books Ltd, Registered Offices:
Harmondsworth, Middlesex, England

First published by Mentor, an imprint of New American Library,
a division of Penguin Putnam Inc.

First Printing, February 1997
10 9 8 7 6 5 4 3

For acknowledgements, please see pages 561–566.

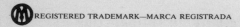 REGISTERED TRADEMARK—MARCA REGISTRADA

Library of Congress Cataloging Card Number: 96-77940

Printed in the United States of America

JAN - - 2002

IN MEMORY OF MY PARENTS,
JERRY W. WARD, SR.
AND
MARY THERIOT WARD,
AND
TO GWENDOLYN BROOKS,
FOR HER BOUNDLESS GENEROSITY.

CONTENTS

III. Voices of Reconstruction
(1865–1910)

IV. The Early Twentieth Century (1910–1960)

V. Voices for a New Age—1960s/1970s

VI. Voices for a New Age— 1980s/1990s

INTRODUCTION

Like the origins of poetry throughout the world, the beginnings of African-American poetry are in speech and song. This fact is of no small consequence. Primacy of the oral and the aural forces us to be active in imagining just how it is that peoples displaced from one part of the world and reassembled in another created a distinctive body of poetry. What is primal about its origins and strongly marked in its continuity as a tradition suggests the value of listening to the poetry as carefully as we read it silently. Listen. The beginning of African-American poetry is the sound of Africans in the complex process of becoming Americans. Those historical moments of transformation are inflected with resistance, the trauma of loss, adaptation, cross-fertilizing, and synthesis.

An African-American poetics emerges from the détente of African languages and cultures with themselves first, and then with encountered European languages and cultures. The initial New World points of becoming (which includes the Afro-Asiatic) remain in deep waters beyond salvage. Nevertheless, the links of African-American poetry to its mixed ancestry recurs in black American oral traditions, in the early inscriptions of Lucy Terry, Jupiter Hamon, Phillis Wheatley, and George Moses Horton; it is to be heard in the sorrow songs, sacred music, blues, and jazz, the penchant for return to African sources among some early and late twentieth-century poets. You hear the ancient links in rap's musical levels. As Eugene Redmond reminds us in *Drumvoices: The Mission of Afro-American Poetry* (1976), we obviously do not know the precise time "when the first African sounds or movements were incorporated into 'white' or Western frames of reference or vice versa; but we do know that it did happen."

Trouble the Water pays tribute to the creative genius of

black folk who have made a tradition of sound and uncommon sense. This anthology honors their insisting that music and speech be fused into a poetry for exploring, coming to know, creating delight and instruction, praising and criticizing, remembering and transforming, and meeting, in the early years of this century, an odd demand: proof of civilization. African-American poetry moves into the new public spheres of the twenty-first century. It absorbs the pre-future of now. It is worthwhile to rediscover how it evolved. It is obligatory to remember it comes from a tradition that, in the words of Margaret Walker, has "remained singularly faithful to the living truth of the human spirit."

> Wade in de water, children
> Wade in de water, children
> God's agwinter trouble de water.

This book is indebted to *The Poetry of the Negro, 1746–1949,* edited by Langston Hughes and Arna Bontemps and to Dudley Randall's *The Black Poets* (1971), models for a difficult enterprise. These collections sought to provide a comprehensive survey of African-American poetic expression. It is easy to survey. It is hard to be comprehensive. Anthologies will not accommodate everything worthy of inclusion, and the fact that no survey of more than two hundred and fifty years of poetry can be definitive is one an editor must accept. Recent anthologies which focus mainly on twentieth-century work—most notably Kevin Powell and Ras Baraka's *In the Tradition* (1992), Michael Harper and Anthony Walton's *Every Shut Eye Ain't Asleep* (1994), E. Ethelbert Miller's *In Search of Color Everywhere* (1994), and Clarence Major's *The Garden Thrives* (1996)—illustrate how the body of poetry that should be read grows larger by the decade. There will always be gaps in representation. Why is poet X not included? Why were poems k, l, and m not reprinted? Well, the permission fee for work by poet X far exceeded the editor's modest budget. Perhaps poems k, l, and m had been frequently anthologized, and the space was assigned to less well-known poets and poems. At best, the editor can only hope an anthology provides work that has both historical importance and aesthetic appeal, that an anthology succeeds in being a useful resource for the study of literature and culture.

In compiling *Trouble the Water,* I was strongly aware that disputes about how to read, how to read a poem, and how to theorize about literary works as features of cultures trouble the contests to open or close the American mind. Moreover, I wanted the collection to be useful to a broad audience: general readers, younger readers who still have the capacity to experience the magic of language, and students and teachers not yet initiated into the priestly prejudices of the academy. It was very important to consider that in the second edition of *The Poetry of the Negro* (1970), Arna Bontemps had suggested the poems of the 1960s should be the answers to questions about the "thoughts and feelings of an aroused folk in a time of trouble." Bontemps was hinting the kind of poetry he and Hughes had included in the first edition was within "the literary traditions of the language that it employs." Poetic works marked by a strong racial idiom (folk seculars, spirituals, blues) were considered outside those literary traditions and were excluded. For Dudley Randall, on the other hand, poetry that might awaken readers from aesthetic tranquillity was very much inside the African-American and American literary traditions. He included such work in *The Black Poets. Trouble the Water* is conceptually closer to Randall's design than Bontemps'. Before one canonizes on the literary/extraliterary axis, it seems desirable to represent the variety and difference that actually does exist. Otherwise, one makes trivial the possibility that **variety** is a crucial feature of our national literature, or that poets at various times address their works to diverse implied audiences.

The manner in which time has been used in structuring this anthology deserves a brief comment. Many anthologies of African-American literature have used such normative categories as eighteenth-century beginnings, the struggle against slavery, the rise of the New Negro, the Harlem Renaissance, the protest years, the Black Arts Movement, and the postmodern to suggest turning points in the growth of the literature. This procedure is quite legitimate. It establishes paradigms for the study of literature. But poets are subversive. They may or may not write works that conform to the dominant ideas of a period. Their works may defy convenient periodicity.

To encourage richer creative and critical responses to the making of the African-American poetic tradition, I have organized the works to emphasize fruitful tensions between poets and history or between individual talents and a narrative always awaiting revision. Within each section, care has been taken to organize the poems according to the birth dates of the poets. Since poets do not always write or publish in their early years, in a few instances, poets who came to public notice later in life may be distanced from their contemporaries. This should remind us that many poets are productive over years that span the divisions. It was tempting to want to organize all the poems by publication dates, but so radical a move would have created unnecessary confusions.

Part I ("Oral Poetry/Slave Creations") marks off a time when works were most often anonymous, when the texts chosen can only represent the "spirit" of a time prior to their being recorded. Part II ("Voices Before Freedom, 1746–1865") draws attention to the poets as enslaved people or free people of color, the acceptance of prevailing modes of writing poetry or some effort to be innovative within accepted forms. The past does impinge upon the present. Readers should bring forward the poetry in Part I for comparison with the self-consciously formal works that yearn for emancipation in Part II. Part III ("Voices of Reconstruction, 1865–1910") emphasizes the poetic voice as a bridge between the late nineteenth-century obligation to deal with an immediate slave past in the same moment it wishes to address the promises of a twentieth-century future. The problem of finding the "right" language for poetry complements DuBois's famed "problem of the color line." It is most poignantly "represented" in the work of Paul Laurence Dunbar and finds temporary resolution in the work of James Weldon Johnson.

The voices in Part IV ("The Early Twentieth Century, 1910–1960") begin with Johnson, whose magisterial introduction to *The Book of American Negro Poetry* (1921) still deserves study for what it says about poetic language and emotion, turn of thought, and the demands of conventions. Johnson set forth the possibility of creating new forms "which will still hold the racial flavor." The poetic forms that embody the intellectual, artistic, and social concerns of African Americans up to the turbulent 1960s are stunning in magnitude, variety, and quality. William Stanley Braithwaite and Countee Cullen use language to register ambivalence about the "rightness" of modernist experimentation. Jean Toomer, Claude McKay, Melvin B. Tolson, and especially Langston Hughes experiment daringly; indeed, Hughes's use of blues and jazz to inform poetic sites of memory is prototypical for the later activity of Bob Kaufman, Ted Joans, and the Beat poets. Anne Spenser, Arna Bontemps, May Miller, and Naomi Long Madgett revitalize the expressive potential of lyric. Sterling Brown, Margaret Walker, Gwendolyn Brooks, and Robert Hayden demonstrate that modernist poetic techniques as well as respect for folk heritage and history are essential in creating art from the raw complexities of African-American life.

The penultimate section, Part V ("Voices for a New Age") begins with the voice of Elma Stuckey, whom E. D. Hirsch noted is one of "the authentic American poets of our century." Her poetry is resonant with concern for history, orality, and the subtle recrafting that enables us, according to Stephen E. Henderson, to "hear the voices of the people who created the spirituals and the blues." The section ends with the recycling voice of Charlie Braxton, who celebrates the necessity of "iambic & trochaic pentameter" to evoke anguish and beauty for those

> just a few generations removed
> from the chains that bind the flesh
> but not the spirit.

We circle back to the poetic work of oral creation, back to Toomer's observation that "one seed becomes/An everlasting song" for the new age and its new voices. Within the historicizing frame of Stuckey and Braxton are the disruptive affirmations of Amiri Baraka, Sonia Sanchez, Askia Muhammad Touré, Ishmael Reed, Sarah Webster Fabio, Haki Madhubuti, and other pioneers of the Black Arts/Black Aesthetic revolution in African-American poetic tradition. Here also is the tradition-conserving work of Mari Evans, Lance Jeffers, Eugene Redmond, Kenneth McClane, Quincy Troupe, Lucille Clifton, Kalamu ya Salaam, Henry Dumas, Carolyn Rodgers, and Sterling D. Plumpp; the distinguished omni-American artistry of Ntozake Shange, Michael Harper,

Wanda Coleman, Rita Dove, Harryette Mullen, and Yusef Komunyakaa. *Trouble the Water* seeks to represent poetic voices moving across the categories and boundaries of more than two centuries, calling and responding both in the private spaces of racialized imperative and in the public spaces of the human necessity we call art.

As the narrator of *Invisible Man* reminds us, history is neither a horizontal nor a vertical line. It is a boomerang. This metaphor has its own invisibility in the continuing evolution of African-American poetry. Giving a judicious hearing to the sounds and formal achievements of the tradition requires being prepared for the boomerang's return. *Trouble the Water* is a sampling of poems (texts) that can be examined for what they reveal about the multiple, necessary, and highly valued functions of African-American art in cultural histories. For those who would continue to ask the tautologous question "IS THE AFRICAN-AMERICAN POEM A WORK OF ART OR A WORK OF EVIDENCE?," *Trouble the Water* is the answer. And for helping me to put it in your hands, I am very grateful to Lawrence Jordan, Rosemary Ahern, Kari Paschall, and Kenny Fountain.

Jerry W. Ward, Jr.
Memphis, Tennessee
August 20, 1996

I

ORAL POETRY/SLAVE CREATIONS

JUBA

JUba dis and JUba dat an
JUba killed my YALlow cat, O JUba,
JUba, JUba, JUba, JUba, JUba.

MISTAH RABBIT

"Mistah Rabbit, Mistah Rabbit, yo tale's
   mighty white."
"Yes, bless God, been gittin outa sight."

Refrain:
Ev'y little soul gwine-a shine, shine,
Ev'y little soul gwine-a shine along.

"Mistah Rabbit, Mistah Rabbit, yo coat's
   mighty gray."
"Yes, bless God, been out fo day."

"Mistah Rabbit, Mistah Rabbit, yo ears mighty
   long."
"Yes, bless God, been put on wrong."

"Mistah Rabbit, Mistah Rabbit, yo ears mighty
   thin."
"Yes, bless God, been splittin the wind."

RAISE A RUCKUS TONIGHT

My ol missus promise me,
When she die she set me free,
Lived so long her haid got ball,
Give up the notion of dyin atall.

Chorus:
Come along, little chillun, come along,
While the moon is shinin' bright.
Git on board, down the river float,
We gonna raise a ruckus tonight.

My ol missus say to me,
John, Ize gonna set you free.
But when dat haid got slick an ball,
Couldn't killed her wid a big green maul.

My ol missus nevah die,
Wid her nose all hooked and skin all dry.
But when ol miss she somehow gone,
She lef po John a-hillin up de corn.

Ol mosser likewise promise me,
When he die he set me free.
But ol mosser go an mak his will,
For to leave me plowin ol Beck still.

Way down yonder in Chittlin Switch,
Bullfrog jump fum ditch to ditch.
Bullfrog jump fum de bottom of de well,
Swore, my Lawd, he jumped fum Hell.

JUBER

Juber up and Juber down,
Juber all around de town,
Juber dis, and Juber dat,
And Juber roun' the simmon vat.
   Hoe corn! hill tobacco!
   Get over double trouble, Juber boys, Juber.

Uncle Phil, he went to mill,
He suck de sow, he starve de pig,
Eat the simmon, gi' me de seed,
I told him I was not in need.
   Hoe corn! hill tobacco!
   Get over double trouble, Juber boys, Juber.

Aunt Kate? look on de high shelf,
Take down de husky dumplin,
I'll eat it wi' my simmon cake.
To cure the rotten belly-ache.
   Hoe corn! hill tobacco!
   Get over double trouble, Juber boys, Juber.

Raccoon went to simmon town,
To choose the rotten from de soun,
Dare he sot upon a sill,
Eating of a whip-poor-will.
    Hoe corn! hill tobacco!
    Get over double trouble, Juber boys, Juber.

MARY, DON YOU WEEP

Mary, don you weep an Marthie don you moan,
Mary, don you weep an Marthie don you moan;
Pharaoh's army got drown-ded,
    Oh Mary don you weep.

I thinks every day an I wish I could,
Stan on de rock whar Moses stood,
Oh Pharaoh's army got drown-ded,
    Oh Mary don you weep.

WHEN-A MAH BLOOD RUNS CHILLY AN COL

Oh, when-a mah blood runs chilly an col, Ize got to go,
Ize got to go,
Oh, when-a mah blood runs chilly an col, Ize got to go,
Way beyond the moon.

Refrain:
Do, Lord, do, Lord, do remember me,
Oh do, Lord, do, Lord, do remember me,
Oh do, Lord, do, Lord, do remember me,
Do, Lord, remember me.

Ef you cain't bear no crosses, you cain't wear no crown,
Ef you cain't bear no crosses, you cain't wear no crown,
Ef you cain't bear no crosses, you cain't wear no crown,
Way beyond the moon.

Ize gotta mother in de Beulah land, she's callin me,
She's callin me, she's callin me,
Ize gotta mother in de Beulah land, she's callin me,
Way beyond de sun.

SOON ONE MAWNIN

Soon one mawnin death come creepin in mah room,
Soon one mawnin death come creepin in mah room,
Soon one mawnin death come creepin in mah room,
Oh mah Lawd, Oh mah Lawd, what shall ah do to be saved?

Death done been heah, took mah mother an gone,
Death done been heah, took mah mother an gone,
Death done been heah, took mah mother an gone,
Oh mah Lawd, Oh mah Lawd, what shall ah do to be saved?

Don't move mah pillow till mah Jesus come,
Don't move mah pillow till mah Jesus come,
Don't move mah pillow till mah Jesus come,
Oh mah Lawd, Oh mah Lawd, what shall ah do to be saved?

I'm so glad I got religion in time,
I'm so glad I got religion in time,
I'm so glad I got religion in time,
Oh mah Lawd, Oh mah Lawd, what shall ah do to be saved?

MOTHERLESS CHILD

Sometimes I feel like a motherless child,
Sometimes I feel like a motherless child,
Sometimes I feel like a motherless child,
A long ways from home,
A long ways from home.

Sometimes I feel like I'm almost gone,
Sometimes I feel like I'm almost gone,
Sometimes I feel like I'm almost gone,
A long ways from home,
A long ways from home.

Sometimes I feel like a feather in the air,
Sometimes I feel like a feather in the air,
Sometimes I feel like a feather in the air,
And I spread my wings and I fly,

I spread my wings and I fly.

NOBODY KNOWS DA TRUBBLE AH SEE

Oh, nobody knows da trubble ah see,
Nobody knows but Jesus.
Nobody knows da trubble ah see,
Glory, Hallelujah!

Sometimes I'm up, sometimes I'm down,
Oh, yes, Lord!
Sometimes I'm almost to the groun',
Oh, yes, Lord!
Although you see me goin along, so,
Oh, yes, Lord!
I have my trubbles here below,
Oh, yes, Lord!

Nobody knows da trubble ah see,
Nobody knows my sorrow.
Nobody knows da trubble ah see,
Glory, Hallelujah!

One day when I was walkin along,
Oh, yes, Lord!
The elements open and his love came down,
Oh, yes, Lord!
I never shall forget dat day,
Oh, yes, Lord!
When Jesus wash my sins away,
Oh, yes, Lord!

Oh, nobody knows da trubble ah see,
Nobody knows my sorrow.
Nobody knows da trubble ah see,
Glory, Hallelujah!

WERE YOU DERE?

Were you dere when dey crucified my Lord?
(Were you dere?)
Were you dere when dey crucified my Lord?
O sometimes it causes me to tremble! tremble! tremble!
Were you dere when dey crucified my Lord?

7

Were you dere when dey nail'd him to da cross?
                 (Were you dere?)
Were you dere when dey nail'd him to da cross?
O sometimes it causes me to tremble! tremble! tremble!
Were you dere when dey nail'd him to da cross?

Were you dere when dey pierced him in da side?
                 (Were you dere?)
Were you dere when dey pierced him in da side?
O sometimes it causes me to tremble! tremble! tremble!
Were you dere when dey pierced him in da side?

Were you dere when da sun refused to shine?
                 (Were you dere?)
Were you dere when da sun refused to shine?
O sometimes it causes me to tremble! tremble! tremble!
Were you dere when da sun refused to shine?

DO, LAWD

O do, Lawd, remember me!
   O do, Lawd, remember me!
O, do remember me, until de year roll round!
   Do, Lawd, remember me!

If you want to die like Jesus died,
   Lay in de grave.
You want to fold your arms and close your
      eyes,
   And die wid a free good will.

For death is a simple ting,
   And he go from door to door,
And he knock down some, and he cripple up
      some,
   And he leave some here to pray.

O do, Lawd, remember me!
   O do, Lawd, remember me!
My old fader's gone till de year roll round;
   Do, Lawd, remember me!

II

Voices Before Freedom
(1746–1865)

Lucy Terry Prince
(1730—1821)

BARS FIGHT, AUGUST 28, 1746

August 'twas, the twenty-fifth,
Seventeen hundred forty-six,
The Indians did in ambush lay,
Some very valient [sic] men to slay,
The names of whom I'll not leave out:
Samuel Allen like a hero fout,
And though he was so brave and bold,
His face no more shall we behold;
Eleazer Hawks was killed outright,
Before he had time to fight,
Before he did the Indians see,
Was shot and killed immediately;
Oliver Amsden, he was slain,
Which caused his friends much grief and pain;
Simeon Amsden they found dead,
Not many rods off from his head;
Adonijah Gillet, we do hear,
Did lose his life, which was so dear;
John Saddler fled across the water,
And so escaped the dreadful slaughter;
Eunice Allen see the Indians comeing [sic],
And hoped to save herself by running,
And had not her petticoats stopt her,
The awful creatures had not cotched her,
And tommyhawked her on the head,
And left her on the ground for dead;
Young Samuel Allen, oh! lack-a-day,
Was taken and carried to Canada.

11

Phillis Wheatley
(c.1753–1784)

ON VIRTUE

O Thou bright jewel in my aim I strive
To comprehend thee. Thine own words declare
Wisdom is higher than a fool can reach.
I cease to wonder, and no more attempt
Thine height t'explore, or fathom thy profound.
But, O my soul, sink not into despair,
Virtue is near thee, and with gentle hand
Would now embrace thee, hovers o'er thine head.
Fain would the heav'n-born soul with her converse,
Then seek, then court her for her promis'd bliss.

    Auspicious queen, thine heav'nly pinions spread,
And lead celestial *Chastity* along;
Lo! now her sacred retinue descends,
Array'd in glory from the orbs above.
Attend me, *Virtue,* thro' my youthful years!
O leave me not to the false joys of time!
But guide my steps to endless life and bliss.
Greatness, or *Goodness,* say what I shall call thee,
To give an higher appellation still,
Teach me a better strain, a nobler lay,
O Thou, enthron'd with Cherubs in the realms of day!

TO THE UNIVERSITY OF CAMBRIDGE,
IN NEW-ENGLAND

While an intrinsic ardor prompts to write,
The muses promise to assist my pen;
'Twas not long since I left my native shore
The land of errors, and *Egyptian* gloom:

12

Father of mercy, 'twas thy gracious hand
Brought me in safety from those dark abodes.

Students, to you 'tis giv'n to scan the heights
Above, to traverse the ethereal space,
And mark the systems of revolving worlds.
Still more, ye sons of science ye receive
The blissful news by messengers from heav'n,
How *Jesus'* blood for your redemption flows.
See him with hands out-stretcht upon the cross;
Immense compassion in his bosom glows;
He hears revilers, nor resents their scorn:
What matchless mercy in the Son of God!
When the whole human race by sin had fall'n,
He deign'd to die that they might rise again,
And share with him in the sublimest skies,
Life without death, and glory without end.

Improve your privileges while they stay,
Ye pupils, and each hour redeem, that bears
Or good or bad report of you to heav'n.
Let sin, that baneful evil to the soul,
By you be shunn'd, nor once remit your guard;
Suppress the deadly serpent in its egg.
Ye blooming plants of human race devine,
An *Ethiop* tells you 'tis your greatest foe;
Its transient sweetness turns to endless pain,
And in immense perdition sinks the soul.

ON BEING BROUGHT FROM
AFRICA TO AMERICA

'Twas mercy brought me from my *Pagan* land,
Taught my benighted soul to understand
That there's a God, that there's a *Saviour* too:
Once I redemption neither sought nor knew.
Some view our sable race with scornful eye,
"Their colour is a diabolic die."
Remember, *Christians, Negros,* black as *Cain,*
May be refin'd, and join th' angelic train.

ON IMAGINATION

Thy various works, imperial queen, we see,
How bright their forms! how deck'd with pomp by thee!
Thy wond'rous acts in beauteous order stand,
And all attest how potent is thine hand.

From *Helicon*'s refulgent heights attend,
Ye sacred choir, and my attempts befriend:
To tell her glories with a faithful tongue,
Ye blooming graces, triumph in my song.

Now here, now there, the roving *Fancy* flies,
Till some lov'd object strikes her wand'ring eyes,
Whose silken fetters all the senses bind,
And soft captivity involves the mind.

Imagination! who can sing thy force?
Or who describe the swiftness of thy course?
Soaring through air to find the bright abode,
Th' empyreal palace of the thund'ring God,
We on thy pinions can surpass the wind,
And leave the rolling universe behind:

From star to star the mental optics rove,
Measure the skies, and range the realms above.
There in one view we grasp the mighty whole,
Or with new worlds amaze th' unbounded soul.

Though *Winter* frowns to *Fancy*'s raptur'd eyes
The fields may flourish, and gay scenes arise;
The frozen deeps may break their iron bands,
And bid their waters murmur o'er the sands.
Fair *Flora* may resume her fragrant reign,
And with her flow'ry riches deck the plain;
Sylvanus may diffuse his honours round,
And all the forest may with leaves be crown'd:
Show'rs may descend, and dews their gems disclose,
And nectar sparkle on the blooming rose.

Such is thy pow'r, nor are thine orders vain,
O thou the leader of the mental train:
In full perfection all thy works are wrought,

14

And thine the sceptre o'er the realms of thought.
Before thy throne the subject-passions bow,
Of subject-passions sov'reign ruler Thou,
At thy command joy rushes on the heart,
And through the glowing veins the spirits dart.

    Fancy might now her silken pinions try
To rise from earth, and sweep th' expanse on high;
From *Tithon*'s *bed now might Aurora* rise,
Her cheeks all glowing with celestial dies,
While a pure stream of light o'erflows the skies.
The monarch of the day I might behold,
And all the mountains tipt with radiant gold,
But I reluctant leave the pleasing views,
Which *Fancy* dresses to delight the *Muse;*
Winter austere forbids me to aspire,
And northern tempests damp the rising fire;
They chill the tides of *Fancy*'s flowing sea,
Cease then, my song, cease the unequal lay.

TO HIS EXCELLENCY
GENERAL WASHINGTON

The following LETTER *and* VERSES *were written by the
famous* Phillis Wheatley, *the African Poetess, and pre-
sented to his Excellency Gen.* Washington.

SIR,
I Have taken the freedom to address your Excellency in
the enclosed poem, and entreat your acceptance, though
I am not insensible of its inaccuracies. Your being ap-
pointed by the Grand Continental Congress to be Generalis-
simo of the armies of North America, together with the
fame of your virtues, excite sensations not easy to sup-
press. Your generosity, therefore, I presume, will pardon the
attempt. Wishing your Excellency all possible success in the
great cause you are so generously engaged in. I am,
      Your Excellency's most obedient humble servant,
           PHILLIS WHEATLEY.

Providence, October 26, 1775
His Excellency Gen. Washington.

CElestial choir! enthron'd in realms of light,
Columbia's scenes of glorious toils I write.
While freedom's cause her anxious breast alarms,
She flashes dreadful in refulgent arms.
See mother earth her offspring's fate bemoan,
And nations gaze at scenes before unknown!
See the bright beams of heaven's revolving light
Involved in sorrows and the veil of night!

The goddess comes, she moves divinely fair,
Olive and laurel binds her golden hair:
Wherever shines this native of the skies,
Unnumber'd charms and recent graces rise.

Muse! bow propitious while my pen relates
How pour her armies through a thousand gates:
As when Eolus heaven's fair face deforms,
Enwrapp'd in tempest and a night of storms;
Astonish'd ocean feels the wild uproar,
The refluent surges beat the sounding shore;
Or thick as leaves in Autumn's golden reign,
Such, and so many, moves the warrior's train.
In bright array they seek the work of war,
Where high unfurl'd the ensign waves in air.
Shall I to Washington their praise recite?
Enough thou know'st them in the fields of fight.
Thee, first in place and honours,—we demand
The grace and glory of thy martial band.
Fam'd for thy valour, for thy virtues more,
Hear every tongue thy guardian aid implore!

One century scarce perform'd its destin'd round,
When Gallic powers Columbia's fury found;
And so may you, whoever dares disgrace
The land of freedom's heaven-defended race!
Fix'd are the eyes of nations on the scales,
For in their hopes Columbia's arm prevails.
Anon Britannia droops the pensive head,
While round increase the rising hills of dead.
Ah! cruel blindness to Columbia's state!
Lament thy thirst of boundless power too late.

Proceed, great chief, with virtue on thy side,
Thy ev'ry action let the goddess guide.
A crown, a mansion, and a throne that shine,
With gold unfading, WASHINGTON! be thine.

Jupiter Hammon
(1711—1806)

An Address to Miss Phillis Wheatly [sic], Ethiopian Poetess, in Boston, who came from Africa at eight years of age, and soon became acquainted with the gospel of Jesus Christ.

1.

O, come, you pious youth! adore
    The wisdom of thy God,
In bringing thee from distant shore,
    To learn His holy word,

2.

Thou mightst been left behind,
    Amidst a dark abode;
God's tender mercy still combined,
    Thou hast the holy word.

3.

Fair Wisdom's ways are paths of peace,
    And they that walk therein,
Shall reap the joys that never cease,
    And Christ shall be their King.

4.

God's tender mercy brought thee here;
    Tossed o'er the raging main;
In Christian faith thou hast a share,
    Worth all the gold of Spain.

5.

While thousands tossed by the sea,
    And others settled down,
God's tender mercy set thee free
    From dangers that come down.

6.

That thou a pattern still might be,
    To youth of Boston town,
The blessed Jesus set thee free
    From every sinful wound.

7.

The blessed Jesus, who came down,
    Unveiled his sacred face,
To cleanse the soul of every wound,
    And give repenting grace.

8.

That we poor sinners may obtain
    The pardon of our sin,
Dear Blessed Jesus, now constrain,
    And bring us flocking in.

9.

Come, you, Phillis, now aspire,
    And seek the living God,
So step by step thou mayst go higher,
    Till perfect in the word.

10.

While thousands moved to distant shore,
    And others left behind,
The blessed Jesus still adore;
    Implant this in thy mind.

11.

Thou hast left the heathen shore;
   Through mercy of the Lord,
Among the heathen live no more;
   Come magnify thy God.

12.

I pray the living God may be,
   The shepherd of thy soul;
His tender mercies still are free,
   His mysteries to unfold.

13.

Thou, Phillis, when thou hunger hast,
   Or pantest for thy God,
Jesus Christ is thy relief,
   Thou hast the holy word.

14.

The bounteous mercies of the Lord
   Are hid beyond the sky,
And holy souls that have His word
   Shall taste them when they die.

15.

These bounteous mercies are from God,
   The merits of His Son;
The humble soul that loves His word
   He chooses for his own.

16.

Come, dear Phillis, be advised
   To drink Samaria's flood;
There nothing that shall suffice
   But Christ's redeeming blood.

17.

While thousands muse with earthly toys,
    And range about the street,
Dear Phillis, seek for heaven's joys,
    Where we do hope to meet.

18.

When God shall send his summons down,
    And number saints together,
Blessed angels chant (triumphant sound),
    Come live with me forever.

19.

The humble soul shall fly to God,
    And leave the things of time,
Start forth as 'twere at the first word,
    To taste things more divine.

20.

Behold! the soul shall waft away,
    Whene'er we come to die,
And leave its cottage made of clay,
    In twinkling of an eye.

21.

Now glory be to the Most High,
    United praises given,
By all on earth, incessantly,
    And all the host of heaven.

1778

George Moses Horton
(c. 1797–c. 1883)

TO ELIZA

Eliza, tell thy lover why
Or what induced thee to deceive me?
   Fare thee well—away I fly—
I shun the lass who thus will grieve me.

Eliza, still thou art my song,
Although by force I may forsake thee;
   Fare thee well, for I was wrong
To woo thee while another take thee.

Eliza, pause and think awhile—
Sweet lass! I shall forget thee never:
   Fare thee well: although I smile,
I grieve to give thee up forever.

Eliza, I shall think of thee—
My heart I shall ever twine about thee;
   Fare thee well—but think of me,
Compell'd to live and die without thee,
   "Fare thee well!—and if forever,
"Still forever fare thee well!"

SLAVERY

When first my bosom glowed with hope,
   I gazed as from a mountain top
    On some delightful plain;
But oh! how transient was the scene—
It fled as though it had not been,
    And all my hopes were vain.

How oft this tantalyzing blaze
    Has led me through deception's maze;
    My friends became my foe—
Then like a plaintive dove I mourned;
To bitter all my sweets were turned,
    And tears began to flow.

Why was the dawning of my birth
Upon this vile, accursed earth,
    Which is but pain to me?
Oh! that my soul had winged its flight,
When I first saw the morning light,
    To worlds of liberty!

Come, melting Pity, from afar,
And break this vast, enormous bar
    Between a wretch and thee;
Purchase a few short days of time,
And bid a vassal rise sublime
    On wings of liberty.

Is it because my skin is black,
That thou should'st be so dull and slack,
    And scorn to set me free?
Then let me hasten to the grave,
The only refuge for the slave,
    Who mourns for liberty.

The wicked cease from troubling there:
No more I'd languish or despair—
    The weary there can rest!
Oppression's voice is heard no more,
Drudg'ry and pain and toil are o'er,
    Yes! there I shall be blest!

The Liberator, March 29, 1834

GEORGE MOSES HORTON, MYSELF

I feel myself in need
    Of the inspiring strains of ancient lore,
My heart to lift, my empty mind to feed,
    And all the world explore.

I know that I am old
    And never can recover what is past,
But for the future may some light unfold
    And soar from ages blast.

I feel resolved to try,
    My wish to prove, my calling to pursue,
Or mount up from the earth into the sky,
    To show what Heaven can do.

My genius from a boy,
    Has fluttered like a bird within my heart,
But could not thus confined her powers employ,
    Impatient to depart.

She like a restless bird,
    Would spread her wings, her power to be
      unfurl'd,
And let her song be loudly heard,
    And dart from world to world.

ON LIBERTY AND SLAVERY

Alas! and am I born for this,
    To wear this slavish chain?
Deprived of all created bliss,
    Through hardship, toil and pain!

How long have I in bondage lain,
    And languished to be free!
Alas! and must I still complain—
    Deprived of liberty.

Oh, Heaven! and is there no relief
    This side the silent grave—

To soothe the pain—to quell the grief
  And anguish of a slave?

Come Liberty, thou cheerful sound,
  Roll through my ravished ears!
Come, let my grief in joys be drowned,
  And drive away my fears.

Say unto foul oppression, Cease:
  Ye tyrants rage no more,
And let the joyful trump of peace,
  Now bid the vassal soar.

Soar on the pinions of that dove
  Which long has cooed for thee,
And breathed her notes from Afric's grove,
  The sound of Liberty.

Oh, Liberty! thou golden prize,
  So often sought by blood—
We crave thy sacred sun to rise,
  The gift of nature's God!

Bid Slavery hide her haggard face,
  And barbarism fly:
I scorn to see the sad disgrace
  In which enslaved I lie.

Dear Liberty! upon thy breast,
  I languish to respire;
And like the Swan unto her nest,
  I'd to thy smiles retire.

Oh, blest asylum—heavenly balm!
  Unto thy boughs I flee—
And in thy shades the storm shall calm,
  With songs of Liberty!

THE SLAVE

What right divine has mortal man received,
    To domineer with uncontroll'd command?
What philosophic wight has thus believed
    That Heaven entailed on him the weaker band?

If Africa was fraught with weaker light,
    Whilst to the tribes of Europe more was given,
Does this impart to them a lawful right
    To counterfeit the golden rule of Heaven?

Did sovereign justice give to robbery birth,
    And bid the fools to theft their rights betray,
To spread the seeds of slavery o'er the earth,
    That you should hold them as your lawful prey?

Why did Almighty God the land divide
    And bid each nation to maintain her own,
Rolling between the deep, the wind and tide,
    With all their rage to make this order known?

The sad phylactory bound on rebel Cain,
    For killing Abel is in blood reveal'd,
For which the soldier falls among the slain,
    A victim on the sanguinary field.

Thus, in the cause of vile and sordid gain,
    To gratify their lust is all the plea;
Like Cain you've your consanguine brother slain,
    And robbed him of his birthright—Liberty.

Why do ye not the Ishmaelites enslave,
    Or artful red man in his rude attire,
As well as with the Black man, split the wave,
    And to his progeny with rage aspire?

SNAPS FOR DINNER, SNAPS FOR BREAKFAST AND SNAPS FOR SUPPER

Come in to dinner, squalls the dame,
    You need it now perhaps;
But hear the husband's loud exclaim,
    I do not like your snaps;
'Tis snaps when at your breakfast meal,
    And snaps when at your spinning wheel,
Too many by a devilish deal,
    For all your words are snaps.

Why do you tarry, tell me why?
    The chamber door she taps;
Eat by yourself, my dear, for I
    Am surfeited with snaps;
For if I cough it is the cry,
    You always snap at supper time,
I'd rather lave in vats of lime,
    Than face you with your snaps.

How gladly would I be a book,
    To your long pocket flaps,
That you my face may read and look,
And learn the worth of snaps;
I'm sorry that I learning lack
    To turn you to an almanac;
Next year I'll hang you on the rack,
    And end the date of snaps.

Daniel A. Payne
(1811—1893)

THE MOURNFUL LUTE OR THE
PRECEPTOR'S FAREWELL

Father and mother, authors of my birth,
Ye dwell in bliss; your son on sinful earth . . .

O, sainted parents, who my life have kept,
Preserved my sinful soul each night I slept;
Since God transported ye to realms of light,
And bade my youth in virtue take delight!
'Twas God. 'Tis he who still preserves my soul,
When foes unite, or waves of trouble roll,
Cared for my childhood, blessed my striving youth;
Me snatched from vice and led in paths of truth.

O, sainted mother, high in glory thou,
If God permits, behold thy Daniel now!
Good Lord, give strength; my feeble mind sustain,
Nor let my sighs ascend to thee in vain . . .

When Ignorance my mind in fetters bound,
He smote the fiend; then beams of light surround;
Broad beams of light described the way of truth,
And bade me lead therein benighted youth.

Oh, here's my bliss, that I the way have shown
To lovely youths which was before unknown;
From scientific shrines plucked golden fire,
And thrilled with notes divine the sacred lyre.

Did I conceive, five rolling years ago,
The luscious fruits which Science can bestow?
Oh, bend in praise devout before his throne!
'Twas God that gave the boon, and God alone.

My sire, when on the bed of death you lay,
Did thy blest soul in fervent accents pray
That I should be what now I feel I am—
Favored of God, preserved from every harm?

Thou didst, my sire; thrice blessed be thy name;
Come, Wisdom, clothe me in thy sacred flame;
Ye scientific truths, my mind control;
And thou, fair Virtue, guide my erring soul.
What's my ambition? What my great desire?
The youthful mind with knowledge to inspire.
Not worlds on worlds for this would I exchange,
Though cruel laws my noble scheme derange.

Soon from the land where first I drew my breath
I go a wanderer on the flying earth!
Where shall I go? O, Thou, my fortune guide,
Who led good Abram with his modest bride.
Him didst thou lead across the eastern wild,
Direct his steps and on his fortune smiled;
In foreign climes spread wide his fruitful boughs,
Made strong his bands and scattered all his foes.

Oh, I had thought the moral plants would grow,
From all the care my talents can bestow,
Like trees of virtue lift their blooming heads,
Where snowy clouds suspend their liquid beds!
Ye lads, whom I have taught with sacred zeal,
For your hard fate I pangs of sorrow feel;
Oh, who shall now your rising talents guide,
Where virtues reign and sacred truths preside?

Ye modest virgins, I have taught your minds
To fly from earth where sinful pleasure binds,
The rugged hill of science to ascend,
Where sacred flames with human fires blend.
Who now shall call your willing, joyful feet
In "wisdom's institute" to learn and meet
Sweet piety and science, gods of light,
Whose precepts lead your erring minds aright?

Who shall for you Minerva's field explore,
Spread open wide fair Nature's roseate door?
Oh, who shall help your op'ning wings to fly

Where virtue sits resplendent in the sky?
O, God of mercy! whither shall I go?
Where turn my steps—to weal, or else to woe?
Speak. I the sacred mandate wait to hear,
Nor shall I ocean dread nor tempest fear.

Eternal Goodness, from thy shining seat
Let Mercy fly to guide my wandering feet.
On distant lands I will thy servant be,
To turn from vice the youthful mind to thee.
Just two revolving moons shall light the shores
When Carolina's laws shall shut the doors
On this fine room, where Science holds his reign,
The humble tutor, hated Daniel Payne.

Oh, that my arms could reach yon burning sun,
And stop his motion till my work be done!
With these small fingers catch the flying moon—
Night should not triumph o'er the dazzling noon.
April should ne'er appear; but I would teach
Each yielding pupil till their minds could reach
The climax of proud science, and their plumes
Could soar where good John Locke or Newton blooms.

Each minute insect and each flying bird,
Each walking beast, whose tuneless notes are heard,
The scaly fish that lives not on the shore,
And man himself, the mighty being explore;
Aspiring mounts and hills, descending dales,
The floating air, when peace or storm prevails;
Oceans and seas, streams and expanding lakes,
When night leaps in, or sweet Aurora wakes.

The flying rays of light, the spangled sky,
On contemplation's wing mount ye on high.
Bright cherubim and flaming seraphim,
All things upon wide earth, th' eternal Him,
Children, all, all are yours! Search, find them out.
Knowledge, where are thy bounds? In depths without.
The heavens, within the heavens, nor time,
Nor vast eternity, the gods sublime,

Can in their sweeping compass e'er embrace!
He reigns o'er angels, guides the human race.

Seek not the joys which sinful earth can give;
They sparkle, perish, for a moment live.
Sweet innocents, behold each moving lip!
From cups of wisdom sacred sweet they sip.
What demon snatches from your hands those books,
And blasts your talents with his withering looks?

I weep. Flow, then, ye sympathetic tears!
Each bitter stream the stamp of sorrow bears.
Oh, who those smiling infants can see
Destined to night, and not lament with me?
Could tears of blood revoke the fierce decree,
The statesman touch and make my pupils free,
I at their feet the crimson tide would pour
Till potent justice swayed the senate floor.

As when a deer does in the pasture graze,
The lion roars—she's filled with wild amaze,
Knows strength unequal for the dreadful fight,
And seeks sweet safety in her rapid flight—
So Payne prepares to leave his native home,
With pigmy purse on distant shores to roam.
Lo! in the skies my boundless storehouse is!
I go reclining on God's promises.

Pupils, attend my last departing wounds;
Ye are my hopes, and ye my mental crowns,
My monuments of intellectual might,
My robes of honor and my armor bright.
Like Solomon, entreat the throne of God;
Light shall descend in lucid columns broad,
And all that man has learned for man can know
In streams prolific shall your minds o'erflow.

Hate sin; love God; religion be your prize;
Her laws obeyed will surely make you wise,
Secure you from the ruin of the vain,
And save your soul from everlasting pain.
Oh, fare you well, for whom my bosom glows
With ardent love, which Christ my savior knows!
'Twas for your good I labored night and day;
For you I wept, and now for you I pray . . .

Charleston, S.C., February 2, 1835

Ann Plato
(c. 1820–?)

TO THE FIRST OF AUGUST

Britannia's isles proclaim
  That freedom is their theme;
And we do view those honored lands
  With soul-delighting mien.

And unto those they held in gloom,
  Gave ev'ry one their right;
They did disdain fell slavery's shade,
  And trust in freedom's light.

Then unto ev'ry British blood,
  Their noble worth revere,
And think them ever noble men,
  And like them hence appear.

And when on Britain's isles remote
  We're then in freedom's bounds,
And while we stand on British ground,
  "You're free—you're free!" resounds.

Lift ye that country's banner high,
  And may it nobly wave,
Until beneath the azure sky,
  Man shall be no more a slave.

And, oh, when youth's ecstatic hour,
  When winds and torrents foam,
And passion's glowing noon are past
  To bless that free born home;

Then let us celebrate the day
  And lay the thought to heart,

31

And teach the rising race the way
 That they may not depart.

ADVICE TO YOUNG LADIES

Day after day I sit and write,
 And thus the moments spend—
The thought that occupies my mind—
 Compose to please my friend.

And then I think I will compose,
 And thus myself engage—
To try to please young ladies' minds,
 Which are about my age.

The greatest word that I can say—
 I think to please, will be,
To try and get your learning young.
 And write it back to me.

But this is not the only thing
 That I can recommend;
Religion is most needful for
 To make in us a friend.

At thirteen years I found a hope,
 And did embrace the Lord;
And since, I've found a blessing great,
 Within his holy word.

Perchance that we may ne'er fulfill,
 The place of aged sires,
But may it with God's holy will,
 Be ever our desires.

James M. Whitfield
(1822—1871)

STANZAS FOR THE FIRST OF AUGUST

From bright West Indies' sunny seas
   Comes, borne upon the balmy breeze,
The joyous shout, the gladsome tone,
   Long in those bloody isles unknown;
Bearing across the heaving wave
The song of the unfettered slave.

No charging squadrons shook the ground,
   When freedom have her claims obtained;
No cannon, with tremendous sound
   The noble patriot's cause maintained;
No famous battle-charger neighed,
No brother fell by brother's blade.

None of these desperate scenes of strife,
   Which mark the woman's proud career,
The awful waste of human life
   Have ever been enacted here;
But truth and justice spoke from heaven,
And slavery's galling chain was riven.

'Twas moral force which broke the chain,
   That bound eight hundred thousand men;
And when we see it snapped in twain,
   Shall we not join in praise then?—
And prayers unto Almighty God,
Who smote to earth the tyrant's rod?

And from those islands of the sea,
   The scenes of blood and crime and wrong,
The glorious anthem of the free

33

Now swells in mighty chorus strong;
Telling th' oppressed, where'er they roam,
Those islands now are freedom's home.

TO CINQUE

All hail! thou truly noble chief,
   Who scorned to live a cowering slave;
Thy name shall stand on history's leaf,
   Amid the mighty and the brave:
Thy name shall shine, a glorious light
   To other brave and fearless men,
Who, like thyself, in freedom's might,
   Shall beard the robber in his den;
Thy name shall stand on history's page,
   And brighter, brighter, brighter glow,
Throughout all time, through every age,
   Till bosoms cease to feel or know
"Created worthy, or human woe."
   Thy name shall nerve the patriot's hand
When, 'mid the battle's deadly strife,
   The glittering bayonet and brand
Are crimsoned with the stream of life:
When the dark clouds of battle roll,
And slaughter reigns without control,
Thy name shall then fresh life impart,
And fire anew each freeman's heart.
Though wealth and power their force combine
   To crush thy noble spirit down,
There is above a power divine
   Shall bear thee up against their frown.

THE NORTH STAR

Star of the North! whose steadfast ray
   Pierces the sable pall of night,
Forever pointing out the way
   That leads to freedom's hallowed light:
The fugitive lifts up his eye
To where thy rays illume the sky.

That steady, calm, unchanging light,
    Through dreary wilds and trackless dells,
Directs his weary steps aright
    To the bright land where freedom dwells;
And spreads, with sympathizing breast,
Her aegis over the oppressed;

Though other stars may round thee burn,
    With larger disk and brighter ray,
And fiery comets round thee turn,
    While millions mark their blazing way;
And the pale moon and planets bright
Reflect on us their silvery light.

Not like that moon, now dark, now bright,
    In phase and place forever changing;
Or planets with reflected light,
    Or comets through the heavens ranging;
They all seem varying in our view,
While thou art ever fixed and true.

So may that other bright North Star,
    Beaming with truth and freedom's light,
Pierce with its cheering ray afar,
    The shades of slavery's gloomy night;
And may it never cease to be
The guard of truth and liberty.

Les Cenelles
(1845)

A MALVINA:
Romance
Air: De la Bonne Vieille (De Béranger)
(B. Valcour)

Belle de grâce et belle de jeunesse,
O Malvina, tu parus à mes yeux;
Quand je te vis, d'une douce allégresse
Mon jeune coeur sentit les premiers feux:
Tu me juras, amante trop cruelle,
Que tu m'aimais—Mais que te dis-je, hélas!
Est-il besoin que ma voix te rappelle
Ce que ton coeur ne te rappelle pas?

Que cette bouche est agréable et pure,
Que ce regard est rempli de candeur!
Pourquoi faut-il que l'infâme imposture
Ait ce sourire aimable et séducteur?
Il m'en souvient qu'avec ce doux sourire
Tu fis serment que tu m'aimais, hélas!
Ce que ta bouche autrefois sut me dire,
Femme, ton coeur ne te le dit-il pas?

Toi que je crus si long temps mon amie,
Quoi, sans remords as-tu pu me trahir?
Ah! je le sens malgré ta perfidie
Mon coeur ne peut encore te haïr.
Souvent, grands dieux! dans mon cruel délire,
Je veux te fuir—que dois-je faire, hélas?
En vain ma bouche ose me le prescrire,
Mais, Malvina, mon coeur ne le dit pas.

LE RETOUR AU VILLAGE AUX PERLES
Romance
(Nelson Desbrosses)

Elle folâtre en ces lieux pleins de charmes,
Tout me le dit, oui, mon coeur le sent bien.
Séjour joyeux, tu bannis mes alarmes,
Dieu des amours, quel bonheur est le mien!

Bosquet fleuri, témoin de notre flamme,
Je te revois, ce n'est point une erreur,
Ruisseau chéri, c'est à toi que mon âme
Veut en ce jour confier son bonheur.

Mais la voilà! comme elle est embellie;
Ah! que d'attraits, que d'aimables appas!
Elle sourit,—combien elle est jolie!
Charmante Emma, je vole sur tes pas.

Mars 1828

UN FRÈRE
Au Tombeau de Son Frère
(25 Septembre 1836)
(Armand Lanusse)

Bien loin de tes parens, sur la rive étrangère,
La Mort a sur ton front fait tournoyer sa faux;
Et moi, je suis venu, dans ma douleur amère,
Demander à ces croix, ces saules, ces tombeaux:
          "Où repose mon frère?—

"C'est donc ici!—pleurons—qu'une larme sincère
Arrose le gazon qui couvre ton cercueil!—
Loin de moi, d'autres mains ont fermé ta paupière
Quand de la vie, hélas! tu franchissais le seuil,
          Mon infortuné frère!—

"A vingt-six ans, Numa, tu finis ta carrière!
Mais tes nombreux amis toujours te pleureront.
Au seul ressouvenir de ton franc caractère

Crois-moi, longtemps encor leurs coeurs palpiteront—
        Dors en paix, mon bon frère!

"Non, je ne doute point de ce divin mystère:
Nous devons tous au ciel, un jour, nous réunir.
Tranquilles et contens auprès de notre mère,
D'un bonheur éternel là nous pourrons jouir.—
        Au revoir, mon cher frère!"

LE CARNAVAL
Chanson
Air: Les oiseaux que l'hiver exile
(Armand Lanusse)

L'hiver, sémillante Palmyre,
Reprend, hélas! son triste cours.
Décembre, les vents, tout conspire
Pour effaroucher les amours.
En les ralliant, la Folie
Donne partout l'heureux signal!—
Bannissons la mélancolie;
Voici le temps du Carnaval.

Dans cette foule où l'on se presse,
Déjà j'entends autour de toi,
Mille amans répéter sans cesse:
"Je t'aime . . . Palmyre, aime moi!—"
Sans craindre d'être inconséquente,
Dis à tous ce refrain banal:
"Je vous aime et serai constante."
Tout est permis en Carnaval.

Mais lorsque ta bouche rieuse
Leur promet amour éternel,
Songe qu'à moi, belle oublieuse,
Tu fis un aveu plus formel.
Pour mieux lier notre existence
Je veux qu'un serment conjugal
Ait pour nous plus de consistance
Qu'une promesse en Carnaval.

ADIEU
(Camille Thierry)

Canal Carondelet, le vent du nord me chasse
        Aujourd'hui de tes bords,
Adieu, je vais chercher près de l'âtre une place
        Pour abriter mon corps.

Sur ton chemin poudreux plus de vertes cigales,
        Plus de beaux papillons,
Rien que le bruit du vent qui vient par intervalles
        Mourir dans les buissons.

Mais semblable à l'amant qui loin de son amante
        Pleure et gémit toujours,
Loin de toi je n'aurai qu'une voix gémissante,
        Et que de mauvais jours!

Je me rappellerai la musique charmante
        Qui sort de tes roseaux,
Lorsqu'en un soir d'été la brise les tourmente,
        Les penche sur tes eaux.

Quand viendra la saison où revient l'hirondelle,
        Où reparait la fleur,
A toi je parlerai de la nymphe cruelle
        Qui rend mon front rêveur.

Oui, je te parlerai de cet amour bizarre
        Que je porte en mon sein,
Et qui me fait parfois, quand mon esprit s'égare,
        Couver un noir dessein!

Si des rêves hideux traversent ma pensée,
        Soulèvent mes douleurs,
C'est que je ne vois point la goutte de rosée
        Qui rafraichit les coeurs.

Poète infortuné, j'ai brisé la mandore
        Que j'avais sous les doigts—
A quoi bon de chantes, quand celle que j'adore
        Reste sourde à ma voix!—

Adieu!—je ne crains pas que les jours de l'absence
      Me fassent t'oublier:
J'aime à me souvenir, et j'aurai souvenance
      De toi, près du foyer!

Frances Ellen Watkins Harper (1825–1911)

THE SLAVE MOTHER

Heard you that shriek? It rose
  So wildly on the air,
It seemed as if a burden'd heart
  Was breaking in despair.

Saw you those hands so sadly clasped—
  The bowed and feeble head—
The shuddering of that fragile form—
  That look of grief and dread?

Saw you the sad, imploring eye?
  Its every glance was pain,
As if a storm of agony
  Were sweeping through the brain.

She is a mother, pale with fear,
  Her boy clings to her side,
And in her kirtle vainly tries
  His trembling form to hide.

He is not hers, although she bore
  For him a mother's pains;
He is not hers, although her blood
  Is coursing through his veins!

He is not hers, for cruel hands
  May rudely tear apart
The only wreath of household love
  That binds her breaking heart.

His love has been a joyous light
    That o'er her pathway smiled,
A fountain gushing ever new,
    Amid life's desert wild.

His lightest word has been a tone
    Of music round her heart,
Their lives a streamlet blent in one—
    Oh, Father! must they part?

They tear him from her circling arms,
    Her last and fond embrace.
Oh! never more may her sad eyes
    Gaze on his mournful face.

No marvel, then, these bitter shrieks
    Disturb the listening air:
She is a mother, and her heart
    Is breaking in despair.

ADVICE TO THE GIRLS

Nay, do not blush! I only heard
    You had a mind to marry;
I thought I'd speak a friendly word,
    So just one moment tarry.

Wed not a man whose merit lies
    In things of outward show,
In raven hair or flashing eyes,
    That please your fancy so.

But marry one who's good and kind,
    And free from all pretence;
Who, if without a gifted mind,
    At least has common sense.

BURY ME IN A FREE LAND

Make me a grave where'er you will,
In a lowly plain or a lofty hill;
Make it among earth's humblest graves,
But not in a land where men are slaves.

I could not rest, if around my grave
I heard the steps of a trembling slave;
His shadow above my silent tomb
Would make it a place of fearful gloom.

I could not sleep, if I heard the tread
Of a coffle-gang to the shambles led,
And the mother's shriek of wild despair
Rise, like a curse, on the trembling air.

I could not rest, if I saw the lash
Drinking her blood at each fearful gash;
And I saw her babes torn from her breast,
Like trembling doves from their parent nest.

I'd shudder and start, if I heard the bay
Of a bloodhound seizing his human prey;
And I heard the captive plead in vain,
As they bound, afresh, his galling chain.

If I saw young girls from their mother's arms
Bartered and sold for their youthful charms,
My eye would flash with a mournful flame,
My death-pale cheek grow red with shame.

I would sleep, dear friends, where bloated Might
Can rob no man of his dearest right;
My rest shall be calm in any grave
Where none can call his brother a slave.

I ask no monument, proud and high,
To arrest the gaze of the passers by;
All that my yearning spirit craves
Is—*Bury me not in a land of slaves!*

THE DYING FUGITIVE

Slowly o'er his darkened features,
Stole the warning shades of death;
And we knew the shadowing angel
Waited for his parting breath.

He had started for his freedom;
And his heart beat firm and high—
But before he won the guerdon,
Came the message—he must die.

He must die, when just before him,
Lay the long'd for, precious prize—
And the hopes that lit him onward,
Faded out before his eyes.

For a while a fearful madness,
Rested on his weary brain;
And he thought the hateful tyrant,
Had rebound his galling chain.

Then he raved in bitter anguish—
"Take me where that good man dwells!"
To a name to freedom precious;—
Lingered mid life's shattered cells.

But as sunshine gently stealing,
O'er the storm-cloud's gloomy track—
Through the tempests of his bosom,
Came the light of reason back.

And without a sigh or murmur
For the home he'd left behind;
Calmly yielded he his spirit,
To the Father of mankind.

Thankful that so near to freedom,
He with eager steps had trod—
E're his ransomed spirit rested,
On the bosom of his God.

VASHTI

She leaned her head upon her hand
   And heard the King's decree—
"My lords are feasting in my halls;
   Bid Vashti come to me.

"I've shown the treasures of my house,
   My costly jewels rare,
But with the glory of her eyes
   No rubies can compare.

"Adorn'd and crown'd I'd have her come,
   With all her queenly grace,
And, 'mid my lords and mighty men,
   Unveil her lovely face.

"Each gem that sparkles in my crown,
   Or glitters on my throne,
Grows poor and pale when she appears,
   My beautiful, my own!"

All waiting stood the chamberlains
   To hear the Queen's reply.
They saw her cheek grow deathly pale,
   But light flash'd to her eye:

"Go, tell the King," she proudly said,
   "That I am Persia's Queen,
And by his crowds of merry men
   I never will be seen.

"I'll take the crown from off my head
   And tread it 'neath my feet,
Before their rude and careless gaze
   My shrinking eyes shall meet.

"A queen unveil'd before the crowd!—
   Upon each lip my name!—
Why, Persia's women all would blush
   And weep for Vashti's shame!

"Go back!" she cried, and waved her hand,
    And grief was in her eye:
"Go, tell the King," she sadly said,
    "That I would rather die."

They brought her message to the King;
    Dark flash'd his angry eye;
'Twas as the lightning ere the storm
    Hath swept in fury by.

Then bitterly outspoke the King,
    Through purple lips of wrath—
"What shall be done to her who dares
    To cross your monarch's path?"

Then spake his wily counsellors—
    "O King of this fair land!
From distant Ind to Ethiop,
    All bow to thy command.

"But if, before thy servants' eyes,
    This thing they plainly see,
That Vashti doth not heed thy will
    Nor yield herself to thee,

"The women, restive 'neath our rule,
    Would learn to scorn our name,
And from her deed to us would come
    Reproach and burning shame.

"Then, gracious King, sign with thy hand
    This stern but just decree,
That Vashti lay aside her crown,
    Thy Queen no more to be."

She heard again the King's command,
    And left her high estate;
Strong in her earnest womanhood,
    She calmly met her fate,

And left the palace of the King,
    Proud of her spotless name—
A woman who could bend to grief.
    But would not bow to shame.

THE MARTYR OF ALABAMA

[The following news item appeared in the newspapers throughout the country, issue of December 27th, 1894:
"Tim Thompson, a little negro boy, was asked to dance for the amusement of some white toughs. He refused, saying he was a church member. One of the men knocked him down with a club and then danced upon his prostrate form. He then shot the boy in the hip. The boy is dead; his murderer is still at large."]

He lifted up his pleading eyes,
    And scanned each cruel face,
Where cold and brutal cowardice
    Had left its evil trace.

It was when tender memories
    Round Beth'lem's manger lay,
And mothers told their little ones
    Of Jesu's natal day.

And of the Magi from the East
    Who came their gifts to bring,
And bow in rev'rence at the feet
    Of Salem's new-born King.

And how the herald angels sang
    The choral song of peace,
That war should close his wrathful lips,
    And strife and carnage cease.

At such an hour men well may hush
    Their discord and their strife,
And o'er that manger clasp their hands
    With gifts to brighten life.

Alas! that in our favored land,
    That cruelty and crime
Should cast their shadows o'er a day,
    The fairest pearl of time.

A dark-browed boy had drawn anear
    A band of savage men,

Just as a hapless lamb might stray
    Into a tiger's den.

Cruel and dull, they saw in him
    For sport an evil chance,
And then demanded of the child
    To give to them a dance.

"Come dance for us," the rough men said;
    "I can't," the child replied,
"I cannot for the dear Lord's sake,
    Who for my sins once died."

Tho' they were strong and he was weak,
    He wouldn't his Lord deny.
His life lay in their cruel hands,
    But he for Christ could die.

Heard they aright? Did that brave child
    Their mandates dare resist?
Did he against their stern commands
    Have courage to resist?

Then recklessly a man (?) arose,
    And dealt a fearful blow.
He crushed the portals of that life,
    And laid the brave child low.

And trampled on his prostrate form,
    As on a broken toy;
Then danced with careless, brutal feet,
    Upon the murdered boy.

Christians! behold that martyred child!
    His blood cries from the ground;
Before the sleepless eye of God,
    He shows each gaping wound.

Oh! Church of Christ arise! arise!
    Lest crimson stain thy hand,
When God shall inquisition make
    For blood shed in the land.

Take sackcloth of the darkest hue,
   And shroud the pulpits round;
Servants of him who cannot lie
   Sit mourning on the ground.

Let holy horror blanch each brow,
   Pale every cheek with fears,
And rocks and stones, if ye could speak,
   Ye well might melt to tears.

Through every fane send forth a cry,
   Of sorrow and regret,
Nor in an hour of careless ease
   Thy brother's wrongs forget.

Veil not thine eyes, nor close thy lips,
   Nor speak with bated breath;
This evil shall not always last,—
   The end of it is death.

Avert the doom that crime must bring
   Upon a guilty land;
Strong in the strength that God supplies,
   For truth and justice stand.

For Christless men, with reckless hands,
   Are sowing round thy path
The tempests wild that yet shall break
   In whirlwinds of God's wrath.

SONGS FOR THE PEOPLE

Let me make the songs for the people,
   Songs for the old and young;
Songs to stir like a battle-cry
   Wherever they are sung.

Not for the clashing of sabres,
   For carnage nor for strife;
But songs to thrill the hearts of men
   With more abundant life.

Let me make the songs for the weary,
　　Amid life's fever and fret,
Till hearts shall relax their tension,
　　And careworn brows forget.

Let me sing for little children,
　　Before their footsteps stray,
Sweet anthems of love and duty,
　　To float o'er life's highway.

I would sing for the poor and aged,
　　When shadows dim their sight;
Of the bright and restful mansions,
　　Where there shall be no night.

Our world, so worn and weary,
　　Needs music, pure and strong,
To hush the jangle and discords
　　Of sorrow, pain, and wrong.

Music to soothe all its sorrow,
　　Till war and crime shall cease;
And the hearts of men grown tender
　　Girdle the world with peace.

III

VOICES OF
RECONSTRUCTION
(1865–1910)

Albery A. Whitman
(1851—1901)

THE LUTE OF AFRIC'S TRIBE

*To the memory of Dr. J. McSimpson, a colored
Author of Anti-Slavery Ballads. Written for
the Zanesville, O., Courier.*

When Israel sate by Babel's stream and wept,
The heathen said, "Sing one of Zion's songs;"
But tuneless lay the lyre of those who slept
Where Sharon bloomed and Oreb vigil kept;
For holy song to holy ears belongs.

So, when her iron clutch the Slave power reached,
And sable generations captive held;
When Wrong the gospel of endurance preached;
The lute of Afric's tribe, tho' oft beseeched,
In all its wild, sweet warblings never swelled.

And yet when Freedom's lispings o'er it stole,
Soft as the breath of undefiled morn,
A wand'ring accent from its strings would stroll—
Thus was our Simpson, man of song and soul,
And stalwart energies, to bless us born.

When all our nation's sky was overcast
With rayless clouds of deepening misery,
His soaring vision mounted thro' the blast,
And from behind its gloom approaching fast,
Beheld the glorious Sun of Liberty.

He sang exultant: "Let her banner wave!"
And cheering senates, fired by his zeal,
Helped snatch their country from rebellion's grave,

Looked through brave tears upon the injured slave,
And raised the battle-arm to break his gyves of steel.

But hushed the bard, his harp no longer sings
The woes and longings of a shackled mind;
For death's cold fingers swept its trembling strings,
And shut the bosom of its murmurings
Forever on the hearing of mankind.

The bird that dips his flight in noonday sun,
May fall, and spread his plumage on the plain;
But when immortal mind its work hath done
On earth, in heaven a nobler work's begun,
And it can never downward turn again.

Of him, whose harp then lies by death unstrung—
A harp that long his lowly brethren cheered,
May'nt we now say that, sainted choirs among,
An everlasting theme inspires his tongue,
Where slaves ne'er groan, and death is never feared?

Yes, he is harping on the "Sea of glass,"
Where saints begin, and angels join the strain;
While Spheres in one profound, eternal bass,
Sing thro' their orbs, illumined as they pass,
And constellations catch the long refrain.

Henrietta Cordelia Ray
(1849–1916)

TO MY FATHER

A leaf from Freedom's golden chaplet fair,
We bring to thee, dear father. Near her shrine
None came with holier purpose, nor was thine
Alone the soul's mute sanction; every prayer
Thy captive brother uttered found a share
In thy wide sympathy; to every sigh
That told the bondman's need thou didst incline.
No thought of guerdon hadst thou but to bear
A long part in Freedom's strife. To see
Sad lives illumined, fetters rent in twain,
Tears dried in eyes that wept for length of days—
Ah! was not that a recompense for thee?
And now where all life's mystery is plain,
Divine approval is thy sweetest praise.

MILTON

O, poet gifted with the sight divine!
To thee 'twas given Eden's groves to pace
With that first pair in whom the human race
Their kinship claim: and angels did incline—
Great Michael, holy Gabriel—to twine
Their heavenly logic, through which thou couldst trace
The rich outpourings of celestial grace
Mingled with argument, around the shrine
Where thou didst linger, vision-rapt, intent
To catch the sacred mystery of Heaven.
Nor was thy longing vain; a soul resolved
To ponder truth supreme to thee was lent;
For thy not *sightless* eyes the veil was riv'n,
Redemption's problem unto thee well solved.

James Edwin Campbell
(1867–1896)

OL' DOC' HYAR

Ur ol' Hyar lib in ur house on de hill,
He hunner yurs ol' an' nebber wuz ill;
He yurs dee so long an' he eyes so beeg,
An' he laigs so spry dat he dawnce ur jeeg;
He lib so long dat he know ebbry tings
'Bout de beas'ses dat walks an' de bu'ds dat sings—
                              Dis Ol' Doc' Hyar,
                              Whar lib up dar
Een ur mighty fine house on ur mighty high hill.

He doctah fur all de beas'ses an' bu'ds—
He put on he specs an' he use beeg wu'ds,
He feel dee pu's' den he look mighty wise,
He pull out he watch an' he shet bofe eyes;
He grab up he hat an' grab up he cane,
Den—"blam!" go de do'—he gone lak de train,
                              Dis Ol' Doc' Hyar,
                              Whar lib up dar
Een ur mighty fine house on ur mighty high hill.

Mistah Ba'r fall sick—dee sont fur Doc' Hyar,
"O, Doctah, come queeck, an' see Mr. B'ar;
He mighty nigh daid des sho' ez you b'on!"
"Too much ur young peeg, too much ur green co'n,"
Ez he put on he hat, said Ol' Doc' Hyar;
"I'll tek 'long meh lawnce, an' lawnce Mistah B'ar,"
                              Said Ol' Doc' Hyar,
                              Whar lib up dar
Een ur mighty fine house on ur mighty high hill.

Mistah B'ar he groaned, Mistah B'ar he growled,
W'ile de ol' Miss B'ar an' de chillen howled;
Doctah Hyar tuk out he sha'p li'l lawnce,
An' pyu'ced Mistah B'ar twel he med him prawnce
Den grab up he hat an' grab up he cane
"Blam!" go de do' an' he gone lak de train,
                                        Dis Ol' Doc' Hyar,
                                        Whar lib up dar
Een ur mighty fine house on ur mighty high hill.

But de vay naix day Mistah B'ar he daid;
Wen dee tell Doc' Hyar, he des scratch he haid:
"Ef pahsons git well ur pahsons git wu's,
Money got ter come een de Ol' Hyar's pu's;
Not wut folkses does, but fur wut dee know
Does de folkses git paid"—an' Hyar larfed low,
                                        Dis sma't Ol' Hyar,
                                        Whar lib up dar
Een de mighty fine house on de mighty high hill!

DE CUNJAH MAN

O chillen, run, de Cunjah man,
Him mouf ez beeg ez fryin' pan,
Him yurs am small, him eyes am raid,
Him hab no toof een him ol' haid,
Him hab him roots, him wu'k him trick,
Him roll him eye, him mek you sick—
    De Cunjah man, de Cunjah man,
    O chillen, run, de Cunjah man!

Him hab ur ball ob raid, raid ha'r,
Him hide it un' de kitchen sta'r
Mam Jude huh pars urlong dat way,
An' now huh hab ur snaik, de say.
Him wrop ur roun' huh buddy tight,
Huh eyes pop out, ur orful sight—
    De Cunjah man, de Cunjah man,
    O chillen, run, de Cunjah man!

Miss Jane, huh dribe him f'um huh do',
An' now huh hens woan' lay no mo';

De Jussey cow huh done fall sick,
Hit all done by de Cunjah trick.
Him put ur root un' 'Lijah's baid,
An' now de man he sho' am daid—
   De Cunjah man, de Cunjah man,
   O chillen, run, de Cunjah man!

Me see him stan' de yudder night
Right een de road een white moon-light;
Him toss him arms, him whirl him 'roun'.
Him stomp him foot urpon de groun';
De snaiks come crawlin', one by one,
Me hyuh um hiss, me break an' run—
   De Cunjah man, de Cunjah man,
   O chillen, run, de Cunjah man!

Joseph Seamon Cotter, Sr.
(1861—1949)

THE WAY-SIDE WELL

A FANCY halts my feet at the way-side well.
It is not to drink, for they say the water is brackish.
It is not to tryst, for a heart at the mile's end
beckons me on.
It is not to rest, for what feet could be weary when
a heart at the mile's end keeps time with their tread?
It is not to muse, for the heart at the mile's end is
food for my being.
I will question the well for my secret by dropping
a pebble into it.
Ah, it is dry.
Strike lightning to the road, my feet, for hearts
are like wells. You may not know they are dry 'til you
question their depths.
Fancies clog the way to Heaven, and saints miss
their crown.

James David Corrothers
(1869—1917)

AT THE CLOSED GATE OF JUSTICE

To be a Negro in a day like this
   Demands forgiveness. Bruised with blow on blow,
Betrayed, like him whose woe dimmed eyes gave bliss,
   Still must one succor those who brought one low,
To be a Negro in a day like this.

To be a Negro in a day like this
   Demands rare patience—patience that can wait
In utter darkness. 'Tis the path to miss,
   And knock, unheeded, at an iron gate,
To be a Negro in a day like this.

To be a Negro in a day like this
   Demands strange loyalty. We serve a flag
Which is to us white freedom's emphasis.
   Ah! one must love when Truth and Justice lag,
To be a Negro in a day like this.

To be a Negro in a day like this—
   Alas! Lord God, what evil have we done?
Still shines the gate, all gold and amethyst,
   But I pass by, the glorious goal unwon,
"Merely a Negro"—in a day like this!

IN THE MATTER OF TWO MEN

One does such work as one will not,
   And well each knows the right;
Though the white storm howls, or the sun is hot,
   The black must serve the white.

And it's, oh, for the white man's softening flesh,
    While the black man's muscles grow!
Well I know which grows the mightier,
    I know; full well I know.

The white man seeks the soft, fat place,
    And he moves and he works by rule.
Ingenious grows the humbler race
    In Oppression's prodding school.
And it's, oh, for a white man gone to seed,
    While the Negro struggles so!
And I know which race develops most,
    I know; yes, well I know.

The white man rides in a palace car,
    And the Negro rides "Jim Crow."
To damn the other with bolt and bar,
    One creepeth so low; so low!
And it's, oh, for a master's nose in the mire,
    While the humbled hearts o'erflow!
Well I know whose soul grows big at this,
    And whose grows small; *I know!*

The white man leases out his land,
    And the Negro tills the same.
One works; one loafs and takes command;
    But I know who wins the game!
And it's, oh, for the white man's shrinking soil,
    As the black's rich acres grow!
Well I know how the signs point out at last,
    I know; ah, well I know!

The white man votes for his color's sake,
    While the black, for his is barred;
(Though "ignorance" is the charge they make),
    But the black man studies hard.
And it's, oh, for the white man's sad neglect,
    For the power of his light let go!
So, I know which man must win at last,
    I know! Ah, Friend, I know!

Paul Laurence Dunbar
(1872–1906)

AN ANTE-BELLUM SERMON

We is gathahed hyeah, my brothahs,
    In dis howlin' wildaness,
Fu' to speak some words of comfo't
    To each othah in distress.
An' we chooses fu' ouah subjic'
    Dis—we'll 'splain it by an' by;
    "An' de Lawd said, 'Moses, Moses,'
    An' de man said, 'Hyeah am I.' "

Now ole Pher'oh, down in Egypt,
    Was de wuss man evah bo'n,
An' he had de Hebrew chillun
    Down dah wukin' in his co'n;
'T well de Lawd got tiahed o' his foolin',
    An' sez he: "I'll let him know—
Look hyeah, Moses, go tell Pher'oh
Fu' to let dem chillun go."
"An' ef he refuse to do it,
    I will make him rue de houah,
Fu' I'll empty down on Egypt
    All de vials of my powah."
Yes, he did—an' Pher'oh's ahmy
    Was n't wuth a ha'f a dime;
Fu' de Lawd will he'p his chillun,
    You kin trust him evah time.

An' yo' enemies may 'sail you
    In de back an' in de front;
But de Lawd is all aroun' you,
    Fu' to ba' de battle's brunt.
Dey kin fo'ge yo' chains an' shackles

F'om de mountains to de sea;
But de Lawd will sen' some Moses
   Fu' to set his chillun free.

An' de lan' shall hyeah his thundah,
   Lak a blas' f'om Gab'el's ho'n,
Fu' de Lawd of hosts is mighty
   When he girds his ahmor on.
But fu' feah some one mistakes me,
   I will pause right hyeah to say,
Dat I'm still a-preachin' ancient,
   I ain't talkin' 'bout to-day.

But I tell you, fellah christuns,
   Things'll happen mighty strange;
Now, de Lawd done dis fu' Isrul,
   An' his ways don't nevah change,
An' de love he showed to Isrul
   Was n't all on Isrul spent;
Now don't run an' tell yo' mastahs
   Dat I's preachin' discontent.

'Cause I isn't; I'se a-judgin'
   Bible people by deir ac's;
I'se a-givin' you de Scriptuah,
   I'se a-handin' you de fac's.
Cose ole Pher'oh b'lieved in slav'ry,
   But de Lawd he let him see,
Dat de people he put bref in,—
   Evah mothah's son was free.

An' dahs othahs thinks lak Pher'oh,
   But dey calls de Scriptuah liar,
Fu' de Bible says "a servant
   Is a-worthy of his hire."
An' you cain't git roun' nor thoo dat,
   An' you cain't git ovah it,
Fu' whatevah place you git in,
   Dis hyeah Bible too 'll fit.

So you see de Lawd's intention,
   Evah sence de worl' began,
Was dat His almighty freedom

Should belong to evah man,
But I think it would be bertah,
  Ef I'd pause agin to say,
Dat I'm talkin' 'bout ouah freedom
  In a Bibleistic way.

But de Moses is a-comin',
  An' he's comin', suah and fas'
We kin hyeah his feet a-trompin',
  We kin hyeah his trumpit blas'.
But I want to wa'n you people,
  Don't you git too brigity;
An' don't you git to braggin'
  'Bout dese things, you wait an' see.

But when Moses wif his powah
  Comes an' sets us chillun free,
We will praise de gracious Mastah
  Dat has gin us liberty;
An' we'll shout ouah halleluyahs,
  On dat mighty reck'nin' day,
When we'se reco'nised ez citiz'—
  Huh uh! Chillun, let us pray!

ODE TO ETHIOPIA

O MOTHER RACE! to thee I bring
This pledge of faith unwavering,
  This tribute to thy glory.
I know the pangs which thou didst feel,
When Slavery crushed thee with its heel,
  With thy dear blood all gory.

Sad days were those—ah, sad indeed!
But through the land the fruitful seed
  Of better times was growing.
The plant of freedom upward sprung,
And spread its leaves so fresh and young—
  Its blossoms now are blowing.

On every hand in this fair land,
Proud Ethiope's swarthy children stand

64

Beside their fairer neighbor;
The forests flee before their stroke,
Their hammers ring, their forges smoke,—
    They stir in honest labour.

They tread the fields where honour calls;
Their voices sound through senate halls
    In majesty and power.
To right they cling; the hymns they sing
Up to the skies in beauty ring,
    And bolder grow each hour.

Be proud, my Race, in mind and soul;
Thy name is writ on Glory's scroll
    In characters of fire.
High 'mid the clouds of Fame's bright sky
Thy banner's blazoned folds now fly,
    And truth shall lift them higher.

Thou hast the right to noble pride,
Whose spotless robes were purified
    By blood's severe baptism.
Upon thy brow the cross was laid,
And labour's painful sweat-beads made
    A consecrating chrism.

No other race, or white or black,
When bound as thou wert, to the rack,
    So seldom stooped to grieving;
No other race, when free again,
Forgot the past and proved them men
    So noble in forgiving.

Go on and up! Our souls and eyes
Shall follow thy continuous rise;
    Our ears shall list thy story
From bards who from thy root shall spring,
And proudly tune their lyres to sing
    Of Ethiopia's glory.

A NEGRO LOVE SONG

Seen my lady home las' night,
   Jump back, honey, jump back.
Hel' huh han' an' sque'z it tight,
   Jump back, honey, jump back.
Hyeahd huh sigh a little sigh,
Seen a light gleam f'om huh eye,
An' a smile go flittin' by—
   Jump back, honey, jump back.

Hyeahd de win' blow thoo de pine,
   Jump back, honey, jump back.
Mockin'-bird was singin' fine,
   Jump back, honey, jump back.
An' my hea't was beatin' so,
When I reached my lady's do',
Dat I could n't ba' to go—
   Jump back, honey, jump back.

Put my ahm aroun' huh wais',
   Jump back, honey, jump back.
Raised huh lips an' took a tase,
   Jump back, honey, jump back.
Love me, honey, love me true?
Love me well ez I love you?
An' she answe'd, " 'Cose I do"—
   Jump back, honey, jump back.

WHEN DE CO'N PONE'S HOT

Dey is times in life when Nature
   Seems to slip a cog an' go,
Jes' a-rattlin' down creation,
   Lak an ocean's overflow;
When de worl' jes' stahts a-spinnin'
   Lak a picaninny's top,
An' yo' cup o' joy is brimmin'
   'Twell it seems about to slop,
An' you feel jes' lak a racah,
   Dat is trainin' fu' to trot—
When yo' mammy says de blessin'
   An' de co'n pone's hot.

When you set down at de table,
   Kin' o' weary lak an' sad,
An' you 'se jes' a little tiahed
   An' purhaps a little mad;
How yo' gloom tu'ns into gladness,
   How yo' joy drives out de doubt
When de oven do' is opened,
   An' de smell comes po'in' out;
Why, de 'lectric light o' Heaven
   Seems to settle on de spot,
When yo' mammy says de blessin'
   An' de co'n pone's hot.

When de cabbage pot is steamin'
   An' de bacon good an' fat,
When de chittlins is a-sputter'n'
   So 's to show you whah dey's at;
Tek away yo' sody biscuit,
   Tek away yo' cake an' pie,
Fu' de glory time is comin',
   An' it's 'proachin' mighty nigh,
An' you want to jump an' hollah,
   Dough you know you'd bettah not,
When yo' mammy says de blessin'
   An' de co'n pone's hot.

I have hyeahd o' lots o' sermons,
   An' I 've hyeahd o' lots o' prayers,
An' I've listened to some singin'
   Dat has tuck me up de stairs
Of de Glory-Lan' an' set me
   Jes' below de Mastah's th'one,
An' have lef' my hea't a-singin'
   In a happy aftah tone;
But dem wu'ds so sweetly murmured
   Seem to tech de softes' spot,
When my mammy says de blessin',
   An' de co'n pone's hot.

WE WEAR THE MASK

We wear the mask that grins and lies,
It hides our cheeks and shades our eyes,—
This debt we pay to human guile;
With torn and bleeding hearts we smile,
And mouth with myriad subtleties.

Why should the world be overwise,
In counting all our tears and sighs?
Nay, let them only see us, while
   We wear the mask.

We smile, but, O great Christ, our cries
To thee from tortured souls arise.
We sing, but oh the clay is vile
Beneath our feet, and long the mile;
But let the world dream otherwise,
   We wear the mask!

SYMPATHY

I KNOW what the caged bird feels, alas!
   When the sun is bright on the upland slopes;
When the wind stirs soft through the springing grass,
And the river flows like a stream of glass;
   When the first bird sings and the first bud opes,
And the faint perfume from its chalice steals—
I know what the caged bird feels!

I know why the caged bird beats his wing
   Till its blood is red on the cruel bars;
For he must fly back to his perch and cling
When he fain would be on the bough a-swing;
   And a pain still throbs in the old, old scars
And they pulse again with a keener sting—
I know why he beats his wing!

I know why the caged bird sings, ah me,
   When his wing is bruised and his bosom sore,—
When he beats his bars and he would be free;
It is not a carol of joy or glee,
   But a prayer that he sends from his heart's deep core,

But a plea, that upward to Heaven he flings—
I know why the caged bird sings!

DOUGLASS

Ah, Douglass, we have fall'n on evil days,
   Such days as thou, not even thou didst know,
   When thee, the eyes of that harsh long ago
Saw, salient, at the cross of devious ways,
And all the country heard thee with amaze.
   Not ended then, the passionate ebb and flow,
   The awful tide that battled to and fro;
We ride amid a tempest of dispraise.

Now, when the waves of swift dissension swarm,
   And Honor, the strong pilot, lieth stark,
Oh, for thy voice high-sounding o'er the storm,
   For thy strong arm to guide the shivering bark,
The blast-defying power of thy form,
   To give us comfort through the lonely dark.

IV

THE EARLY TWENTIETH CENTURY
(1910–1960)

James Weldon Johnson
(1871–1938)

THE CREATION

And God stepped out on space,
And he looked around and said:
I'm lonely—
I'll make me a world.

And far as the eye of God could see
Darkness covered everything,
Blacker than a hundred midnights
Down in a cypress swamp.

Then God smiled,
And the light broke,
And the darkness rolled up on one side,
And the light stood shining on the other,
And God said: That's good!

Then God reached out and took the light in his hands,
And God rolled the light around in his hands
Until he made the sun;
And he set that sun a-blazing in the heavens.
And the light that was left from making the sun
God gathered it up in a shining ball
And flung it against the darkness,
Spangling the night with the moon and stars.
Then down between
The darkness and the light
He hurled the world;
And God said: That's good!

Then God himself stepped down—
And the sun was on his right hand,

And the moon was on his left;
The stars were clustered about his head,
And the earth was under his feet.
And God walked, and where he trod
His footsteps hollowed the valleys out
And bulged the mountains up.

Then he stopped and looked and saw
That the earth was hot and barren.
So God stepped over to the edge of the world
And he spat out the seven seas—
He batted his eyes, and the lightnings flashed—
He clapped his hands, and the thunders rolled—
And the waters above the earth came down,
The cooling waters came down.

Then the green grass sprouted,
And the little red flowers blossomed,
The pine tree pointed his finger to the sky,
And the oak spread out his arms,
The lakes cuddled down in the hollows of the ground,
And the rivers ran down to the sea;
And God smiled again,
And the rainbow appeared,
And curled itself around his shoulder.

Then God raised his arm and he waved his hand
Over the sea and over the land,
And he said: Bring forth! Bring forth!
And quicker than God could drop his hand,
Fishes and fowls
And beasts and birds
Swam the rivers and the seas,
Roamed the forests and the woods,
And split the air with their wings.
And God said: That's good!

Then God walked around,
And God looked around
On all that he had made.
He looked at his sun,
And he looked at his moon,
And he looked at his little stars;

He looked on his world
With all its living things,
And God said: I'm lonely still.

Then God sat down—
On the side of a hill where he could think;
By a deep, wide river he sat down;
With his head in his hands,
God thought and thought,
Till he thought: I'll make me a man!

Up from the bed of the river
God scooped the clay;
And by the bank of the river
He kneeled him down;
And there the great God Almighty
Who lit the sun and fixed it in the sky,
Who flung the stars to the most far corner of the night,
Who rounded the earth in the middle of his hand;
This Great God,
Like a mammy bending over her baby,
Kneeled down in the dust
Toiling over a lump of clay
Till he shaped it in his own image;

Then into it he blew the breath of life,
And man became a living soul.
Amen. Amen.

LIFT EVERY VOICE AND SING

Lift every voice and sing
Till earth and heaven ring,
Ring with the harmonies of Liberty;
Let our rejoicing rise
High as the listening skies,
Let it resound loud as the rolling sea.
Sing a song full of the faith that the dark past has taught us,
Sing a song full of the hope that the present has brought us,
Facing the rising sun of our new day begun
Let us march on till victory is won.

Stony the road we trod,
Bitter the chastening rod,
Felt in the days when hope unborn had died;
Yet with a steady beat,
Have not our weary feet
Come to the place for which our fathers sighed?
We have come over a way that with tears has been watered,
We have come, treading our path through the blood of the
    slaughtered,
Out from the gloomy past,
Till now we stand at last
Where the white gleam of our bright star is cast.

God of our weary years,
God of our silent tears,
Thou who has brought us thus far on the way;
Thou who has by Thy might
Led us into the light,
Keep us forever in the path, we pray.
Lest our feet stray from the places, our God, where we met
    Thee,
Lest, our hearts drunk with the wine of the world, we forget
    Thee;
Shadowed beneath Thy hand,
May we forever stand.
True to our God,
True to our native land.

THE WHITE WITCH

O brothers mine, take care! Take care!
The great white witch rides out tonight,
Trust not your prowess nor your strength;
Your only safety lies in flight;
For in her glance there is a snare,
And in her smile there is a blight.

The great white witch you have not seen?
Then, younger brothers mine, forsooth,
Like nursery children you have looked
For ancient hag and snaggle-tooth;
But no, not so; the witch appears
In all the glowing charms of youth.

Her lips are like carnations red,
Her face like new-born lilies fair,
Her eyes like ocean waters blue,
She moves with subtle grace and air,
And all about her head there floats
The golden glory of her hair.

But though she always thus appears
In form of youth and mood of mirth,
Unnumbered centuries are hers,
The infant planets saw her birth;
The child of throbbing Life is she,
Twin sister to the greedy earth.

And back behind those smiling lips,
And down within those laughing eyes,
And underneath the soft caress
Of hand and voice and purring sighs,
The shadow of the panther lurks,
The spirit of the vampire lies.

For I have seen the great white witch,
And she has led me to her lair,
And I have kissed her red, red lips
And cruel face so white and fair;
Around me she has twined her arms,
And bound me with her yellow hair.

I felt those red lips burn and sear
My body like a living coal;
Obeyed the power of those eyes
As the needle trembles to the pole;
And did not care although I felt
The strength go ebbing from my soul.

Oh! she has seen your strong young limbs,
And heard your laughter loud and gay,
And in your voices she has caught
The echo of a far-off day,
When man was closer to the earth;
And she has marked you for her prey.

She feels the old Antæan strength
In you, the great dynamic beat
Of primal passions, and she sees
In you the last besieged retreat
Of love relentless, lusty, fierce,
Love pain-ecstatic, cruel-sweet.

O, brothers mine, take care! Take care!
The great white witch rides out tonight.
O, younger brothers mine, beware!
Look not upon her beauty bright;
For in her glance there is a snare,
And in her smile there is a blight.

O BLACK AND UNKNOWN BARDS

O black and unknown bards of long ago,
How came your lips to touch the sacred fire?
How, in your darkness, did you come to know
The power and beauty of the minstrels' lyre?
Who first from midst his bonds lifted his eyes?
Who first from out the still watch, lone and long,
Feeling the ancient faith of prophets rise
Within his dark-kept soul, burst into song?

Heart of what slave poured out such melody
As "Steal away to Jesus"? On its strains
His spirit must have nightly floated free,
Though still about his hands he felt his chains.
Who heard great "Jordan roll"? Whose starward eye
Saw chariot "swing low"? And who was he
That breathed that comforting, melodic sigh,
"Nobody knows de trouble I see"?

What merely living clod, what captive thing,
Could up toward God through all its darkness grope,
And find within its deadened heart to sing
These songs of sorrow, love and faith, and hope?
How did it catch that subtle undertone,
That note in music heard not with the ears?
How sound the elusive reed so seldom blown,
Which stirs the soul or melts the heart to tears.

78

Not that great German master in his dream
Of harmonies that thundered amongst the stars
At the creation, ever heard a theme
Nobler than "Go down, Moses." Mark its bars
How like a mighty trumpet-call they stir
The blood. Such are the notes that men have sung
Going to valorous deeds; such tones there were
That helped make history when Time was young.

There is a wide, wide wonder in it all,
That from degraded rest and servile toil
The fiery spirit of the seer should call
These simple children of the sun and soil.
O black slave singers, gone, forgot, unfamed,
You—you alone, of all the long, long line
Of those who've sung untaught, unknown, unnamed,
Have stretched out upward, seeking the divine.

You sang not deeds of heroes or of kings;
No chant of bloody war, no exulting paean
No arms-won triumphs; but your humble strings
You touched in chord with music empyrean.
You sang far better than you knew; the songs
That for your listeners' hungry hearts sufficed
Still live—but more than this to you belongs:
You sang a race from wood and stone to Christ.

William Stanley Braithwaite
(1878–1962)

DEL CASCAR

DEL CASCAR, Del Cascar
Stood upon a flaming star,
Stood and let his feet hang down
Till in China the toes turned brown.

And he reached his fingers over
The rim of the sea, like sails from Dover,
And caught a Mandarin at prayer,
And tickled his nose in Orion's hair.

The sun went down through crimson bars,
And left his blind face battered with stars—
But the brown toes in China kept
Hot the tears Del Cascar wept.

SCINTILLA

I KISSED a kiss in youth
    Upon a dead man's brow;
And that was long ago,—
    And I'm a grown man now.

It's lain there in the dust,
    Thirty years and more;—
My lips that set a light
    At a dead man's door.

RHAPSODY

I am glad daylong for the gift of song,
For time and change and sorrow;
For the sunset wings and the world-end things
Which hang on the edge of tomorrow.
I am glad for my heart whose gates apart
Are the entrance-place of wonders,
Where dreams come from the rush and din
Like sheep from the rains and thunders.

Angelina Weld Grimké
(1880—1958)

GRASS FINGERS

Touch me, touch me,
Little cool grass fingers,
Elusive, delicate grass fingers.
With your shy brushings,
Touch my face—
My naked arms—
My thighs—
My feet.
Is there nothing that is kind?
You need not fear me.
Soon I shall be too far beneath you,
For you to reach me, even,
With your tiny, timorous toes.

A MONA LISA

1.

I should like to creep
Through the long brown grasses
    That are your lashes;

I should like to poise
    On the very brink
Of the leaf-brown pools
    That are your shadowed eyes;
I should like to cleave
    Without sound,
Their glimmering waters,
    Their unrippled waters,

I should like to sink down
    And down
       And down. . . .
          And deeply drown.

2.

Would I be more than a bubble breaking?
    Or an ever-widening circle
    Ceasing at the marge?
Would my white bones
    Be the only white bones
Wavering back and forth, back and forth
    In their depths?

THE BLACK FINGER

I have just seen a most beautiful thing
    Slim and still,
    Against a gold, gold sky,
    A straight black cypress,
    Sensitive,
    Exquisite,
    A black finger
    Pointing upwards.
Why, beautiful still finger, are you black?
And why are you pointing upwards?

Anne Spencer
(1882—1975)

AT THE CARNIVAL

Gay little Girl-of-the-Diving-Tank,
I desire a name for you,
Nice, as a right glove fits;
For you—who amid the malodorous
Mechanics of this unlovely thing,
Are darling of spirit and form.
I know you—a glance, and what you are
Sits-by-the-fire in my heart.
My Limousine-Lady knows you, or
Why does the slant-envy of her eyes mark
Your straight air and radiant inclusive smile?
Guilt pins a fig-leaf; Innocence is its own adorning.
The bull-necked man knows you—this first time
His itching flesh sees form divine and vibrant health,
And thinks not of his avocation.
I came incuriously—
Set on no diversion save that my mind
Might safely nurse its brood of misdeeds
In the presence of a blind crowd.
The color of life was gray.
Everywhere the setting seemed right
For my mood!

Here the sausage and garlic booth
Sent unholy incense skyward;
There a quivering female-thing
Gestured assignations, and lied
To call it dancing;
There, too, were games of chance
With chances for none;
But oh! the Girl-of-the-Tank, at last!

84

Gleaming Girl, how intimately pure and free
The gaze you send the crowd,
As though you know the dearth of beauty
In its sordid life.
We need you—my Limousine-Lady,
The bull-necked man, and I.
Seeing you here brave and water-clean,
Leaven for the heavy ones of earth,
I am swift to feel that what makes
The plodder glad is good; and
Whatever is good is God.
The wonder is that you are here;
I have seen the queer in queer places,
But never before a heaven-fed
Naiad of the Carnival-Tank!
Little Diver, Destiny for you,
Like as for me, is shod in silence;
Years may seep into your soul
The bacilli of the usual and the expedient;
I implore Neptune to claim his child to-day!

LETTER TO MY SISTER

It is dangerous for a woman to defy the gods;
To taunt them with the tongue's thin tip,
Or strut in the weakness of mere humanity,
Or draw a line daring them to cross;
The gods own the searing lightning,
The drowning waters, tormenting fears
And anger of red sins.

Oh, but worse still if you mince timidly—
Dodge this way or that, or kneel or pray,
Be kind, or sweat agony drops
Or lay your quick body over your feeble young;
If you have beauty or none, if celibate
Or vowed—the gods are Juggernaut,
Passing over . . . over . . .

This you may do:
Lock your heart, then, quietly,
And lest they peer within,

85

Light no lamp when dark comes down
Raise no shade for sun;
Breathless must your breath come through
If you'd die and dare deny
The gods their god-like fun.

Georgia Douglas Johnson
(1886—1966)

THE HEART OF A WOMAN

The heart of a woman goes forth with the dawn,
As a lone bird, soft winging, so restlessly on,
Afar o'er life's turrets and vales does it roam
In the wake of those echoes the heart calls home.

The heart of a woman falls back with the night,
And enters some alien cage in its plight,
And tries to forget it has dreamed of the stars
While it breaks, breaks, breaks on the sheltering bars.

I WANT TO DIE WHILE YOU LOVE ME

I want to die while you love me,
 While yet you hold me fair,
While laughter lies upon my lips
 And lights are in my hair.

I want to die while you love me,
 And bear to that still bed,
Your kisses turbulent, unspent
 To warm me when I'm dead.

I want to die while you love me
 Oh, who would care to live
Till love has nothing more to ask
 And nothing more to give!

I want to die while you love me
 And never, never see
The glory of this perfect day
 Grow dim or cease to be.

ESCAPE

Shadows, shadows,
Hug me round
So that I shall not be found
By sorrow:
She pursues me
Everywhere,
I can't lose her
Anywhere.

Fold me in your black
Abyss,
She will never look
In this,—
Shadows, shadows,
Hug me round
In your solitude
Profound.

THE RIDDLE

White men's children spread over the earth—
A rainbow suspending the drawn swords of birth,
Uniting and blending the races in one
The world man—cosmopolite—everyman's son!

He channels the stream of the red blood and blue,
Behold him! A Triton—the peer of the two;
Unriddle this riddle of "outside in"
White men's children in black men's skin.

Fenton Johnson
(1888—1958)

THE BANJO PLAYER

There is music in me, the music of a peasant people.
I wander through the levee, picking my banjo and singing my
    songs of the cabin and the field. At the Last Chance Saloon
    I am as welcome as the violets in March;
    there is always food and drink for me there, and the dimes
    of those who love honest music. Behind the railroad tracks
    the little children clap their hands and love me as they love
    Kris Kringle.
But I fear that I am a failure.
    Last night a woman called me a troubadour.
    What is a troubadour?

TIRED

I am tired of work; I am tired of building up somebody else's
    civilization.
Let us take a rest, M'Lissy Jane.
I will go down to the Last Chance Saloon, drink a gallon or two
    of gin, shoot a game or two of dice and sleep the rest of
    the night on one of Mike's barrels.
You will let the old shanty go to rot, the white people's clothes
    turn to dust, and the Calvary Baptist Church sink to the
    bottomless pit.
You will spend your days forgetting you married me and your
    nights hunting the warm gin Mike serves the ladies in the
    rear of the Last Chance Saloon.
Throw the children into the river; civilization has given us too
    many. It is better to die than to grow up and find that you
    are colored.

Pluck the stars out of the heavens. The stars mark our destiny.
   The stars marked my destiny.
I am tired of civilization.

WHO IS THAT A-WALKING IN THE CORN?

Who is that a-walking in the corn?
I have looked to East and looked to West
But nowhere could I find Him who walks
   Master's cornfield in the morning.

Who is that a-walking in the corn?
Is it Joshua, the son of Nun?—
Or King David come to fight the giant
   Near the cornfield in the morning?

Who is that a-walking in the corn?
Is it Peter jangling Heaven's keys?—
Or old Gabriel come to blow his horn
   Near the cornfield in the morning?

Who is that a-walking in the corn?
I have looked to East and looked to West
But nowhere could I find Him who walks
   Master's cornfield in the morning.

Claude McKay
(1889–1948)

HARLEM SHADOWS

I hear the halting footsteps of a lass
    In Negro Harlem when the night lets fall
Its veil. I see the shapes of girls who pass
    To bend and barter at desire's call.
Ah, little dark girls who in slippered feet
Go prowling through the night from street to street!

Through the long night until the silver break
    Of day the little gray feet know no rest;
Through the lone night until the last snow-flake
        Has dropped from heaven upon the earth's
        white breast,
The dusky, half-clad girls of tired feet
Are trudging, thinly shod, from street to street.

Ah, stern harsh world, that in the wretched way
    Of poverty, dishonor and disgrace,
Has pushed the timid little feet of clay,
    The sacred brown feet of my fallen race!
Ah, heart of me, the weary, weary feet
In Harlem wandering from street to street.

IF WE MUST DIE

If we must die, let it not be like hogs
Hunted and penned in an inglorious spot,
While round us bark the mad and hungry dogs,
Making their mock at our accursed lot.
If we must die, O let us nobly die,
So that our precious blood may not be shed

In vain; then even the monsters we defy
Shall be constrained to honor us though dead!
O kinsmen! we must meet the common foe!
Though far outnumbered let us show us brave,
And for their thousand blows deal one deathblow!
What though before us lies the open grave?
Like men we'll face the murderous, cowardly pack,
Pressed to the wall, dying, but fighting back!

TIGER

The white man is a tiger at my throat,
Drinking my blood as my life ebbs away,
And muttering that his terrible striped coat
Is Freedom's and portends the Light of Day.
Oh white man, you may suck up all my blood
And throw my carcass into potter's field,
But never will I say with you that mud
Is bread for Negroes! Never will I yield.

Europe and Africa and Asia wait
The touted New Deal of the New World's hand!
New systems will be built on race and hate,
The Eagle and the Dollar will command.
Oh Lord! My body, and my heart too, break—
The tiger in his strength his thirst must slake!

AMERICA

Although she feeds me bread of bitterness,
And sinks into my throat her tiger's tooth,
Stealing my breath of life, I will confess
I love this cultured hell that tests my youth!
Her vigor flows like tides into my blood,
Giving me strength erect against her hate.
Her bigness sweeps my being like a flood.
Yet as a rebel fronts a king in state,
I stand within her walls with not a shred
Of terror, malice, not a word of jeer.
Darkly I gaze into the days ahead,

And see her might and granite wonders there,
Beneath the touch of Time's unerring hand,
Like priceless treasures sinking in the sand.

THE WHITE HOUSE

Your door is shut against my tightened face,
And I am sharp as steel with discontent;
But I possess the courage and the grace
To bear my anger proudly and unbent.
The pavement slabs burn loose beneath my feet,
A chafing savage, down the decent street;
And passion rends my vitals as I pass,
Where boldly shines your shuttered door of glass.
Oh, I must search for wisdom every hour,
Deep in my wrathful bosom sore and raw,
And find in it the superhuman power
To hold me to the letter of your law!
Oh, I must keep my heart inviolate
Against the potent poison of your hate.

Jean Toomer
(1894–1967)

SONG OF THE SON

Pour O pour that parting soul in song,
O pour it in the sawdust glow of night,
Into the velvet pine-smoke air tonight,
And let the valley carry it along.
And let the valley carry it along.

O land and soil, red soil and sweet-gum tree,
So scant of grass, so profligate of pines,
Now just before an epoch's sun declines
Thy son, in time, I have returned to thee.
Thy son, I have in time returned to thee.

In time, for though the sun is setting on
A song-lit race of slaves, it has not set;
Though late, O soil, it is not too late yet
To catch thy plaintive soul, leaving, soon gone,
Leaving, to catch thy plaintive soul soon gone.

O Negro slaves, dark purple ripened plums,
Squeezed, and bursting in the pine-wood air,
Passing, before they stripped the old tree bare
One plum was saved for me, one seed becomes

An everlasting song, a singing tree,
Caroling softly souls of slavery,
What they were, and what they are to me,
Caroling softly souls of slavery.

GEORGIA DUSK

The sky, lazily disdaining to pursue
   The setting sun, too indolent to hold
   A lengthened tournament for flashing gold,
Passively darkens for night's barbeque,

A feast of moon and men and barking hounds.
   An orgy for some genius of the South
   With blood-hot eyes and cane-lipped scented mouth,
Surprised in making folk-songs from soul sounds.

The sawmill blows its whistle, buzz-saws stop,
   And silence breaks the bud of knoll and hill,
   Soft settling pollen where plowed lands fulfill
Their early promise of a bumper crop.

Smoke from the pyramidal sawdust pile
   Curls up, blue ghosts of trees, tarrying low
   Where only chips and stumps are left to show
The solid proof of former domicile.

Meanwhile, the men, with vestiges of pomp,
   Race memories of king and caravan,
   High-priests, an ostrich, and a juju-man,
Go singing through the footpaths of the swamp.

Their voices rise . . the pine trees are guitars,
   Strumming, pine-needles fall like sheets of rain . .
   Their voices rise . . the chorus of the cane
Is caroling a vesper to the stars . .

O singers, resinous and soft your songs
   Above the sacred whisper of the pines,
   Give virgin lips to cornfield concubines,
Bring dreams of Christ to dusky cane-lipped throngs.

IMPRINT FOR RIO GRANDE

The Indians beat drums, sing and dance to assert
   themselves as human beings (or to surrender
   themselves?) in the vast universe that comes to earth in
   New Mexico.

Perhaps, too, they have quiet rituals which swing the body-mind to acquiescence, that the faculties the outer world knows nothing of, may gain the wakefulness which relates a man to higher worlds.

When I leave places that men call great and return to the State of which I am curiously native, I beat thoughts against the drum of mind, sing music that never leaves my instruments, and dance without gestures to assert myself (or to surrender myself?) in the same universe that comes to the same earth.

There are some things so basic that they are seldom mentioned between men. Yet they come out now and again, and it is one of these I honestly inscribe upon that ether, the memory of earth, above the Rio Grande, from Taos and above Taos, to Santa Fe and below Santa Fe.

There is an Exile in me, and sometimes I am him, and when I am, the mountains of the Southwest, each cliff and peak, all ridges and even the flat lands arise from an ancient deluge that I may be engulfed again, or crushed, or driven out.

You there who have seen me but did not realize the Exile, who have seen this body of a man and a human mask walking plazas in Taos and Santa Fe and the main street of Española, how could you know my feeling that the earth and all her Nature, that heaven and all its gods were gunning for cosmic outlaws, you and I being of the driven band?

Adobe walls are friendly to the touch because hands put them there, but I recall times when I was my exile in New Mexico, when even within these walls, and friends around, and piñon burning in the fireplace, the walls exposed me to at-one-ment or extinction.

And there is a Being in me. Sometimes, though rarely, I am him, and when I am, there is such marvel in the Rio Grande, such ecstasy of inner sun to outer sun, or inner breath to the blazing winds, that I and everyone seem re-born upon that ark which still rides high, straight above the mesas of all sunken lands.

I remember one twilight I walked into Santa Fe, and you were walking with me, but did not know it—or did you? You, the beings of many people who have no names to distinguish you as on plazas. We moved

96

together, descending as from a hill, yet ascending in
spiral, and came upon the essence of piñon as it arose
from the houses into an air so marvelous that even
Being took it in and was enhanced.

So I know that the struggle of Being and Exile, the
central contest which no man resolves until he gives
utter allegiance to the radiant, can be won and
celebrated by mended instruments, as that of us which
belongs to it rises, and blends with the vast universe
that comes to earth in New Mexico.

Joseph Seamon Cotter, Jr.
(1895—1919)

THE BAND OF GIDEON

The band of Gideon roam the sky,
The howling wind is their war-cry,
The thunder's roll is their trump's peal,
And the lightning's flash their vengeful steel.
  Each black cloud
  Is a fiery steed.
  And they cry aloud
  With each strong deed,
"The sword of the Lord and Gideon."

And men below rear temples high
And mock their God with reasons why,
And live in arrogance, sin and shame,
And rape their souls for the world's good name.
  Each black cloud
  Is a fiery steed.
  And they cry aloud
  With each strong deed,
"The sword of the Lord and Gideon."

The band of Gideon roam the sky
And view the earth with baleful eye,
In holy wrath they scourge the land
With earth-quake, storm and burning brand.
  Each black cloud
  Is a fiery steed.
  And they cry aloud
  With each strong deed,
"The sword of the Lord and Gideon."

The lightnings flash and the thunders roll,
And "Lord have mercy on my soul,"
Cry men as they fall on the stricken sod,
In agony searching for their God.

      Each black cloud
      Is a fiery steed.
      And they cry aloud
      With each strong deed,
"The sword of the Lord and Gideon."

And men repent and then forget
That heavenly wrath they ever met.
The band of Gideon yet will come
And strike their tongues of blasphemy

      Each black cloud
      Is a fiery steed.
      And they cry aloud
      With each strong deed,
"The sword of the Lord and Gideon."

IS IT BECAUSE I AM BLACK?

Why do men smile when I speak,
And call my speech
The whimperings of a babe
That cries but knows not what it wants?
Is it because I am black?

Why do men sneer when I arise
And stand in their councils,
And look them eye to eye,
And speak their tongue?
Is it because I am black?

RAIN MUSIC

On the dusty earth-drum
   Beats the falling rain;
Now a whispered murmur,
   Now a louder strain.

Slender, silvery drumsticks,
   On an ancient drum,
Beat the mellow music
   Bidding life to come.

Chords of earth awakened,
   Notes of greening spring,
Rise and fall triumphant
   Over every thing.

Slender, silvery drumsticks
   Beat the long tatoo—
God the Great Musician
   Calling life anew.

Melvin B. Tolson
(1898–1966)

HARLEM

Diamond Canady
Was stabbed in bed by Little Eva Winn.
Deacon Phineas Bloom
Confessed his adultery on his deathbed.

Dusky Bards,
Heirs of eons of Comedy and Tragedy,
Pass along the streets and alleys of Harlem
Singing ballads of the Dark World:

> *When a man has lost his taste fer you,*
> *Jest leave dat man alone.*
> *Says I . . . a dawg won't eat a bone*
> *If he don't want de bone.*

> *I likes de Eyetalian . . . I likes de Jew . . .*
> *I likes de Chinaman, but I don't like you.*

> *Happy days are here again.*
> *Dat's sho' one great big lie.*
> *Ain't had a beefsteak in so long*
> *My belly wants to cry.*

Preacher called to bless my home
An' keep it free from strife.
Preacher called to bless my home
An' keep it free from strife.
Now I's got a peaceful home
An' de preacher's got my wife.

White cops sho' will beat you up, littlest thing you do.
Black cops make Black Boy feel proud, but dey'll beat you too!

> *Rather be a hobo, Lawd,*
> *Wid a stinkin' breath*
> *Dan live in de Big House*
> *Workin' folks to death.*

My two-timin' Mama says to me:
Daddy, did I let you down?
Gonna break dat woman's goddamn neck
Befo' I leaves dis town.

> *Black Boy, sing an' clown an' dance,*
> *Strutt yo' low-down nigger stuff.*
> *White Folks sho' will tip you big*
> *If you flatters 'em enough.*

Frederick Judson
Made cigars that pleased General Ulysses Grant.
Soldier Boy
Was decorated by Pancho Villa.
Poker Face Duncan
Killed his rival with a billiard ball.

Vergil Ragsdale,
Dishwasher poet at Mr. Maranto's café,
Who wrote the epic *An African Tragedy*
Burned as trash by Big Sadie's husband . . .
Vergil Ragsdale, the consumptive,
Gulped down a glass of molten gin,
Leaned tipsily against the bar in Duke Huggins's Subway,
Scanned with fever-bright eyes
The horizon of uncouth black faces,
And declaimed in funereal cadences:

"Harlem, O Harlem,
I shall not see the quiet Dawn
When the yellow and brown and black proletarians
Swarm out of stinking dives and fire-trap tenements,
Pour through canyon-streets,
Climb Strivers' Row and Sugar Hill,
Erase the liveried flunkies,
And belly laugh in the rich apartments of the Big Niggers.

102

"I shall not see the unwashed mob
Hoofing the Lindy Hop in Madame Alpha Devine's drawing
    room,
Guzzling champagne in Banker Calverton's library,
Bouncing their unperfumed butts upon Miss Briffault's
    silken beds,
Gorging the roast chicken and eclairs in Editor Speare's
    kitchen.

"Harlem, O Harlem,
City of the Big Niggers,
Graveyard of the Dark Masses,
Soapbox of the Red Apocalypse . . .
I shall be forgotten like you
Beneath the Debris of Oblivion."

Radicals, prizefighters, actors and deacons,
Beggars, politicians, professors and redcaps,
Bulldikers, Babbitts, racketeers and jig-chasers,
Harlots, crapshooter, workers and pink-chasers,
Artists, dicties, Pullman porters and messiahs . . .
The Curator has hung the likenesses of all
In *A Gallery of Harlem Portraits*.

UNCLE RUFUS

The Harlem Advocate fell between his legs.
The story was incredible!
Taking off his glasses,
Uncle Rufus rubbed the lenses and thought . . . thought.

Yes, his son had always been a prodigal son,
Drinking home brew and chasing sin-loving women
And staying away from church at revival times.

Then he had gone to Selma, Alabama,
With that Blackwood woman
Who had lived with a dozen different sweet men.

The Harlem Advocate said
Eddie had cut up the Blackwood woman in a dance hall;

And, when the jury had found him guilty,
He'd struck the prosecuting attorney on the jaw;
And it had taken the jurors and a deputy sheriff
To pin him to the floor and handcuff him.

Uncle Rufus bowed his head and groaned.
He remembered now that people used to say
Eddie was a little off . . . a little off.

"De boy musta been crazy," Uncle Rufus mused aloud.
"Yes, he musta been crazy . . .
Him hittin' a white lawyah
In a white man's courthouse,
Befo' a white jedge an' a white jury
Down in Alabama."

MADAME ALPHA DEVINE

Madame Alpha Devine she made a million
Straight'nin' out de kinks in woolly hair.
If I had a lotion to turn Black Folks white,
I'd be a billionaire!

Alpha Devine had a vision
Over a steaming washtub on Captain Webb's plantation
At Bitter Ridge, Arkansas . . .
A vision of the Negro Woman Beautiful.

In the Jim Crow cemetery near the Bedrock Baptist Church
She prayed on her mother's sunken grave at midnight;
And a white-robed seraph appeared,
Giving her the formula for the Devine Hair Grower
And commanding her to go into a far city.

The Madame Alpha Devine Manufacturing Company, Inc.,
Has made a fortune for its owner,
Whose business genius established
The Alpha Devine Academy of Beauty Culture,
Which trains colored beauticians.

Black gals use de straight'nin' iron.
White gals use de curlin' rod.

Why cain't folks be satisfied
Wid'de handiwork of God?

Madame Alpha Devine goes about the country
In her sumptuous limousine,
Lecturing to worshipping dark ladies.

Madame Alpha Devine tells them
That God has not always blessed her with a mansion on the
    Hudson,
That she came from the poverty-stricken masses,
That she knows the grime and drudgery of their lives,
That God sent her forth with the Devine Hair Grower
To make kinky hair straight
And short hair luxuriant . . .
The crowning glory of the Negro Woman Beautiful!

May Miller
(1899—1995)

CALVARY WAY

How did you feel, Mary,
Womb heavy with Christ Child,
Tasting the dust of uncertain journey?
Were you afraid?
When, winding the swaddling clothes,
You laid Him in the manger,
Were you afraid?
Could you trace nail holes
Under His curling fingers,
Thorn pricks on the forehead?
Could you trace them?

I should bear a warm brown baby,
A new dark world of wonder;
But I fear the nails that pierce the spirit,
The unseen crosses.
How did you feel, Mary,
On the road beyond the star-lit manger,
Up the hill to crucifixion?
Were you afraid?

THE WRONG SIDE OF THE MORNING

We wake on the wrong side of the morning
From a nightmare of wings
And mushrooms of huge death.
Weep for us whose lives are caged
In concrete, for our straw images
Seen through glass walls
Are you and you tomorrow.

Weep for yourselves then
Dismayed by that vouchsafed you.
Cry down the gods of science
Dedicated to eternity for walls
While denying youth its prophecy.

They are the idle rosy with words
That look where once a light burned
And reiterate tomorrow, tomorrow;
The dead will rise again;
Some appointed star may rekindle
The ash heap and the broken.
They prate to lull one another
And deceive you . . . Look.
Their eyes are glass eyes of teddy bears;
Their voices those of last year's snow men.

We know, we know
Though we speak in no tongue of fire
And beg no absolution,
Yet warn the stranger to this hour
Beyond a time of anger.
Weep a misshapen future
And the antic place where heights stood
Now so terribly crashed and fragmented.
Here will the hoped-for progeny range
Seeking a green sill
Where unsmiling they only scuff
Dead leaves before splintered doors.

THE SCREAM

I am a woman controlled,
Remember this; I never scream,
Yet I stood a form apart
Watching my other frenzied self
Beaten by words and wounds
Make in silence a mighty scream—
A scream that the wind took up
And thrust through the bars of night
Beyond all reason's final rim.

Out where the sea's last murmur dies
And the gull's cry has no sound,
Out where city voices fade,
Stilled in a lyric sleep
Where silence is its own design,
My scream hovered a ghost denied
Wanting the shape of lips.

WHERE IS THE GUILT

At last I am acquitted
My body heavy with shame.
I dip myself in the dark river,
Wash again, and once more,
What is the mass that floats from me
Down the dark river?

I am not guilty!
I am not guilty!
I tell the white birds
Flying low over my head.
(But they're busy with each other.)
Lovers, accept me, you lovers!
I call to the pair
Swept by in a canoe's rhythm.
(No answer, no matter,
I'll never see them again.)

I return to the waters
Trampling the hollow sedges
That do not bother to answer
Even persistent winds.
Only the river responds
Promising no unholy footprint.

Marcus B. Christian
(1900—1976)

SELASSIE AT GENEVA

They could have stayed the iron hand of might
And fought for right down to the earth's last man,
But louder voices brayed into the night,
So, jackals ended what the League began.
Now suave-voiced diplomats drone on and on;
Geneva's air is rife with fear and hate,
While at the council table fights alone
The fallen ruler of a member State.
Pile lies upon wrongs, ring the curtain down
Upon the closing scene of this last act;
The King of Kings now yields his ancient crown
To those who signed the Non-Aggression Pact,
As weaker nations vanish, one by one . . .
Blow, bugles! Armageddon has begun!

"GO DOWN, MOSES!"
(Berlin, 1938)

In great Berlin, each weary night on night,
Go frightened souls who even fear to sleep,
As racial hatred rears its ugly might,
And terrors in their cloaks of darkness creep.
The while men tramp the streets with hopes all gone,
The Gods of Greed, with lashing whips of hate,
Drive maddened Nordics onward—ever on—
To slay and plunder in the name of "State."

O Moses, who, in mounting fury, killed
Proud Egypt's son who wronged the Israelite,
The spirit of the Pharaohs is not stilled,

For the first-born still dies by day and night;
So go you where crazed Aryan hate holds sway
And smite with flame the Pharaohs of today.

THE CRAFTSMAN

I ply with all the cunning of my art
This little thing, and with consummate care
I fashion it—so that when I depart,
Those who come after me shall find it fair
And beautiful. It must be free of flaws—
Pointing no laborings of weary hands;
And there must be no flouting of the laws
Of beauty—as the artist understands.
Through passion, yearnings infinite—yet dumb—
I lift you from the depths of my own mind
And gild you with my soul's white heat to plumb
The souls of future men. I leave behind
This thing that in return this solace gives:
"He who creates true beauty ever lives."

Sterling A. Brown
(1901–1989)

SOUTHERN ROAD

Swing dat hammer—hunh—
Steady, bo';
Swing dat hammer—hunh—
Steady, bo';
Ain't no rush, bebby,
Long ways to go.

Burner tore his—hunh—
Black heart away;
Burner tore his—hunh—
Black heart away;
Got me life, bebby,
An' a day.

Gal's on Fifth Street—hunh—
Son done gone;
Gal's on Fifth Street—hunh—
Son done gone;
Wife's in de ward, bebby,
Babe's not bo'n.

My ole man died—hunh—
Cussin' me;
My ole man died—hunh—
Cussin' me;
Ole lady rocks, bebby,
Huh misery.

Doubleshackled—hunh—
Guard behin';
Doubleshackled—hunh—

Guard behin';
Ball an' chain, bebby,
On my min'.

White man tells me—hunh—
Damn yo' soul;
White man tells me—hunh—
Damn yo' soul;
Got no need, bebby,
To be tole.

Chain gang nevah—hunh—
Let me go;
Chain gang nevah—hunh—
Let me go;
Po' los' boy, bebby,
Evahmo'. . . .

MA RAINEY

I

When Ma Rainey
Comes to town,
Folks from anyplace
Miles aroun',
From Cape Girardeau,
Poplar Bluff,
Flocks in to hear
Ma do her stuff;
Comes flivverin' in,
Or ridin' mules,
Or packed in trains,
Picknickin' fools. . . .
That's what it's like,
Fo' miles on down,
To New Orleans delta
An' Mobile town,
When Ma hits
Anywheres aroun'.

II

Dey comes to hear Ma Rainey from de little river settlements,
From blackbottom cornrows and from lumber camps;
Dey stumble in de hall, jes a-laughin' an' a-cacklin',
Cheerin' lak roarin' water, lak wind in river swamps.

An' some jokers keeps deir laughs a-goin' in de crowded
    aisles,
An' some folks sits dere waitin' wid deir aches an' miseries,
Till Ma comes out before dem, a-smilin' gold-toofed smiles
An' Long Boy ripples minors on de black an' yellow keys.

III

O Ma Rainey,
Sing yo' song;
Now you's back
Whah you belong,
Git way inside us,
Keep us strong. . . .

O Ma Rainey,
Li'l an' low;
Sing us 'bout de hard luck
Roun' our do';
Sing us 'bout de lonesome road
We mus' go. . . .

IV

I talked to a fellow, an' the fellow say,
"She jes' catch hold of us, somekindaway.
She sang Backwater Blues one day:

> *'It rained fo' days an' de skies was dark as night,*
> *Trouble taken place in de lowlands at night.*

> *'Thundered an' lightened an' the storm begin to roll*
> *Thousan's of people ain't got no place to go.*

> *'Den I went an' stood upon some high ol' lonesome hill,*
> *An' looked down on the place where I used to live.'*

113

An' den de folks, dey natchally bowed dey heads an' cried,
Bowed dey heavy heads, shet dey moufs up tight an' cried,
An' Ma lef' de stage, an' followed some de folks outside."

Dere wasn't much more de fellow say:
She jes' gits hold of us dataway.

STRONG MEN

The young men keep coming on
The strong men keep coming on.
             SANDBURG

They dragged you from homeland,
They chained you in coffles,
They huddled you spoon-fashion in filthy hatches,
They sold you to give a few gentlemen ease.

They broke you in like oxen,
They scourged you,
They branded you,
They made your women breeders,
They swelled your numbers with bastards. . . .
They taught you the religion they disgraced.

You sang:
    Keep a-inchin' along
    Lak a po' inch worm. . . .

You sang:
    Bye and bye
    I'm gonna lay down dis heaby load. . . .

You sang:
    Walk togedder, chillen,
    Dontcha git weary. . . .
      The strong men keep a-comin' on
      The strong men git stronger.

They point with pride to the roads you built for them,
They ride in comfort over the rails you laid for them.

They put hammers in your hands
And said—Drive so much before sundown.

You sang:
    Ain't ho hammah
    In dis lan',
    Strikes lak mine, bebby,
    Strikes lak mine.

They cooped you in their kitchens,
They penned you in their factories,
They gave you the jobs that they were too good for,
They tried to guarantee happiness to themselves
By shunting dirt and misery to you.

You sang:
    Me an' muh baby gonna shine, shine
    Me an' muh baby gonna shine.
        The strong men keep a-comin' on
        The strong men git stronger. . . .

They bought off some of your leaders
You stumbled, as blind men will . . .
They coaxed you, unwontedly soft-voiced. . . .
You followed a way.
Then laughed as usual.

They heard the laugh and wondered;
Uncomfortable,
Unadmitting a deeper terror. . . .
        The strong men keep a-comin' on
        Gittin' stronger. . . .

What, from the slums
Where they have hemmed you,
What, from the tiny huts
They could not keep from you—
What reaches them
Making them ill at ease, fearful?
Today they shout prohibition at you
"Thou shalt not this"
"Thou shalt not that"
"Reserved for whites only"
You laugh.

One thing they cannot prohibit—
>
> The strong men . . . coming on
> The strong men gittin' stronger.
> Strong men. . . .
> Stronger. . . .

TRANSFER

I

It must have been that the fellow was tongue-tied,
Or absent-minded, or daft with the heat,
But howsoeverbeit he didn't say sir,
So they took and bounced him out on the street.

And then the motorman brained him with his crank,
And the conductor clubbed him with his gun,
But before they could place the nickels on his eyes,
The cops rushed up to see justice done.

The city-court judge was merciful to him:
Gave him just four years and suspended his fine,
For bruising white knuckles, inciting to riot,
And holding up traffic on the Peachtree line.

When the boy came to, he was still right skittish,
They figured they had got him rid of his harm,
By beating his head, and displacing his jawbone,
So they made him a trusty on the prison-farm.

II

But one day a red sun beat on the red hills
And he was in the pasture, haltering a mare,
And something went snap in his trusty old head
And he started a-riding away from there.

When he got to Atlanta, the folks took him in,
And fed him and clothed him, and hid him away;
And let him out only when the cops disappear
From the streets of Darktown at the dusk of day:

116

Then he goes to the car-stop and takes his stand,
And some call him daffy, and some call him smart,
But all have heard the one text he's been preaching,
And some have the whole sermon down by heart:

"I stayed in my place, and my place stayed wid me,
Took what was dished, said I liked it fine:
Figgered they would see that I warn't no trouble,
Figgered this must be the onliest line.

"But this is the wrong line we been ridin',
This route doan git us where we got to go.
Got to git transferred to a new direction.
We can stand so much, then doan stan no mo'."

CROSSING

This is not Jordan River
There lies not Canaan
There is still
One more wide river to cross.

This is the Mississippi
And the stars tell us only
That this is not the road.

We do not know
If any have reached that Canaan
We have received no word.

Behind us the belling pack
Beyond them the hunters
Before us the dismal swamp.

We do not know. . . .

We have exchanged Louisiana for Mississippi
Merely
Georgia for Florida
Carolina for Tennessee.

We have passed, repassed
So many rivers

117

Okmulgee, Chattahoochee,
St. Mary's, Mississippi,
Alabama, Tennessee,
Mississippi.

We have leapt
From swamp land
Into marshes
We have won through
To bloodred clay
To gravel and rock
To the baked lands
To the scorched barrens.

And we grow footsore
And muscle weary
Our faces grow sullen
And our hearts numb

We do not know. . . .

We know only
That there lies not Canaan
That this is no River Jordan.

Still are we motherless children
Still are we dragging travelers
Alone, and a long ways from home.

Still with the hard earth for our folding bed
Still with our head pillowed upon a rock

And still
With one more river,
Oh, one wide river to cross.

Clarissa Scott Delany
(1901–1927)

THE MASK

So detached and cool she is
No motion e'er betrays
The secret life within her soul,
The anguish of her days.

She seems to look upon the world
With cold ironic eyes,
To spurn emotion's fevered sway,
To scoff at tears and sighs.

But once a woman with a child
Passed by her on the street,
And once she heard from casual lips
A man's name, bitter-sweet.

Such baffled yearning in her eyes,
Such pain upon her face!
I turned aside until the mask
Was slipped once more in place.

INTERIM

The night was made for rest and sleep,
For winds that softly sigh;
It was not made for grief and tears;
So then why do I cry?

The wind that blows through leafy trees
Is soft and warm and sweet;

For me the night is a gracious cloak
To hide my soul's defeat.

Just one dark hour of shaken depths,
Of bitter black despair—
Another day will find me brave,
And not afraid to dare.

Langston Hughes
(1902–1967)

THE NEGRO SPEAKS OF RIVERS

I've known rivers:
I've known rivers ancient as the world and older than the
flow of human blood in human veins.

My soul has grown deep like the rivers.

I bathed in the Euphrates when dawns were young.
I built my hut near the Congo and it lulled me to sleep.

I looked upon the Nile and raised the pyramids above it.
I heard the singing of the Mississippi when Abe Lincoln
went down to New Orleans, and I've seen its muddy
bosom turn all golden in the sunset.

I've known rivers:
Ancient, dusky rivers.

My soul has grown deep like the rivers.

MOTHER TO SON

Well, son, I'll tell you:
Life for me ain't been no crystal stair.
It's had tacks in it,
And splinters,
And boards torn up,
And places with no carpet on the floor—
Bare.
But all the time
I'se been a-climbin' on,

And reachin' landin's,
And turnin' corners,
And sometimes goin' in the dark
Where there ain't been no light.
So boy, don't you turn back.
Don't you set down on the steps
'Cause you finds it's kinder hard
Don't you fall now—
For I'se still goin', honey,
I'se still climbin',
And life for me ain't been no crystal stair.

THEME FOR ENGLISH B

The instructor said,

> *Go home and write*
> *a page tonight.*
> *And let that page come out of you—*
> *Then, it will be true.*

I wonder if it's that simple?
I am twenty-two, colored, born in Winston-Salem.
I went to school there, then Durham, then here
to this college on the hill above Harlem.
I am the only colored student in my class.
The steps from the hill lead down into Harlem,
through a park, then I cross St. Nicholas,
Eighth Avenue, Seventh, and I come to the Y,
the Harlem Branch Y, where I take the elevator
up to my room, sit down, and write this page:

It's not easy to know what is true for you or me
at twenty-two, my age. But I guess I'm what
I feel and see and hear, Harlem, I hear you:
hear you, hear me—we two—you, me, talk on this page.
(I hear New York, too.) Me—who?

Well, I like to eat, sleep, drink, and be in love.
I like to work, read, learn, and understand life.
I like a pipe for a Christmas present,
or records—Bessie, bop, or Bach.

I guess being colored doesn't make me *not* like
the same things other folks like who are other races.
So will my page be colored that I write?
Being me, it will not be white.
But it will be
a part of you, instructor.
You are white—
yet a part of me, as I am a part of you.
That's American.
Sometimes perhaps you don't want to be a part of me.
Nor do I often want to be a part of you.
But we are, that's true!
As I learn from you,
I guess you learn from me—
although you're older—and white—
and somewhat more free.

This is my page for English B.

Arna Bontemps
(1902—1973)

A BLACK MAN TALKS OF REAPING

I have sown beside all waters in my day.
I planted deep, within my heart the fear
That wind or fowl would take the grain away.
I planted safe against this stark, lean year.

I scattered seed enough to plant the land
In rows from Canada to Mexico
But for my reaping only what the hand
Can hold at once is all that I can show.

Yet what I sowed and what the orchard yields
My brother's sons are gathering stalk and root,
Small wonder then my children glean in fields
They have not sown, and feed on bitter fruit.

NOCTURNE AT BETHESDA

I thought I saw an angel flying low,
I thought I saw the flicker of a wing
Above the mulberry trees; but not again.
Bethesda sleeps. This ancient pool that healed
A host of beared Jews does not awake.

This pool that once the angels troubled does not move
No angel stirs it now, no Saviour comes
With healing in His hands to raise the sick
And bid the lame man leap upon the ground.

The golden days are gone. Why do we wait
So long upon the marble steps, blood

Falling from our open wounds? and why
Do our black faces search the empty sky?
Is there something we have forgotten? some precious thing
We have lost, wandering in strange lands?

There was a day, I remember now,
I beat my breast and cried, "Wash me God,
Wash me with a wave of wind upon
The barley; O quiet One, draw near, draw near!
Walk upon the hills with lovely feet
And in the waterfall stand and speak.

"Dip white hands in the lily pool and mourn
Upon the harps still hanging in the trees
Near Babylon along the river's edge,
But oh, remember me, I pray, before
The summer goes and rose leaves lose their red."

The old terror takes my heart, the fear
Of quiet waters and of faint twilights.
There will be better days when I am gone
And healing pools where I cannot be healed.
Fragrant stars will gleam forever and ever
Above the place where I lie desolate.

Yet I hope, still I long to live.
And if there can be returning after death
I shall come back. But it will not be here;
If you want me you must search for me
Beneath the palms of Africa. Or if

I am not there then you may call to me
Across the shining dunes, perhaps I shall
Be following a desert caravan.

I may pass through centuries of death
With quiet eyes, but I'll remember still
A jungle tree with burning scarlet birds.
There is something I have forgotten, some precious thing.
I shall be seeking ornaments of ivory,
I shall be dying for a jungle fruit.

    You do not hear, Bethesda.
O still green water in a stagnant pool!

Love abandoned you and me alike.
There was a day you held a rich full moon
Upon your heart and listened to the words
Of men now dead and saw the angels fly.
There is a simple story on your face;
Years have wrinkled you. I know, Bethesda!
You are sad. It is the same with me.

GOLGOTHA IS A MOUNTAIN

Golgotha is a mountain, a purple mound
Almost out of sight.
One night they hanged two thieves there,
And another man.
Some women wept heavily that night;
Their tears are flowing still. They have made a river;
Once it covered me.
Then the people went away and left Golgotha
Deserted.
Oh, I've seen many mountains:
Pale purple mountains melting in the evening mists and
blurring on the borders of the sky.

I climbed old Shasta and chilled my hands in its summer
snows.
I rested in the shadow of Popocatepetl and it whispered
to me of daring prowess.
I looked upon the Pyrenees and felt the zest of warm
exotic nights.
I slept at the foot of Fujiyama and dreamed of legend and
of death.
And I've seen other mountains rising from the wistful
moors like the breasts of a slender maiden.
Who knows the mystery of mountains!
Some of them are awful, others are just lonely.

Italy has its Rome and California has San Francisco,
All covered with mountains.
Some think these mountains grew
Like ant hills
Or sand dunes.
That might be so—

I wonder what started them all!
Babylon is a mountain
And so is Nineveh,
With grass growing on them;
Palaces and hanging gardens started them.
I wonder what is under the hills
In Mexico
And Japan!
There are mountains in Africa too.
Treasure is buried there:
Gold and precious stones
And moulded glory.
Lush grass is growing there
Sinking before the wind.
Black men are bowing
Naked in that grass
Digging with their fingers.
I am one of them:
Those mountains should be ours.
It would be great
To touch the pieces of glory with our hands.
These mute unhappy hills,
Bowed down with broken backs,
Speak often one to another:
"A day is as a year," they cry,
"And a thousand years as one day."
We watched the caravan
That bore our queen to the courts of Solomon;
And when the first slave traders came
We bowed our heads.
"Oh, Brothers, it is not long!
Dust shall yet devour the stones
But we shall be here when they are gone."
Mountains are rising all around me.
Some are so small they are not seen;
Others are large.
All of them get big in time and people forget
What started them at first.
Oh the world is covered with mountains!
Beneath each one there is something buried:
Some pile of wreckage that started it there.
Mountains are lonely and some are awful.

One day I will crumble.
They'll cover my heap with dirt and that will make a
   mountain.
I think it will be Golgotha.

Gwendolyn Bennett
(1902—1981)

SONNETS

1

He came in silvern armour, trimmed with black—
A lover come from legends long ago—
With silver spurs and silken plumes a-blow,
And flashing sword caught fast and buckled back
In a carven sheath of Tamarack.
He came with footsteps beautifully slow,
And spoke in voice meticulously low.
He came and Romance followed in his track. . . .

I did not ask his name—I thought him Love;
I did not care to see his hidden face.
All life seemed born in my intaken breath;
All thought seemed flown like some forgotten dove.
He bent to kiss and raised his visor's lace . . .
All eager-lipped I kissed the mouth of Death.

2

Some things are very dear to me—
Such things as flowers bathed by rain
Or patterns traced upon the sea
Or crocuses where snow has lain . . .
The iridescence of a gem,
The moon's cool opalescent light,
Azaleas and the scent of them,
And honeysuckles in the night.
And many sounds are also dear—
Like winds that sing among the trees
Or crickets calling from the weir
Or Negroes humming melodies.
But dearer far than all surmise
Are sudden tear-drops in your eyes.

Countee Cullen
(1903–1946)

HERITAGE

(For Harold Jackman)

What is Africa to me:
Copper sun or scarlet sea,
Jungle star or jungle track,
Strong bronzed men, or regal black
Women from whose loins I sprang
When the birds of Eden sang?
One three centuries removed
From the scenes his fathers loved,
Spicy grove, cinnamon tree,
What is Africa to me?

So I lie, who all day long
Want no sound except the song
Sung by wild barbaric birds
Goading massive jungle herds,
Juggernauts of flesh that pass
Trampling tall defiant grass
Where young forest lovers lie,
Plighting troth beneath the sky.
So I lie, who always hear,
Though I cram against my ear
Both my thumbs, and keep them there,
Great drums throbbing through the air.
So I lie, whose fount of pride,
Dear distress, and joy allied,
Is my somber flesh and skin,
With the dark blood dammed within
Like great pulsing tides of wine
That, I fear, must burst the fine
Channels of the chafing net
Where they surge and foam and fret.

Africa? A book one thumbs
Listlessly, till slumber comes.
Unremembered are her bats
Circling through the night, her cats
Crouching in the river reeds,
Stalking gentle flesh that feeds
By the river brink; no more
Does the bugle-throated roar
Cry that monarch claws have leapt
From the scabbards where they slept.
Silver snakes that once a year
Doff the lovely coats you wear,
Seek no covert in your fear
Lest a mortal eye should see;
What's your nakedness to me?
Here no leprous flowers rear
Fierce corollas in the air;
Here no bodies sleek and wet,
Dripping mingled rain and sweat,
Tread the savage measures of
Jungle boys and girls in love.
What is last year's snow to me,
Last year's anything? The tree
Budding yearly must forget
How its past arose or set—
Bough and blossom, flower, fruit,
Even what shy bird with mute
Wonder at her travail there,
Meekly labored in its hair.
One three centuries removed
From the scenes his fathers loved,
Spice grove, cinnamon tree,
What is Africa to me?

So I lie, who find no peace
Night or day, no slight release
From the unremittant beat
Made by cruel padded feet
Walking through my body's street.
Up and down they go, and back,
Treading out a jungle track.
So I lie, who never quite
Safely sleep from rain at night—

I can never rest at all
When the rain begins to fall;
Like a soul gone mad with pain
I must match its weird refrain;
Ever must I twist and squirm,
Writhing like a baited worm,
While its primal measures drip
Through my body, crying, "Strip!
Doff this new exuberance.
Come and dance the Lover's Dance!"
In an old remembered way
Rain works on me night and day.

Quaint, outlandish heathen gods
Black men fashion out of rods,
Clay, and brittle bits of stone,
In a likeness like their own,
My conversion came high-priced;
I belong to Jesus Christ,
Preacher of humility;
Heathen gods are naught to me.

Father, Son, and Holy Ghost,
So I make an idle boast;
Jesus of the twice-turned cheek,
Lamb of God, although I speak
With my mouth thus, in my heart
Do I play a double part.
Ever at Thy glowing altar
Must my heart grow sick and falter,
Wishing He I served were black,
Thinking then it would not lack
Precedent of pain to guide it,
Let who would or might deride it;
Surely then this flesh would know
Yours had borne a kindred woe.
Lord, I fashion dark gods, too,
Daring even to give You
Dark despairing features where,
Crowned with dark rebellious hair,
Patience wavers just so much as
Mortal grief compels, while touches
Quick and hot, of anger, rise

To smitten cheek and weary eyes.
Lord, forgive me if my need
Sometimes shapes a human creed.

All day long and all night through,
One thing only must I do:
Quench my pride and cool my blood,
Lest I perish in the flood.
Lest a hidden ember set
Timber that I thought was wet
Burning like the dryest flax,
Melting like the merest wax,
Lest the grave restore its dead.
Not yet has my heart or head
In the least way realized
They and I are civilized.

FROM THE DARK TOWER

(To Charles S. Johnson)

We shall not always plant while others
    reap
The golden increment of bursting fruit,
Not always countenance, abject and mute,
That lessser men should hold their brothers
    cheap;
Not everlastingly while others sleep
Shall we beguile their limbs with mellow
    flute,
Not always bend to some more subtle brute;
We were not made eternally to weep.

The night whose sable breast relieves the
    stark,
White stars is no less lovely being dark,
And there are buds that cannot bloom at all
In light, but crumplc, pitcous, and fall;
So in the dark we hide the heart that bleeds,
And wait, and tend our agonizing seeds.

SCOTTSBORO, TOO, IS WORTH ITS SONG

(A poem to American poets)

I said:
Now will the poets sing,—
Their cries go thundering
Like blood and tears
Into the nation's ears,
Like lightning dart
Into the nation's heart.
Against disease and death and all things fell,
And war,
Their strophes rise and swell
To jar
The foe smug in his citadel.

Remembering their sharp and pretty
Tunes for Sacco and Vanzetti,
I said:
Here too's a cause divinely spun
For those whose eyes are on the sun,
Here in epitome
Is all disgrace
And epic wrong,
Like wine to brace
The minstrel heart, and blare it into song.

Surely, I said,
Now will the poets sing.
    But they have raised no cry.
    I wonder why

KARENGE YA MARENGE

Wherein are words sublime or noble? What
Invests one speech with haloed eminence,
Makes it the sesame for all doors shut,
Yet in its like sees but impertinence?
Is it the hue? Is it the cast of eye,
The curve of lip or Asiatic breath,
Which mark a lesser place for Gandhi's cry
Than "Give me liberty or give me death!"

134

Is Indian speech so quaint, so weak, so rude,
So like its land enslaved, denied, and crude,
That men who claim they fight for liberty
Can hear this battle-shout impassively,
Yet to their arms with high resolve have sprung
At those same words cried in the English tongue?

August 19, 1942

Jonathan Henderson Brooks
(1904–1945)

THE RESURRECTION

His friends went off and left Him dead
In Joseph's subterranean bed,
Embalmed with myrrh and sweet aloes,
And wrapped in snow-white burial clothes.

Then shrewd men came and set a seal
Upon His grave, lest theives should steal
His lifeless form away, and claim
For Him an undeserving fame.

"There is no use," the soldiers said,
"Of standing sentries by the dead."
Wherefore, they drew their cloaks around
Themselves, and fell upon the ground,
And slept like dead men, all night through,
In the pale moonlight and chilling dew.

A muffled whiff of sudden breath
Ruffled the passive air of death.

He woke, and raised Himself in bed;
　　Recalled how He was crucified;
Touched both hands' fingers to His head,
　　And lightly felt His fresh-healed side.

Then with a deep, triumphant sigh,
He coolly put His grave-clothes by—
Folded the sweet, white winding sheet,
　　The toweling, the linen bands,
　　The napkin, all with careful hands—
And left the borrowed chamber neat.

His steps were like the breaking day:
  So soft across the watch He stole,
  He did not wake a single soul,
Nor spill one dewdrop by the way.

Now Cavalry was loveliness:
  Lilies that flowered thereupon
Pulled off the white moon's pallid dress,
  And put the morning's vesture on.

"Why seek the living among the dead?
He is not here," the angel said.

The early winds took up the words,
And bore them to the lilting birds,
The leafing trees, and everything
That breathed the living breath of spring.

THE LAST QUARTER MOON
OF THE DYING YEAR

The last quarter moon of the dying year,
Pendant behind a naked cottonwood tree
On a frosty, dawning morning
With the back of her silver head
Turned to the waking sun.
Quiet like the waters
Of Galilee
After the Lord had bid them
"Peace, be still."
O silent beauty, indescribable!

Dead, do they say?
Would God that I shall seem
So beautiful in death.

Frank Marshall Davis
(1905–1987)

ROBERT WHITMORE

Having attained success in business
possessing three cars
one wife and two mistresses
a home and furniture
talked of by the town
and thrice ruler of the local Elks
Robert Whitmore
died of apoplexy
when a stranger from Georgia
mistook him
for a former Macon waiter.

ARTHUR RIDGEWOOD, M.D.

He debated whether
as a poet
to have dreams and beans
or as a physician
have a long car and caviar.
Dividing his time between both
he died from a nervous breakdown
caused by worry
from rejection slips
and final notices from the Finance company.

GILES JOHNSON, PH.D.

Giles Johnson
had four college degrees
knew the whyfore of this
the wherefore of that
could orate in Latin
and cuss in Greek
and, having learned such things
he died of starvation
because he wouldn't teach
and he couldn't porter.

DUKE ELLINGTON

Comes now
Taste of firecrackers
in my mouth
Sound of honey
In my ear—
Gentlemen
I dig you!

Hum a hymn for the happy hip
Every hipster
completely happy
Send 'em on a banana balloon
Riding toward a grapefruit moon

Conjure man of music
Magician of sharps and flats
Inventor of forty nine new ways
　　to bend a chord, shape a note
Crazy painter brushing kaleidoscopic sounds
　　on aural canvas
Mad sculptor melting metronomes
　　into liquid mobiles
Pardon me: wasn't that a black-maned lion
　　pawing party piano in a Park Avenue
　　penthouse?
Who gathers the goldred orchids
　　raining on the jukebox sea?

Someday someone
should give a dance for the band
Let the instruments dress
and have a ball
I'd like to ease
around slow, you know
with the alto sax
in a tight silk gown
and no bra
You take her tenor sister
But keep an eye
on baritone brother
He can be mighty mean—
If somebody gave
a dance for the band
who'd make music?
A fine fat quail
with rhythm in her tail
and hungry hips
for the long trombone?

Music cascades from brass and reeds
        in a rhythmic rainbow waterfall
Coiled snakes of biting notes
        spring from bass and drums
Through it all the piano darts
        like a boisterous bumblebee
And a cool cat falls
to his knees
shouting hot hosannas
in a jingling jangling
jiving jargon
to a jazz jehovah

Light the cannon crackers
I have a taste for the exploding hot;
Turn on the cool
Give me the sound of honey
in my ear—
Gentlemen
I am gassed!

LITTLE AND BIG

Little people often make big heroes—
From the unknown ranks
Of the population swellers;
From the Joes and Janes distinguished
Only by Social Security numbers
Giants spring;
Giants whose names
Soon become a familiar taste
in the mental mouths of the world.

Sometimes those born big
Go with a slim sputter
And all the hymns money can buy
Praises hymned in printers' ink
Cannot magnify
Fizz into boom.

Richard Wright
(1908–1960)

I HAVE SEEN BLACK HANDS

I am black and I have seen black hands, millions and
    millions of them—
Out of millions of bundles of wool and flannel tiny black
    fingers have reached restlessly and hungrily for life.
Reached out for the black nipples at the black breasts of
    black mothers,
And they've held red, green, blue, yellow, orange, white,
    and purple toys in the childish grips of possession.
And chocolate drops, peppermint sticks, lollypops,
    wineballs, ice cream cones, and sugared cookies in
    fingers sticky and gummy,
And they've held balls and bats and gloves and marbles
    and jack-knives and sling-shots and spinning tops in
    the thrill of sport and play,
And pennies and nickels and dimes and quarters and
    sometimes on New Year's, Easter, Lincoln's Birthday,
    May Day, a brand new green dollar bill,
They've held pens and rulers and maps and tablets and
    books in palms spotted and smeared with ink,
And they've held dice and cards and half-pint flasks and
    cue sticks and cigars and cigarettes in the pride of
    new maturity . . .

II

I am black and I have seen black hands, millions and
    millions of them—
They were tired and awkward and calloused and grimy
    and covered with hangnails,
And they were caught in the fast-moving belts of
    machines and snagged and smashed and crushed,
And they jerked up and down at the throbbing machines

massing taller and taller the heaps of
gold in the banks of bosses,
And they piled higher and higher the steel, iron, the
lumber, wheat, rye, the oats, corn, the cotton, the
wool, the oil, the coal, the meat, the fruit, the glass,
and the stone until there was too much to be used,
And they grabbed guns and slung them on their
shoulders and marched and groped in trenches and
fought and killed and conquered nations who were
customers for the goods black hands had made.
And again black hands stacked goods higher and higher
until there was too much to be used,
And then the black hands held trembling at the factory
gates the dreaded lay-off slip,
And the black hands hung idle and swung empty and
grew soft and got weak and bony from
unemployment and starvation,
And they grew nervous and sweaty, and opened and
shut in anguish and doubt and hesitation and
irresolution . . .

III

I am black and I have seen black hands, millions and
millions of them—
Reaching hesitantly out of days of slow death for the
goods they had made, but the bosses warned that
the goods were private and did not belong to them,
And the black hands struck desperately out in defence of
life and there was blood, but the enraged bosses
decreed that this too was wrong,
And the black hands felt the cold steel bars of the prison
they had made, in despair tested their strength and
found that they could neither bend nor break them,
And the black hands lifted palms in mute and futile
supplication to the sodden faces of mobs wild in
the revelries of sadism,
And the black hands strained and clawed and struggled
in vain at the noose that tightened about the black
throat,
And the black hands waved and beat fearfully at the tall
flames that cooked and charred the black flesh . . .

143

I am black and I have seen black hands
Raised in fists of revolt, side by side with the white fists
    of white workers,
And some day—and it is only this which sustains me—
Some day there shall be millions and millions of them,
On some red day in a burst of fists on a new horizon!

BETWEEN THE WORLD AND ME

And one morning while in the woods I stumbled
    suddenly upon the thing,
Stumbled upon it in a grassy clearing guarded by scaly
    oaks and elms.
And the sooty details of the scene rose, thrusting
    themselves between the world and me. . . .

There was a design of white bones slumbering forgottenly
    upon a cushion of ashes.
There was a charred stump of a sapling pointing a blunt
    finger accusingly at the sky.
There were torn tree limbs, tiny veins of burnt leaves, and
    a scorched coil of greasy hemp;
A vacant shoe, an empty tie, a ripped shirt, a lonely hat,
    and a pair of trousers stiff with black blood.
And upon the trampled grass were buttons, dead matches,
    butt-ends of cigars and cigarettes, peanut shells, a
    drained gin-flask, and a whore's lipstick;
Scattered traces of tar, restless arrays of feathers, and the
    lingering smell of gasoline.
And through the morning air the sun poured yellow
    surprise into the eye sockets of a stony skull. . . .

And while I stood my mind was frozen with a cold pity
    for the life that was gone.
The ground gripped my feet and my heart was circled by
    icy walls of fear—
The sun died in the sky; a night wind muttered in the
    grass and fumbled the leaves in the trees; the woods
    poured forth the hungry yelping of hounds; the
    darkness screamed with thirsty voices; and the
    witnesses rose and lived:

The dry bones stirred, rattled, lifted, melting themselves
      into my bones.
The grey ashes formed flesh firm and black, entering into
      my flesh.

The gin-flask passed from mouth to mouth; cigars and
      cigarettes glowed, the whore smeared the lipstick red
      upon her lips,
And a thousand faces swirled around me, clamoring that
      my life be burned. . . .

And then they had me, stripped me, battering my teeth
      into my throat till I swallowed my own blood.
My voice was drowned in the roar of their voices, and my
      black wet body slipped and rolled in their hands as
      they bound me to the sapling.
And my skin clung to the bubbling hot tar, falling from
      me in limp patches.
And the down and quills of the white feathers sank into
      my raw flesh, and I moaned in my agony.
Then my blood was cooled mercifully, cooled by a
      baptism of gasoline.
And in a blaze of red I leaped to the sky as pain rose like
      water, boiling my limbs.
Panting, begging I clutched childlike, clutched to the hot
      sides of death.
Now I am dry bones and my face a stony skull staring in
      yellow surprise at the sun. . . .

RED CLAY BLUES

> I miss that red clay, Lawd, I
> Need to feel it on my shoes.
> Says miss that red clay, Lawd, I
> Need to feel it on my shoes.
> I want to see Georgia, cause I
> Got them red clay blues.
>
> Pavement's hard on my feet. I'm
> Tired o'this concrete street.
> Pavement's hard on my feet, I'm
> Tired o'this city street.

Goin' back to Georgia where
That red clay can't be beat.

I want to tramp in the red mud, Lawd, and
Feel the red clay round my toes.
I want to wade in the red mud,
Feel that red clay suckin' at my toes.
I want my little farm back and I
Don't care where that landlord goes.

I want to be in Georgia, when the
Big storms start to blow.
Yes I want to be in Georgia when that
Big storm starts to blow.
I want to see the landlords runnin' cause I
Wonder where they gonna go!

I got them red clay blues.

Robert Hayden
(1913—1980)

HOMAGE TO THE EMPRESS OF THE BLUES

Because there was a man somewhere in a candystripe silk shirt,
gracile and dangerous as a jaguar and because a woman moaned
for him in sixty-watt gloom and mourned him Faithless Love
Twotiming Love Oh Love Oh Careless Aggravating Love,

> She came out on the stage in yards of pearls, emerging like
> a favorite scenic view, flashed her golden smile and sang.

Because grey laths began somewhere to show from underneath
torn hurdygurdy lithographs of dollfaced heaven;
and because there were those who feared alarming fists of snow
on the door and those who feared the riot-squad of statistics,

> She came out on the stage in ostrich feathers, beaded satin,
> and shone that smile on us and sang.

RUNAGATE RUNAGATE

I.

Runs falls rises stumbles on from darkness into darkness
and the darkness thicketed with shapes of terror
and the hunters pursuing and the hounds pursuing
and the night cold and the night long and the river
to cross and the jack-muh-lanterns beckoning beckoning
and blackness ahead and when shall I reach that somewhere
morning and keep on going and never turn back and keep on going

> Runagate
> > Runagate
> > > Runagate

147

Many thousands rise and go
many thousands crossing over

O mythic North
O star-shaped yonder Bible city

Some go weeping and some rejoicing
some in coffins and some in carriages
some in silks and some in shackles

Rise and go or fare you well

No more auction block for me
no more driver's lash for me

If you see my Pompey, 30 yrs of age,
new breeches, plain stockings, negro shoes;
if you see my Anna, likely young mulatto
branded E on the right cheek, R on the left,
catch them if you can and notify subscriber.
Catch them if you can, but it won't be easy.
They'll dart underground when you try to catch them,
plunge into quicksand, whirlpools, mazes,
turn into scorpions when you try to catch them.

And before I'll be a slave
I'll be buried in my grave

North star and bonanza gold
I'm bound for the freedom, freedom-bound
and oh Susyanna don't you cry for me

Runagate

Runagate

II.

Rises from their anguish and their power,

Harriet Tubman,

woman of earth, whipscarred,
a summoning, a shining

148

Mean to be free

And this was the way of it, brethren brethren,
way we journeyed from Can't to Can.
Moon so bright and no place to hide,
the cry up and the patterollers riding,
hound dogs belling in bladed air.
And fear starts a-murbling, Never make it,
we'll never make it. *Hush that now*,
and she's turned upon us, levelled pistol
glinting in the moonlight:
Dead folks can't jaybird-talk, she says;
you keep on going now or die, she says.

Wanted   Harriet Tubman   alias The General
alias Moses   Stealer of Slaves

In league with Garrison   Alcott   Emerson
Garrett   Douglass   Thoreau   John Brown

Armed and known to be Dangerous

Wanted   Reward   Dead or Alive

Tell me, Ezekiel, oh tell me do you see
mailed Jehovah coming to deliver me?

Hoot-owl calling in the ghosted air,
five times calling to the hants in the air.
Shadow of a face in the scary leaves,
shadow of a voice in the talking leaves:

Come ride-a my train

Oh that train, ghost-story train
through swamp and savanna movering movering,
over trestles of dew, through caves of the wish,
Midnight Special on a subre track movering movering,
first stop Mercy and the last Hallelujah.

Come ride-a my train

Mean mean mean to be free.

FREDERICK DOUGLASS

When it is finally ours, this freedom, this liberty, this beautiful
and terrible thing, needful to man as air,
usable as earth; when it belongs at last to all,
when it is truly instinct, brain matter, diastole, systole,
reflex action; when it is finally won; when it is more
than the gaudy mumbo jumbo of politicians:
this man, this Douglass, this former slave, this Negro
beaten to his knees, exiled, visioning a world
where none is lonely, none hunted, alien,
this man, superb in love and logic, this man
shall be remembered. Oh, not with statues' rhetoric,
not with legends and poems and wreaths of bronze alone,
but with the lives grown out of his life, the lives
fleshing his dream of the beautiful, needful thing.

O DAEDALUS, FLY AWAY HOME

(For Maia and Julie)

Drifting night in the Georgia pines,
coonskin drum and jubilee banjo.
     Pretty Malinda, dance with me.

Night is juba, night is conjo.
     Pretty Malinda, dance with me.

Night is an African juju man
weaving a wish and a weariness together
     to make two wings.

     O fly away home fly away

Do you remember Africa?

     O cleave the air fly away home

My gran, he flew back to Africa,
just spread his arms and
     flew away home.

150

Drifting night in the windy pines;
night is a laughing, night is a longing.
    Pretty Malinda, come to me.

Night is a mourning juju man
weaving a wish and a weariness together
    to make two wings.

O fly away home fly away

Owen Dodson
(1914–1983)

THE SIGNIFYING DARKNESS

There was an evil darkness way before
The war rose clear, a darkness before that dawn,
Before that midnight and that evening dusk:
A signifying darkness too few saw

When there was blazing light unfree
Of sun and unblown candle or artificial;
The darkness of skin and shame in it,
The darkness of condescension, greed and charity.

O, could you watch this map of prejudice:
How sharp the acid rivers eat,
The valleys deplore, the mountains scorn—
Then you would see Paris and Metz as victories less

For all their wide appeal and joy.
You would see here the black wet face
Of a dark mother staring at the blood
Ruin dust and bone and dead that was her boy.

POEM FOR PEARL'S DANCERS
Scene: A Slave Auction

On my back they've written history, Lord,
On my back they've lashed out hell.

My eyes run blood,
The faces I see are blood,
My toes can't dig no deeper in the dirt.

When my children get to reading, Lord,
On my back they'll read my tale.

My lips taste blood,
And in they souls they's blood.
My tongue can't joy no future in this blood.

When my children get to shouting, Lord,
All around they'll shout this scene.

When my children get to manhood, Lord,
When my children get to standing straight,
Lord, Lord, Lord,
When that time come rolling down!

Margaret Walker
(1915–)

FOR MY PEOPLE

For my people everywhere singing their slave songs
     repeatedly: their dirges and their ditties and their blues
     and jubilees, praying their prayers nightly to an
     unknown god, bending their knees humbly to an
     unseen power;

For my people lending their strength to the years, to the
     gone years and the now years and the maybe years,
     washing ironing cooking scrubbing sewing mending
     hoeing plowing digging planting pruning patching
     dragging along never gaining never reaping never
     knowing and never understanding.

For my playmates in the clay and dust and sand of Alabama
     backyards playing baptizing and preaching and doctor
     and jail and soldier and school and mama and cooking
     and playhouse and concert and store and hair and Miss
     Choomby and company;

For the cramped bewildered years we went to school to learn
     to know the reasons why and the answers to and the
     people who and the places where and the days when, in
     memory of the bitter hours when we discovered we
     were black and poor and small and different and nobody
     cared and nobody wondered and nobody understood;

For the boys and girls who grew in spite of these things to
     be man and woman, to laugh and dance and sing and
     play and drink their wine and religion and success, to
     marry their playmates and bear children and then die
     of consumption and anemia and lynching;

For my people thronging 47th Street in Chicago and Lenox
   Avenue in New York and Rampart Street in New
   Orleans, lost disinherited dispossessed and happy
   people filling the cabarets and taverns and other
   people's pockets needing bread and shoes and milk and
   land and money and something—something all our own;

For my people walking blindly spreading joy, losing time
   being lazy, sleeping when hungry, shouting when
   burdened, drinking when hopeless, tied, and shackled
   and tangled among ourselves by the unseen creatures
   who tower over us omnisciently and laugh;

For my people blundering and groping and floundering in
   the dark of churches and schools and clubs and
   societies, associations and councils and committees and
   conventions, distressed and disturbed and deceived and
   devoured by money-hungry glory-craving leeches,
   preyed on by facile force of state and fad and novelty, by
   false prophet and holy believer;

For my people standing staring trying to fashion a better way
   from confusion, from hypocrisy and misunderstanding,
   trying to fashion a world that will hold all the people,
   all the faces, all the adams and eves and their countless
   generations;

Let a new earth rise. Let another world be born. Let a
   bloody peace be written in the sky. Let a second
   generation full of courage issue forth; let a people
   loving freedom come to growth. Let a beauty full of
   healing and a strength of final clenching be the pulsing
   in our spirits and our blood. Let the martial songs be
   written, let the dirges disappear. Let a race of men now
   rise and take control.

WE HAVE BEEN BELIEVERS

We have been believers believing in the black gods of an old
   land, believing in the secrets of the seeress and the
   magic of the charmers and the power of the devil's evil
   ones.

And in the white gods of a new land we have been believers
   believing in the mercy of our masters and the beauty of
   our brothers, believing in the conjure of the humble
   and the faithful and the pure.

Neither the slaves' whip nor the lynchers' rope nor the
   bayonet could kill our black belief. In our hunger we
   beheld the welcome table and in our nakedness the
   glory of a long white robe. We have been believers in
   the new Jerusalem.

We have been believers feeding greedy grinning gods, like a
   Moloch demanding our sons and our daughters, our
   strength and our wills and our spirits of pain. We have
   been believers, silent and stolid and stubborn and
   strong.

We have been believers yielding substance for the world.
   With our hands have we fed a people and out of our
   strength have they wrung the necessities of a nation.
   Our song has filled the twilight and our hope has
   heralded the dawn.

Now we stand ready for the touch of one fiery iron, for the
   cleansing breath of many molten truths, that the eyes
   of the blind may see and the ears of the deaf may hear
   and the tongues of the people be filled with living fire.

Where are our gods that they leave us asleep? Surely the
   priests and the preachers and the powers will hear.
   Surely now that our hands are empty and our hearts too
   full to pray they will understand. Surely the sires of
   the people will send us a sign.

We have been believers believing in our burdens and our
   demigods too long. Now the needy no longer weep and

pray; the long-suffering arise, and our fists bleed
against the bars with a strange insistency.

LINEAGE

My grandmothers were strong.
They followed plows and bent to toil.
They moved through fields sowing seed.
They touched earth and grain grew.
They were full of sturdiness and singing.
My grandmothers were strong.

My grandmothers are full of memories
Smelling of soap and onions and wet clay
With veins rolling roughly over quick hands
They have many clean words to say.
My grandmothers were strong.
Why am I not as they?

AMOS, 1963

Amos is a Shepherd of suffering sheep;
A pastor preaching in the depths of Alabama
Preaching social justice to the Southland
Preaching to the poor a new gospel of love
With the words of a god and the dreams of a man
Amos is our loving Shepherd of the sheep
Crying out to the stricken land
"You have sold the righteous for silver
And the poor for a pair of shoes.
My God is a mighty avenger
And He shall come with His rod in His hand."
Preaching to the persecuted and the disinherited millions
Preaching love and justice to the solid southern land
Amos is a Prophet with a vision of brotherly love
With a vision and a dream of the red hills of Georgia
"When Justice shall roll down like water
And Righteousness like a mighty stream."
Amos is our Shepherd standing in the Shadow of our God
Tending his flocks all over the hills of Albany
And the seething streets of Selma and of bitter Birmingham.

BALLAD OF THE HOPPY-TOAD

Ain't been on Market Street for nothing
With my regular washing load
When the Saturday crowd went stomping
Down the Johnny-jumping road

Seen Sally Jones come running
With a razor at her throat,
Seen Deacon's daughter lurching
Like a drunken alley goat.

But the biggest for my money,
And the saddest for my throw
Was the night I seen the goopher man
Throw dust around my door.

Come sneaking round my doorway
In a stovepipe hat and coat;
Come sneaking round my doorway
To drop the evil note.

I run down to Sis Avery's
And told her what I seen
"Root-worker's out to git me
What you reckon that there mean?"

Sis Avery she done told me,
"Now honey go on back
I knows just what will hex him
And that old goopher sack."

Now I done burned the candles
Till I seen the face of Jim
And I done been to Church and prayed
But can't get rid of him.

Don't want to burn his picture
Don't want to dig his grave
Just want to have my peace of mind
And make that dog behave.

Was running through the fields one day
Sis Avery's chopping corn
Big horse come stomping after me
I knowed then I was gone.

Sis Avery grabbed that horse's mane
And not one minute late
Cause trembling down behind her
I seen my ugly fate.

She hollered to that horse to "Whoa!
I gotcha hoppy-toad."
And yonder come the goopher man
A-running down the road.

She hollered to that horse to "Whoa"
And what you wanta think?
Great-God-a-mighty, that there horse
Begun to sweat and shrink.

He shrunk up to a teeny horse
He shrunk up to a toad
And yonder come the goopher man
Still running down the road.

She hollered to that horse to "Whoa"
She said, "I'm killing him.
Now you just watch this hoppy-toad
And you'll be rid of Jim."

The goopher man was hollering
"Don't kill that hoppy-toad."
Sis Avery she said "Honey,
You bout to lose your load."

That hoppy-toad was dying
Right there in the road
And goopher man was screaming
"Don't kill that hoppy-toad."

The hoppy-toad shook one more time
And then he up and died
Old goopher man fell dying, too.
"O hoppy-toad," he cried.

HARRIET TUBMAN

Dark is the face of Harriet,
Darker still her fate
Deep in the dark of Southern wilds
Deep in the slaves' hate.

Fiery thc eye of Harriet,
Fiery, dark, and wild;
Bitter, bleak, and hopeless
Is the bonded child.

Stand in the fields, Harriet,
Stand alone and still
Stand before the overseer
Mad enough to kill.

This is slavery, Harriet,
Bend beneath the lash;
This is Maryland, Harriet,
Bow to poor white trash.

You're a field hand, Harriet,
Working in the corn;
You're a grubber with the hoe
And a slave child born.

You're just sixteen, Harriet,
And never had a beau;
Your mother's dead long time ago,
Your daddy you don't know.

This piece of iron's not hard enough
To kill you with a blow,
This piece of iron can't hurt you,
Just let you slaves all know.

I'm still the overseer,
Old marster'll believe my tale;
I know that he will keep me
From going to the jail.

Get up, bleeding Harriet,
I didn't hit you hard;
Get up, bleeding Harriet,
And grease your head with lard.

Get up, sullen Harriet,
Get up and bind your head.
Remember this is Maryland
And I can beat you dead.

How far is the road to Canada?
How far do I have to go?
How far is the road from Maryland
And the hatred that I know?

I stabbed that overseer;
I took his rusty knife;
I killed that overseer;
I took his lowdown life.

For three long years I waited,
Three years I kept my hate,
Three years before I killed him,
Three years I had to wait.

Done shook the dust of Maryland
Clean off my weary feet;
I'm on my way to Canada
And Freedom's golden street.

I'm bound to git to Canada
Before another week
I come through swamps and mountains,
I waded many a creek.

Now tell my brothers yonder
That Harriet is free;
Yes, tell my brothers yonder
No more auction block for me.

Come down from the mountain, Harriet,
Come down to the valley at night,
Come down to your weeping people
And be their guiding light.

Sing Deep Dark River of Jordan,
Don't you want to cross over today?
Sing Deep Wide River of Jordan,
Don't you want to walk Freedom's way?

I stole down in the nighttime,
I come back in the day,
I stole back to my Maryland
To guide the slaves away.

I met old marster yonder
A-coming down the road,
And right past me in Maryland
My old marster strode.

I passed beside my marster
And covered up my head;
My marster didn't know me
I guess he heard I'm dead.

I wonder if he thought about
That overseer's dead;
I wondered if he figured out
He ought to know this head?

You'd better run, brave Harriet,
There's ransom on your head;
You better run, Miss Harriet,
They want you live or dead.

Been down in valleys yonder
And searching round the stills,
They got the posse after you,
A-riding through the hills.

They got the bloodhounds smelling,
They got their guns cocked too;
You better run, bold Harriet,
The white man's after you.

They got ten thousand dollars
Put on your coal-black head;

They'll give ten thousand dollars;
They're mad because you fled.

I wager they'll be riding
A long, long time for you.
Yes, Lord, they'll look a long time
Till Judgment Day is due.

I'm Harriet Tubman, people,
I'm Harriet the slave,
I'm Harriet, free woman,
And I'm free within my grave.

> Come along, children, with Harriet
> Come along, children, come along
> Uncle Sam is rich enough
> To give you all a farm.

I killed the overseer.
I fooled old marster's eyes,
I found my way to Canada
With hundreds more besides.

> Come along to Harpers Ferry
> Come along to brave John Brown
> Come along with Harriet, children,
> Come along ten million strong.

I met the mighty John Brown
I knew Fred Douglass too
Enlisted Abolitionists
Beneath the Union Blue.

I heard the mighty trumpet
That sent the land to war;
I mourned for Mister Lincoln
And saw his funeral car.

> Come along with Harriet, children,
> Come along to Canada.
> Come down to the river, children,
> And follow the northern star.

I'm Harriet Tubman, people,
I'm Harriet, the slave,
I'm Harriet, free woman,
And I'm free beyond my grave.

Come along to freedom, children,
Come along ten million strong;
Come along with Harriet, children,
Come along ten million strong.

I HEAR A RUMBLING. . . .

I hear a rumbling underground.
I hear a rumbling. . . .
I hear my brothers underground
I hear a rumbling.

I hear an earthquake underground
I hear a rumbling.
I hear the red man underground
I hear a rumbling.

I hear the dead men from their graves
I hear them speaking
I hear the starving underground
I hear the rumbling

I hear Chicanos underground
I hear them grumbling
I hear the prisoners underground
I hear a rumbling

I hear a rumble and a grumble
I hear a rumbling
I hear the yellow and the brown men
I hear a rumbling

There are rockets in the air
There *is* a rumbling
There is lightning in the sky
There *is* a rumbling

I hear my children crying "Bread"
I hear my children crying "Peace"
I hear the farmers crying "Bread"
I hear the soldiers crying "Peace"

There is a rumbling. . . .

Guns and butter will not help.
We want Peace.
Dollars in the marketplace
We want Bread.

When the volcanoes erupt
We want Peace.
Bread and Peace are not enough;
Freedom too.

I hear a rumbling. . . .

They have boxed us in a coffin
Underground
They have chained us to a rock
Underground.

How long will their prices rise
to the skies?
How long must my children cry
to the skies?

How long will my people starve
Underground?
How long will the prisoners cry
Underground?

Christ is coming, so they say
In the skies.
Worlds will all be blown away
To the skies.

Will the earthquake underground
And the lighting in the skies
Peace and Bread and Freedom come
And the dead below arise?

There's a rumbling in the air
There's a lighting in the skies
There's a rumbling and a grumbling
And the walls of prisons breaking.

I hear rumbling underground
I hear rumbling.
Don't you hear the children crying?
Don't you hear the mothers weeping?

Blown to bits this craven crowd
Underground?
Blown to bits these plastic people
Underground?

Will you laugh or shout or cry?
Will you gloat and scream and die?
From the people everywhere
I have heard them here and there

Give us Freedom give us Peace
Give us Bread and Freedom, too
I hear rumbling underground
Peace and Bread and Freedom, too.

We will seize the power-mad
Everywhere
We will seize the guns and bread
Everywhere.

Give us Freedom, Give us Peace
I hear rumbling underground
Bread and Peace and Freedom too
I hear rumbling underground.

Margaret Esse Danner
(1915—1984)

AND THROUGH THE CARIBBEAN SEA

We, like shades that were first conjured up
by an African witch-doctor's ire,
(indigo for the drum and the smoke of night,

tangerine for the dancing smudged fire)
have been forced to exist in a huge kaleidoscope world.
We've been shifting with time and sifting through
    space,

at each whimsical turn of the hands that have thrown
the kaleidoscope, until any pattern or place
or shade is our own.

The indigo sifted from its drum-like vein
toward the blue of the sky that the Goths attained.
The tangerine became the orange of the tango, again

the red of the Susy Q., and each time the turning
    invaded
one pattern, a new one was formed
and in forming each pattern, we traded.

Until, who questions whether we'd be prone to yearn
for a Louis Quinze frame, a voodoo fire,
Rococo, Baroque, an African mask or a Gothic spire
or any style of any age or any place or name.

THIS IS AN AFRICAN WORM

This is an African worm
but then a worm in any land
is still a worm.

It will not stride, run, stand up
before the butterflies, who
have passed their worm-like state.

It must keep low, not lift its head.
I've had the dread experience, I know.
A worm can do no thing but crawl.

Crawl, and wait.

Gwendolyn Brooks
(1917–)

THE MOTHER

Abortions will not let you forget.
You remember the children you got that you did not
    get,
The damp small pulps with a little or with no hair,
The singers and workers that never handled the air.
You will never neglect or beat
Them, or silence or buy with a sweet.
You will never wind up the sucking-thumb
Or scuttle off ghosts that come.
You will never leave them, controlling your luscious
    sigh,
Return for a snack of them, with gobbling mother-eye.

I have heard in the voices of the wind the voices of my
    dim killed children.
I have contracted. I have eased
My dim dears at the breasts they could never suck.
I have said, Sweets, if I sinned, if I seized
Your luck
And your lives from your unfinished reach,
If I stole your births and your names,
Your straight baby tears and your games,
Your stilted or lovely loves, your tumults, your mar-
    riages, aches, and your deaths,
If I poisoned the beginnings of your breaths,
Believe that even in my deliberateness I was not de-
    liberate.
Though why should I whine,
Whine that the crime was other than mine?—
Since anyhow you are dead.
Or rather, or instead,
You were never made.

But that too, I am afraid,
Is faulty: oh, what shall I say, how is the truth to be
    said?
You were born, you had body, you died.
It is just that you never giggled or planned or cried.

Believe me, I loved you all.
Believe me, I knew you, though faintly, and I loved, I
    loved you
All.

MY DREAMS, MY WORKS,
MUST WAIT TILL AFTER HELL

I hold my honey and I store my bread
In little jars and cabinets of my will.
I label clearly, and each latch and lid
I bid, Be firm till I return from hell.
I am very hungry. I am incomplete.
And none can tell when I may dine again.
No man can give me any word but Wait,
The puny light. I keep eyes pointed in;
Hoping that, when the devil days of my hurt
Drag out to their last dregs and I resume
On such legs as are left me, in such heart
As I can manage, remember to go home,
My taste will not have turned insensitive
To honey and bread old purity could love.

WHAT SHALL I GIVE MY CHILDREN?

What shall I give my children? who are poor,
Who are adjudged the leastwise of the land,
Who are my sweetest lepers, who demand
No velvet and no velvety velour;
But who have begged me for a brisk contour,
Crying that they are quasi, contraband
Because unfinished, graven by a hand
Less than angelic, admirable or sure.
My hand is stuffed with mode, design, device.
But I lack access to my proper stone.

170

And plenitude of plan shall not suffice
Nor grief nor love shall be enough alone
To ratify my little halves who bear
Across an autumn freezing everywhere.

FIRST FIGHT. THEN FIDDLE.

First fight. Then fiddle. Ply the slipping string
With feathery sorcery; muzzle the note
With hurting love; the music that they wrote
Bewitch, bewilder. Qualify to sing
Threadwise. Devise no salt, no hempen thing
For the dear instrument to bear. Devote
The bow to silks and honey. Be remote
A while from malice and from murdering.
But first to arms, to armor. Carry hate
In front of you and harmony behind.
Be deaf to music and to beauty blind.
Win war. Rise bloody, maybe not too late
For having first to civilize a space
Wherein to play your violin with grace.

THE EGG BOILER

Being you, you cut your poetry from wood.
The boiling of an egg is heavy art.
You come upon it as an artist should,
With rich-eyed passion, and with straining heart.
We fools, we cut our poems out of air,
Night color, wind soprano, and such stuff.
And sometimes weightlessness is much to bear.
You mock it, though, you name it Not Enough.
The egg, spooned gently to the avid pan,
And left the strict three minutes, or the four,
Is your Enough and art for any man.
We fools give courteous ear—then cut some more,
Shaping a gorgeous Nothingness from cloud.
You watch us, eat your egg, and laugh aloud.

MALCOLM X

For Dudley Randall

Original.
Ragged-round.
Rich-robust.

He had the hawk-man's eyes.
We gasped. We saw the maleness.
The maleness raking out and making guttural the air
and pushing us to walls.

And in a soft and fundamental hour
a sorcery devout and vertical
beguiled the world.

He opened us—
who was a key,

who was a man.

TO THOSE OF MY SISTERS
WHO KEPT THEIR NATURALS

*Never to look
a hot comb in the teeth.*

Sisters!
I love you.
Because you love you.
Because you are erect.
Because you are also bent.
In season, stern, kind.
Crisp, soft—in season.
And you withhold.
And you extend.
And you Step out.
And you go back.
And you extend again.
Your eyes, loud-soft, with crying and
        with smiles,
are older than a million years.

172

And they are young.
You reach, in season.
You subside, in season.
And All
below the richrough righttime of your hair.
You have not bought Blondine.
You have not hailed the hot-comb recently.
You never worshipped Marilyn Monroe.
You say: Farrah's hair is hers.
You have not wanted to be white.
Nor have you testified to adoration of that
    state
with the advertisement of imitation
(*never* successful because the hot-comb is
    laughing too.)

But oh the rough dark Other music!
the Real,
the Right.
The natural Respect of Self and Seal!
        Sisters!
Your hair is Celebration in the world!

THE NEAR-JOHANNESBURG BOY

> *In South Africa the Black*
> *children ask each other:*
> *"Have you been detained yet?*
> *How many times have you been*
> *detained?"*

> *The herein boy does not live*
> *in Johannesburg. He is not*
> *allowed to live there. Perhaps*
> *he lives in Soweto.*

My way is from woe to wonder.
A Black boy near Johannesburg, hot
in the Hot Time.

Those people
do not like Black among the colors.
They do not like our

173

calling our country ours.
They say our country is not ours.

Those people.
Visiting the world as I visit the world.
Those people.
Their bleach is puckered and cruel.

It is work to speak of my Father. My Father.
His body was whole till they Stopped it.
Suddenly.
With a short shot.
But, before that, physically tall and among us,
he died every day. Every moment.
My Father. . . .
First was the crumpling.
No. First was the Fist-and-the-Fury.
Last was the crumpling. It is
a little used rag that is Under, it is not,
it is not my Father gone down.

About my Mother. My Mother
was this loud laugher
below the sunshine, below the starlight at festival.
My Mother is still this loud laugher!
Still moving straight in the Getting-It-Done (as she names
   it.)
Oh a strong eye is my Mother.
Except when it seems we are lax in our looking.

Well, enough of slump, enough of Old Story.
Like a clean spear of fire
I am moving. I am not still. I am ready
to be ready.
I shall flail
in the Hot Time.

Tonight I walk with
a hundred of playmates to where
the hurt Black of our skin is forbidden.
There, in the dark that is our dark, there,
a-pulse across earth that is our earth, there,
there exulting, there Exactly, there redeeming, there

Roaring Up
(oh my Father)
we shall forge with the Fist-and-the-Fury:
we shall flail in the Hot Time:
we shall
we shall

KOJO
"I AM A BLACK"

According to my Teachers,
I am now an African-American.

They call me out of my name.

BLACK is an open umbrella.
I am Black and A Black forever.

I am one of The Blacks.

We are Here, we are There.
We occur in Brazil, in Nigeria, Ghana,
in Botswana, Tanzania, in Kenya,
in Russia, Australia, in Haiti, Soweto,
in Grenada, in Cuba, in Panama, Libya,
in England and Italy, France.

We are graces in any places.
I am Black and A Black
forever.

I am other than Hyphenation.

I say, proudly, MY PEOPLE!
I say, proudly, OUR PEOPLE!

Our People do not disdain to eat yams or melons or grits
or to put peanut butter in stew.

I am Kojo. In West Afrika Kojo
means Unconquerable. My parents

named me the seventh day from my birth
in Black spirit, Black faith, Black communion.
I am Kojo. I am A Black.
And I Capitalize my name.

Do not call me out of my name.

ULYSSES
"RELIGION"

At home we pray every morning, we
get down on our knees in a circle,
holding hands, holding Love,
and we sing Hallelujah.

Then we go into the World.

Daddy *speeds,* to break bread with his Girl Friend.
Mommy's a Boss. And a lesbian.
(She too has a nice Girl Friend.)

My brothers and sisters and I come to school.
We bring knives pistols bottles, little boxes, and cans.

We talk to the man who's cool at the playground gate.
Nobody Sees us, nobody stops our sin.

Our teachers feed us geography.
We spit it out in a hurry.

Now we are coming home.

At home, we pray every evening, we
get down on our knees in a circle,
holding hands, holding Love.

And we sing Hallelujah.

MERLE
"UNCLE SEAGRAM"

My uncle likes me too much.

I am five and a half years old, and in kindergarten.
In kindergarten everything is clean.

My uncle is six feet tall, with seven bumps on his chin.
My uncle is six feet tall, and he stumbles.
He stumbles because of his Wonderful Medicine
packed in his pocket all times.
Family is ma and pa and my uncle,
three brothers, three sisters, and me.

Every night at my house we play checkers and dominoes.
My uncle sits *close*.
There aren't any shoes or socks on his feet.
Under the table a big toe tickles my ankle.
Under the oilcloth his thin knee beats into mine.
And mashes. And mashes.

When we look at TV
my uncle picks *me* to sit on his lap.
As I sit, he gets hard in the middle.
I squirm, but he keeps me, and kisses my ear.

I am not even a girl.

Once, when I went to the bathroom,
my uncle noticed, came in, shut the door,
put his long white tongue in my ear,
and whispered "We're Best Friends, and Family,
and we know how to keep Secrets."

My uncle likes me too much. I am worried.

I do not like my uncle anymore.

Samuel Allen
(1917–)

TO SATCH *

Sometimes I feel like I will *never* stop
Just go on forever
Till one fine mornin
I'm gonna reach up and grab me a handfulla stars
Swing out my long lean leg
And whip three hot strikes burnin down the heavens
And look over at God and say
How about that!

*The career of Satchel Paige, the legendary baseball pitcher,
extended into five decades.

HARRIET TUBMAN
aka Moses

High in the darkening heavens
   the wind swift, the storm massing
the giant arrow rose, a crackling arch, a sign
   above the fleeing band of people,
toy figures in the canebrake
   below.

Far in the distance, moving quickly,
came the patterrollers
bloodhounds loping, silent.

Minutes before, one of the fleeing band had fallen,
the others for a moment waited
but he did not rise.

A small dark woman stood above him.
His words were slow to come and more a groan:

> Can't make it, just can't make it
> You all go head without me.

Moses pulled out her revolver and she quietly said:

> Move or die.
>
> You ain't stoppin now
> You *can't* stop now
> You gonna move
> move or die.
>
> If you won't go on
> Gonna risk us all—
> Ahma send your soul to glory, I said move!
>
> Long time now, I got if figgered out
> Ev'ry child a God got a double right, death
> or liberty, Move, now
> or you will die.

Listen to me

Way back yonder
　　down in bondage
　　　　on my knee
Th' moment that He gave his promise—
I was free

(Walk, children)

He said that when destruction rages
He *is* a rock—
　　the Rock of Ages
Declared that when the tempest ride
He just come mosey
　　straight—
　　　to my side.

(Don't you get weary)

Promised me the desprit hour
be the signal for His power
Hounddogs closin on the track

Sunlight

and the thunderclap!

(How you get weary!)

Bloodhounds quickenin on the scent
Over my head, yesss
   the heavens rent!

O He's a father He *is* a mother
A sister He will
   be your brother
Supplies the harvest, He raises up the grain
O don't you feel—it's fallin now
   the blessed rain.

Don't make no diffunce if you weary
Don't mean a hoot owl if you scared
He was with us in the six troubles
He won't desert you in the seventh.

Get on up now

That's it, no need a gettin weary
There is a glory there!

   There be a great rejoicin
      no more sorrow
      shout 'n *nev*vuh tire
      a great camp meetin
        in that land.

By fire in heaven she was guided
saved by stream
   and by water reed
By her terrible grimace of faith
   beautiful and defiant,
Till, for a moment
   in the long journey
   came the first faint glimpse
   of the stars   the everlasting stars   shining clear
   over the free
             cold
               land.

FROM PAUL VESEY'S LEDGER

As King grew cold on a Memphis slab
the crowds of office workers
    surged into the streets,
in the shadow of the White House
    racing for the parking lots,
fleeing, in the first shadows of dusk
     for the suburbs.

The lot attendant, sprinting to keep pace,
    stopped for a moment,
    astounded by the frantic rush, accelerating
    like an old Chaplin movie.
Slowly, he shook his head,
    'Look at those mothers run'
and, softly,
    'Easy, baby, you ain't going nowheres.'

But they swept through the streets possessed
heedless, beneath the pillars of rage
mounting in huge billows
    a darkening slab
    over the already smoldering city.

Malcolm gave a choice

The choice he gave was fair,
    of ballots or ballistics.
He recognized equations
    superior force is equal to
    superior force
and made a promise four square
    Ahma tear, great Gawd
    this buildin down.

Malcolm said I am
    the way I am the light
what you could have done
you should have done
now there is no more time
soon the mummy dust of death
    will settle on you.

The guilty, where they gonna run?
The sinner, can he hide?
You will be blinded still
    In the winding sheet
    of your last journey.
Insight and prophecy
    Ahma tear
the hope of generations
    Ahma tear
yield now only foolscap
    on a wintry sea.

Malcolm gave a choice
    it was fair
a ballot or a bullet
    it will tear
agreed to an equation
    made a promise four square
superior force is equal to
    Ahma tear, great Gawd
    Ahma tear this buildin *down* Ahma tear.

Naomi Long Madgett
(1923–)

HOMAGE

Consider the eternal Cat,
Bird-watcher supreme,
Who alone among the fluttering things
Waits and is sure.
Incapable of flight and yet secure,
He knows it isn't wings
One needs to soar (or to redeem
The rabbit from the hat).

Their doom foreshadowed when he sees a feather fall,
He knows they do not know
Salvation is the *use* of idle things
Like songs and wings
They think they owe
To time and trust and the redemptive All.

MORTALITY

This is the surest death
Of all the deaths I know.
The one that halts the breath,
The one that falls with snow
Are nothing but a peace
Before the second zone.
For Aprils never cease
To resurrect their own,
And in my very veins
Flows blood as old as Eve.
The smallest cell contains
Its privileged reprieve.

But vultures recognize
This single mortal thing
And watch with hungry eyes
When hope starts staggering.

KIN

(For Jill)

Something has passed between us more than blood,
keener than bone that locks us into rhythms
of chin and cheek and brow. When diamond glints
of sun bounce from your mountains
my wings in shadow soar;
when rutted clay entraps your feet
my own steps slog in kindred snares.

Leaves of one vine entwine us utterly
nourished by juices of a common earth.
Your seasons shake me louder than the sounds of chance,
deeper than solitudes of birth.

EXITS AND ENTRANCES

Through random doors we wandered
into passages disguised as paradise
and out again, discarding,
embracing hope anew, discarding again:
exits and entrances to many houses.

Without joy we sang,
without grace we danced,
our hump-back rhythms colliding
with our sanity,
our beauty blanching in a hostile sun.

How should we, could we
sing our song in a strange land?

Through random doors we have come
home to our kingdom, our own battleground,
not with harps, not with trumpets even,

but armed with the invincible sword and shield
of our own names and faces.

PHILLIS

I hardly remember my mother's face now,
But I still feel
At my bosom a chill wind
Stirring strange longings for the sturdy back
I used to lean against for warmth and comfort
When I had grown too tall to ride.

And I am blinded by
The glint of sunlight
Striking golden fire from the flint
Of seafoamed rocks below me
On some island not too far from home.

After that, the only light I saw
Was a few wayward chinks of day
That somehow slanted into the airless tomb
Where chains confined me motionless to a dank wall.

Then the sun died and time went out completely.
In that new putrid helltrap of the dead
And dying, the stench
Of vomit, sweat, and feces
Mingled with the queasy motion
Of the ship until my senses failed me . . .

I do not know how many weeks or months
I neither thought nor felt, but I awoke
One night—or day, perhaps—
Revived by consciousness of sound.

I heard
The pounding of the waves against the shipside
And made believe its rhythm
Was the speech of tribal drums
Summoning in acute need the spirit
Of my ancestors. I dreamed I saw
Their carven images arrayed

In ceremonial austerity. I thought I heard
Their voices thundering an answer
To my supplication: "Hold fast.
Sur/vive   sur/vive   sur/*vive*!"
And then I slept again . . .

Once more the sunlight came, but not the same
As I remembered it. Now it sat silver-cold
Upon the indifferent New England coast. Still
It was good to see the sun at all.
And it was something
To find myself the bright dark mascot
Of a blind but well-intentioned host—
A toy, a curiosity, a child
Taking delight in anyone's attention
After so long a death.

As I grew older, it was not enough.
That native lifesong once again burst free,
Spilled over sands of my acquired rituals—
Urged me to match the tribal rhythms
That had so long sustained me, that must
Sustain me still. I learned to sing
A dual song:

> *My fathers will forgive me if I lie*
> *For they instructed me to live, not die.*
> *"Grief cannot compensate for what is lost,"*
> *They told me. "Win, and never mind the cost.*
> *Show to the world the face the world would see;*
> *Be slave, be pet, conceal your Self—but be."*

Lurking behind the docile Christian lamb,
Unconquered lioness asserts: "I am!"

V

Voices for a New Age— 1960s/1970s

Elma Stuckey
(1907—1988)

LONG COTTON ROW

Lord, don't set that sun
On the long cotton row,
Look like I done chopped
'til I can't chop no mo'.

Shoo that sun over there
Right behind that cloud,
Then when breeze come 'long
I be mighty proud.

That'll make the day mo' easy,
Won't seem so long gettin' through,
And if I ain't too broken down
I'll sho be praisin' You,
That's if I ain't too broken down . . .

THE BIG GATE

*Slaves often stood out of earshot of
the master, down at the gate to the path leading
to the great house, and told
tall tales. . . .*

I

We's gathered here to tell our tales
'bout how we treat Ole Marse,
Some tales be big, some tales be small,
Sometimes the tales be sparse.

189

II

First of all I tell my tale.
None of you was 'round
When I pick up my fist and say,
"I'll knock you to the ground."

I say, "Old Marse, I owns you,
You knows that you is mine."
That man, he whimper like a dog,
Ain't nothin' in his spine.

Now if Ole Marse come up here
To raise hell like the dickens,
I'll chase him right between you all
And scatter you like chickens.

III

There ain't no Marse can trick me,
I'se always on the ball,
I take my fist and knock 'em dead
And don't care where they fall.

Last one I whupped, here come Miss,
She say, "Marse on the flo'!
What happen' to your Marsa?
Don't say that you don't know."

I say, "Ole Miss, I do my work
Like you done told me to,
I call you when I see him fall,
What else I s'pose to do?"

IV

I'm stuck wid Marse, he stuck wid me.
He tried to sell me twice,
The traders say, "Hell no, not Bose,
Not Bose at any price."

The secret is, I'se on the block
And so I thumbs my nose.

Marse do not see but traders see,
That's why they don't want Bose.

V

Shucks, I ain't scared o' Marse,
I treat him like a snake.
I twist his neck and stomp his tail
And curl him 'round my rake.

I talks to him like I is boss
And talk like he is slave.
If any Tom is at this gate
I put him in his grave.

VI

Ole Miss' tell Marse to beat me!
I is in puzzlement.
She knows I is de mean one,
Ain't broken and ain't bent.

I run smack-dab into dat man
And choke 'im like de devil,
Ole Missus look and clap de hands,
Say, "Boys, go git de shovel!"

VII

We s'pose to listen at this gate
But no one's heard me yet.
I got a tale to beat all tales—
Don' b'lieve me? What you bet?

I kilt Old Marse and buried him—
You think I lie? I ain't—
If you see somethin' look like Marse
Just pay no mind, that's haint.

VIII

From miles around they knowed me,
Plantation to plantation.

I is most stubborn slave of all,
I'se hell and all damnation.

Nobody rule this brawny man,
Nobody try to whip 'im.
If S.O.B. stand up to me
I sho' to hell will lick 'im.

I'se bad, real bad, Marse knows I'se bad,
Bet you don't see 'im comin',
And if you see Old Marse at all
You see his back, he runnin'.

IX

Look folks, pay me some 'tention
'bout what I got to say,
Y'all just so glad that Marse is dead
And buried yesterday.

Nobody ask one question,
What kilt him, made him sick?
Since you ain't ask, I shut my mouth
'bout why he died so quick.

X

I'se wishin' I could drown Ole Marse,
He plays into my hand,
Come at me when I'm fishin'
And come er-raisin' sand.

We grapple and we struggle,
We hit the river bed,
We down there where no one can see
And so I push his head.

Now that's the last I seen of him,
Don't blame no mess on me
Because I swim up to the top
And he float out to sea.

XI

Marse give us head, he give us tail
And then he give us middlins,
He give us ears, he give us feet
And then he give us chittlins.

I slip and burn the smoke house down,
Ole Marse rage and cuss,
He knowed we et the hams and ribs
that done been cooked for us.

XII

Had three Marsas in my time,
Each one was scared of me,
But being white they had to bluff
'cause other slaves would see.

They knew they could not whip me
But each just had to try,
And I done warned, "You lift that whip,
You kiss this world goodbye."

They raised the whip, I kept my word,
They never lay a lick on me,
I betcha you can find three graves
And I ain't on no tree.

XIII

Little bit of lye each day
Stirred easy in his whiskey.
Now he am in de family plot,
That way it were not risky.

XIV

Ole Marse would whup me in de field,
He says I is de lazies',
I smart 'nough to choke him good
And now he pushin' daisies.

XV

My trouble were not with Old Marse,
It were with Marsa's Missis.
She make me climb in bed with her
And say it bettern' his is.

XVI

Hot weather come, I fan that man
'til he drop off to sleep.
I scratch my head and figure how
To make his sleep be deep.

I gather up some poison weeds
And beat them into dust,
And fan it close while he am sleep
And that am fair and just.

One night that dust hit home on him,
He did not cough or hack,
But keeled and died with crooked neck,
Doc called it heart attack.

XVII

I sing and dance for my Old Marse,
I holler and I whoop,
He think I happy and I is
'bout to fly the coop.

XVIII

Ole Marse, he had stud nigger,
Dat nigger hit de lick!
Ole Missus heard about him
And now she big as tick.

XIX

I put spiders in the pot,
Black widows to be sho'
They et and praise me highly,
I'se glad to see them go.

XX

I goes up to the big house
Before Ole Missus rise,
I stand right over Missus' bed
And catch her by surprise.

I say, "Git up, you lazy thing,
Git up and cook for me."
She buck her eyes 'til they pop out,
So scared she cannot see.

I tell her, "You no mo' Miss Anne,
To me you plain old Annie.
Call me Miss Lue and do it quick
Or else I whip your fannie."

She say, "I'm white and I can't cook,
My white lips can't say Miss."
I say, "I slap you side your head—
Now you take that and this!"

Here come Ole Marse from other room,
"Miss Lue, if what I see
Is that you slap old Annie's face,
Hit one more lick for me."

XXI

Saint Peter tell me watch his gate,
Don't let no bad 'uns in,
And so I put my hands on hips
To stop each one that sin.

I see Ole Marsa treckin' 'long,
He trudgin' up the line,
And so I says unto myself,
At last your meat is mine.

He at the gate, he see me there,
He rear way back and swell,
I slam that gate and say to him,
"You git the hell to hell!"

XXII

Everyone done told a tale,
The last tale fall on me,
I got no right talking here
'cause y'all know I'se free.

I sho' don't chop no cotton
And I don't pick none too,
Marsa is so scared of me
I is the "Booger Boo."

I goes this way and that way
And never need no pass,
Ole Marse look down, cap in hand,
He know he bet' not sass.

Marse a lush head son of a gun,
I just now caught him plastered.
Go on y'all, lay in the shade,
'cause I done kilt the bastard.

REBEL

I break the hoe, I break the plow
And here he come, that hellion.
I say right then unto myself,
This a one-man rebellion.

I stand foursquare and face Old Marse,
He call me crazy nigger,
I rush him and I take his gun
And then I pull the trigger.

My time is come and I don't care
If they hang me from a tree,
By bein' crazy like a fox
I sent Marse 'head of me.

SOUTHERN BELLE

Ole Missus is a vile one,
Got everything, she rich!
But walk around house niggers
Buck naked, not a stitch.

I don't know what she provin',
Ole Marsa love the shacks,
There's something in them quarters
That his Ole Missus lacks.

THIS IS IT

I holler hallelujah,
I jump up and I shout,
Ain't gettin' on my knees no more,
Done just 'bout wore 'em out.

Things go 'long about the same,
I try to do what's right,
I can't please Marse and can't please God,
I reckon He is white.

I always prayed to the Lord
That things be turned about,
Ain't gettin' on my knees no more,
Done just 'bout wore 'em out.

LET THEM COME

Let them come
As they usually do by night
With eyes of blue steel
And hearts of stone,

Let them come
As they usually do in throngs
With whiskey breath and
Tobacco dripping mouths
To take one black,

Let them wait
As they usually do
Squatting on haunches
Lusting for blood,

Let them come, let them come,
Not a one would dare
Come alone.

DEFENSE

De fence they keep on talking 'bout
Must gonna be powerful strong.
Done taken all them soldier boys,
Must gonna be powerful long.

Done ask us all to help with it
And I can't figger why
Unless that it's gonna be
A fence that's mighty high.

De forest we been savin'
Will be split up for de rails.
We got to make it strong they say
And hammer it with nails.

They say de enemy is awful,
Say he likely to commence
For to messin' with the country
If he break in through de fence.

If he ever charge at me
Just like he ain't got no sense,
I ain't gonna stand there like er fool,
One of us gonna jump de fence.

TEMPTATION

I was offered roses,
There were thorns,
I did not reach.

I was offered jewels:
lustrous pearls, dazzling rubies
and beautiful sapphires,
I was not impressed,
Again, I did not reach.

I was offered longevity,
I did not reach
for old age and its problems.
Alas, I was offered peace,
quiet and rest.
With all my heart and soul
I reached—and
embraced death.

RIBBONS AND LACE

For A. Clifford Brown

Aint Rachel was an ex-slave,
Mulatto, midwife, and infidel who lived
In Shelby County, Tennessee.
Like a witch riding in on a broom,
She would appear at our house,
Never knocking at the door or announcing herself.
We would happen to look around and there
She was with her little brown dog, Pup,
And her little black bag.

She was a tiny woman with long straight
Mixed gray hair drawn back from her
Forehead which was covered with a damp
Rag filled with gypsum weed to ward off headaches.
Her nose was like a beak and her thin lips curled
Over scattered teeth.
Aint Rachel kept a twig in one corner of her mouth
Which she would now and then dip in her snuff box.
One long tooth protruded.

It was brown from snuff dipping
And it was difficult to tell which was twig
And which was tooth.
Her eyes were like slits and were somber-looking.

Pup seems to have taken on her expression:
He had eyes like slits that had a somber appearance.
Pup was always close to her skirts and
Where they stood or sat they looked
As if they had grown there.
To hear her laugh was frightening:
Her expression at such times never changed.

During winter or summer, Aint Rachel
Wore the same type of clothes,
Several long black skirts and a man's
Suit coat buttoned up and fastened at
The neck with a safety pin.
She would say on a hot day,
"De same thing keep out de cold, keep out de heat."
There was a nutmeg on a string around
Her neck, and tied around her waist was
A blue check apron with a big pocket
In which she carried her snuff box and fresh eggs.

We were small children and would whisper about Aint
Rachel. Mamma would make us go into the next room
And we would push and shove to look thru
The keyhole at her.
We were fascinated by her little black bag
And wondered if there was a baby in it.
Mamma and Papa always used the doctor
To bring babies but it made no difference to Aint Rachel.
Whenever Mamma was pregnant, she came
And sat around, hoping to "ketch de baby."
She'd say to Mamma, "You like
Er settin' hen, can't come out, so I
Come to see you."
We heard other fragments of conversation,
"I jes fed Pup his gun powder and sweet milk.
If anybody bothers me, Pup will *bardaciously*
Et em' up. I can't tarry long,
Gotta go see Martha who swallowed er punkin seed."
She looked at her black bag and said,
"She'll be needin' me soon."

Aint Rachel had another practice, claiming she
Could "fix" any woman so she would get pregnant.

She got quite a bit of money from a white man
Whose wife never conceived.
He was angry and brought his wife back
And was told by Aint Rachel:
"Tell 'er to come inside and I'll zamin' her."
Aint Rachel put the woman on the kitchen
Table and when she finished zaminin' her
Told him, "Aint a thing in de
World wrong wid your wife.
All she need ter
Do is ter change mens."

When mamma asked Aint Rachel to
Come to church sometime,
She answered: "De church is alright till de
Folks git in. Anyway, if its er God
Up there, whuts He hidin' fuh?
Ought to come out in de open.
Yez, de church is full uv washpot
Prayin.' Dat's all 'tis, en He aint hearin' it."
She told how slaves used to turn down
An iron pot, put a stick under it,
Then lie on the ground beside
The pot and pray.
This was done so the pot
Could catch the sound without
Ole Marsa hearing it.
"Hah, de prayers didn't git no further dan de wash pot.
I aint studdin' bout God.
He did't know my mamma en
He don't know me.
My pappy, my slave master, took me from
My mamma at birth and I wuz raised at de big house.
Where wuz God when I was took from my mamma?
Hah, hidin' out!"

Aint Rachel talked about her life
As a child at the big house.
She said that things then were easy,
That she was never sent to the fields to work.
A frequent remark of hers was: "I played
Like er kitten and minded ole missus children."
She added that her father was a doctor

"En made er pet uv me.
Later, my pappy use ter take me
On his rounds ter see de sick.
While he was inside tendin' de sick,
I sat outside and held de hosses.
My pappy used ter give big balls,
And when I grew up I use to dance
Fer de folks, all dressed up
In ribbons en lace.
Got de dresses in my trunk to prove it.
I'll dress up in 'em sometimes—ribbons en lace.

"Yez, my pappy wuz er real doctor.
Why dese newfangled doctors uv today
Will cut yer heart out en call it er tumor.
I'm bettern most uv em, en I
Make es good er medicine as de next one."
When mamma asked her how
She got her medical training,
She was indignant, answering, "Didn't
I set outside en hold de hosses?
Well I'm gwine now, Pup wants ter go."
Even though Pup appeared to be asleep,
With one motion she and Pup got up
And sailed off with Pup practically
Riding the hem of her skirts.

Some days Aint Rachel would talk about white folks,
Which she especially enjoyed doing when
She hadn't been paid for delivering a white baby.
She'd fuss and fume, "I'll 'sick' Pup
On 'em if they ever come 'round me!
Dey lie and de truth aint in 'em.
Claim dey give us freedom, didn't dey?
Dey give it ter us locked in er box
En de white man kept de key.
Try ter bust de box open, like hittin' on dynamite.
Like Pup barkin' et de moon.
Das how far off yer freedom is."

The next day she'd take the Negro for her topic.
Smiling, she'd say, "I'm straddle
De fence and can talk erbout de white en de black.

202

I'll neer jin Hemp's church,
He's er parson wid concubines.
Undertaker Riggin' will never bury my body;
He's es crooked es er barrel uv snakes.
Now you take Mr. Wilson,
I married him cause he could read."
Each Sunday during Mr. Wilson's
Lifetime, he bathed, dressed
And sat on the front porch and read the paper.
She'd have him sit in the opening
Between the vines so that he could be seen reading.

As we grew older, we were sent to the
Store and had to pass Aint Rachel's house.
Her yard was filled with fig, elderberry,
Mulberry, and peach trees.
There was gypsum weed, sage, mint,
Tansy, and other herbs from which she made medicine.
A bayou swirled and curved through her yard.
There were roosters crowing, hens
Cackling and chicken coops scattered around.

Though the board of health had been after her
To put in a bathroom,
She still had a privy half-hidden by the vines and trees.
She had "sicked" Pup on the man from the board of health
But Pup only wagged his tail.
She excused him by saying,
"I hadn't fed him his gun powder and sweet milk."

Aint Rachel's house was frame and right on the ground,
With two steps leading to the porch.
The windows were covered with shutters and
There was a lattice across the porch covered with vines,
So we could never be sure whether she was
Sitting behind the lattice.
When all at once she would call us,
Afraid, we would hold hands.
Yet we were fascinated by her and would
Sit on the steps as close to her as we could get.

Once she told us she had hoodooed old man Joe Thomas.
She prophesied he would die in a day or so and

Took three sips from a level dipper of
Water and called out "Joe Thomas" three times,
Tossed the water over her left shoulder,
Letting it fall on the ground, then told us,
"I put 'em right back in de ground
Whar he come from."
A few weeks later, when Mr. Thomas died
Aint Rachel took credit for his death.
Not long thereafter, she showed a wisp
Of a woman's hair, put it in an empty
Snuff box and told us, "Someday
If I get mad enough, I'll throw
De snuff box in de bayou. When I do dat,
A certain woman gwine crazy es er bed bug."

Once Aint Rachel asked us, "Wanna see inside my house?"
It sounded sinister but we were lured
Inside a room with half-closed shutters.
There were odd shaped tables, chairs and a high
Bed with a bright colored quilt.
A large picture of Mr. Wilson hung over
The bed and his eyes seemed to follow us.
There were some small plantation pictures
Hanging on the walls.
As we looked at a picture of Negroes
Picking cotton, Aint Rachel said, "My folks."
We saw pictures of white people standing
In front of a big colonial house and
She said, "My folks. But I don't take no stock in 'em."
When we asked to see inside her trunk,
She told us, "Never been opened since Mr. Wilson died."
That scared us and we didn't want to see
Her dresses trimmed in ribbons and lace.

We returned to the porch and asked her
To tell us some tales of slavery.
The one I liked best was about
Her half-brother, Jim.
She said that Jim was a hard working
Man and swore as he chopped cotton
Under the blazing sun.

He would accuse God of "sicking"
The sun on the long rows of cotton.

Aint Rachel related his strange deathbed wish:
He wanted his hoe buried with him.
She smiled and said, "I guess he gwine ter chop his way into
heaben."

On Halloween night, the question was, "Is Aint Rachel out
tonight?"
Just as if she were a lion.
All at once she'd appear, her long skirts
Floating in the air.
She did't need a mask,
All she had to do was come out.
She'd chase us with Pup at our heels barking furiously.
We screamed with fear and delight.

Years passed and somehow I was no
longer afraid of Aint Rachel.
I would sit on her steps as I had as a child.
She could hardly get around because of rheumatism
and great age.
Still, she liked to hear of new babies in the neighborhood.
She'd look at her gnarled hands and remark,
"Dey ketched and spanked er many baby."
Once in a while someone would come for medicine.
She was proud that people remembered her
Medicine and continued to sing her praises as a doctor.
And she continued to let Pup romp
In her backyard until one day he lay
Exhausted at her back door.
Aint Rachel brought him inside and doctored on him
But, despite her medicine, Pup died
A few days later.
I was there when he died and tried
To console her, but her voice was
Filled with sadness as she praised Pup,
"Yez, Pup wuz de best dat ever lived.
He *bardaciously* ate up anybody dat bothered me.
De grave don't mean nothin' ter Pup.
He'll come out if he's er mind ter."
I helped her inside the house and realized that
She was seriously ill.

Mamma and others took food to her but she barely ate.
Though she wore her head rag, she complained of headaches.

Eventually Lena, a niece of hers who came to
Take care of her, asked her if she wanted
Reverend Hemp to come and pray for her.
Mention of his name almost gave Aint Rachel a stroke.
She screamed, "If he come 'round me,
I'll call Pup from de grave!"
She didn't want a doctor and still
Thought her medicine was "es good es de next ones."
However, the doctor came, left some pills
And told Lena that Aint Rachel would not last much longer.

She grew weaker and slept most of the time.
One morning, she just slept away.
When we heard about it, undertaker Riggin
Was carrying her body out.
Aint Rachel's words came back to me:
"He's es crooked es er barrel uv snakes."
The neighborhood was saddened and frightened—
Children hung onto their mothers' skirts.
Suddenly her house had a strange, deserted look
And for the first time we noticed that
Weeds had almost overtaken it.

The day of the funeral came and undertaker
Riggin's place was filled with white and Negro people.
Reverend Hemp walked in, his cane over one arm,
His celluloid collar turned backward.
He wore a frock-tail coat and carried a tattered Bible.
A murmur went through the crowd.
No one seemed to know how it was
That Rev. Hemp was to preach the funeral.
Then there was complete silence.
Reverend Hemp's eyes had a yellowish
Cast and he was feeble from old age.
He placed his feet wide apart to brace himself
And broke the silence by bellowing out:
"Dars great rejoicin' in heaben dis moanin'!
Ah say dars grate rejoicin' in heaben dis moanin'!
Ah tell ya, er lost sheep is found!
De angels is singin', Ah tell ya . . ."
He was off to a good start.

Soon we heard someone coming past
The parlour talking gibberish and laughing

In a high thin voice.
I recalled the words, "If I get
mad enough, I'll throw de snuff
Box in de bayou. When I do dat,
Er certain woman gwine crazy es er bed bug."
My mind was wandering, reviewing the
Many hours spent with Aint Rachel.
From somewhere far off came the
Sound of a dog barking and I recalled
The words: "De grave don't mean
Nothin' to Pup; he'll come out if hc's er mind ter."

The choir was singing "Just As I Am"
And Reverend Hemp was wiping perspiration
From his face as I joined the others
To view Aint Rachel.
Some were crying softly and some were screaming
"Aint Rachel's gone, gone!"
She looked so tiny, so frail,
So strange.
She was all dressed up in ribbons and lace.

Dudley Randall
(1914–)

ROSES AND REVOLUTIONS

Musing on roses and revolutions,
I saw night close down on the earth like a great dark wing,
and the lighted cities were like tapers in the night,
and I heard the lamentations of a million hearts
regretting life and crying for the grave,
and I saw the Negro lying in the swamp with his face
　　blown off,
and in northern cities with his manhood maligned and felt
　　the writhing
of his viscera like that of the hare hunted down or the
　　bear at bay,
and I saw men working and taking no joy in their work
and embracing the hard-eyed whore with joyless excitement
and lying with wives and virgins in impotence.

And as I groped in darkness
and felt the pain of millions,
gradually, like day driving night across the continent,
I saw dawn upon them like the sun a vision
of a time when all men walk proudly through the earth
and the bombs and missiles lie at the bottom of the ocean
like the bones of dinosaurs buried under the shale of eras,
and men strive with each other not for power or the
　　accumulation of paper
but in joy create for others the house, the poem, the game
　　of athletic beauty.

Then washed in the brightness of this vision,
I saw how in its radiance would grow and be nourished
　　and suddenly
burst into terrible and splendid bloom
the blood-red flower of revolution.

LEGACY: MY SOUTH

What desperate nightmare rapts me to this land
Lit by a bloody moon, red on the hills,
Red in the valleys? Why am I compelled
To tread again where buried men have trod,
To shed my tears where blood and tears have flowed?
Compulsion of the blood and of the moon
Transports me. I was molded from this clay.
My blood must ransom all the blood shed here,
My tears redeem the tears. Cripples and monsters
Are here. My flesh must make them whole and hale.
I am the sacrifice.

　　　　　　　See where the halt
Attempt again and again to cross a line
Their minds have drawn, but fear snatches them back
Though health and joy wait on the other side.
And there another locks himself in a room
And throws away the key. A ragged scarecrow
Cackles an antique lay, and cries himself
Lord of the world. A naked plowman falls
Famished upon the plow, and overhead
A lean bird circles

CORAL ATOLL

No wedding ring of doges, this white cirque that lies
dazzling, immaculate, upon the blue
of wide Pacific. High the airman sees
small ships crawl past it, and the surf exclaim
upon that O in foam less shining white.

No spiny island hurled out of the deep
by birthpangs of an earthquake is this round,
or green plateau that's sentient with warm life.
Things without thought, unvisioned and undreamed,
through mute numb years under the swaying tides
have died into a perfect form that sings.

Lance Jeffers
(1919–1985)

MY BLACKNESS IS THE BEAUTY OF THIS LAND

My blackness is the beauty of this land,
my blackness,
tender and strong, wounded and wise,
my blackness:
I, drawling black grandmother, smile muscular and sweet,
unstraightened white hair soon to grow in earth,
work-thickened hand thoughtful and gentle on grandson's
    head,
my heart is bloody-razored by a million memories' thrall:

> remembering the crook-necked cracker who spat
>   on my naked body,
> remembering the splintering of my son's spirit
>   because he remembered to be proud
> remembering the tragic eyes in my daughter's
>   dark face when she learned her color's meaning,

and my own dark rage a rusty knife with teeth to gnaw
    my bowels,
my agony ripped loose by anguished shouts in Sunday's
    humble church,
my agony rainbowed to ecstasy when my feet oversoared
    Montgomery's slime,

ah, this hurt, this hate, this ecstasy before I die,
and all my love a strong cathedral!
My blackness is the beauty of this land!

Lay this against my whiteness, this land!
Lay me, young Brutus stamping hard on the cat's tail,
gutting the Indian, gouging the nigger,

booting Little Rock's Minniejean Brown in the buttocks
    and boast, my sharp white teeth derision-bared as I
    the conqueror crush!
Skyscraper-I, white hands burying God's human clouds
    beneath the dust!
Skyscraper-I, slim blond young Empire
    thrusting up my loveless bayonet to rape the sky,
then shrink all my long body with filth and in the gutter lie
as lie I will to perfume this armpit garbage,
While I here standing black beside
wrench tears from which the lies would suck the salt
to make me more American than America . . .
But yet my love and yet my hate shall civilize this land,
this land's salvation.

WHEN I KNOW THE POWER OF MY BLACK HAND

I do not know the power of my hand,
I do not know the power of my black hand.

I sit slumped in the conviction that I am powerless,
tolerate ceilings that make me bend.
My godly mind stoops, my ambition is crippled;
I do not know the power of my hand.

I see my children stunted,
my young men slaughtered,
I do not know the mighty power of my hand.

I see the power over my life and death in
another man's hands, and sometimes
I shake my woolly head and wonder:

    Lord have mercy! What would it be like . . . to be free?

But when I know the mighty power of my black hand
    I will snatch my freedom from the tyrant's mouth,
know the first taste of freedom on my eager tongue,
sing the miracle of freedom with all the force
    of my lungs,
christen my black land with exuberant creation,
stand independent in the hall of nations,

root submission and dependence from the soil of my soul
and pitch the monument of slavery from my back when
I know the mighty power of my hand!

TRELLIE

From the old slave shack I chose my lady,
from the harsh garden of the South,
from the South's black children,
from the old slaves bending between the rows of cotton,
from Charlie James whose soul was African in
    the unredeeming Southern sun,
from the song of slaves who choked the sky like
    chitlins down their throats,
from the woman dark who stood and leaned back as
    Southern women do, her stomach out, her shoulders
    back,
    and wombed the grandeur of her poetry in song as
    long and deep as prehistoric night,
in song as causeful as the fiery center of the earth,
in love as muscular as the thighs of
    darkskinned god who cradled Africa to his chest,
in love as nippled as the milk that flows from Nile to sea:

She lies beside me in the night
    who is the greatness of the slaves without their fear,
she is the anger of this day and elegant pride
    that touched the child who walked three miles to
    school and saw white children's bus leave her trampling
    in the dust:

There is a beauty here that I aspire:
there is a grandeur here that I require:
the Southern loam to throw into the sandbags of my soul:
some other rapture that my song must lyre,
some woolier head to batter the entombment of my fire:
to lay my stunted heart upon the pyre and blow upon
    my godliness till it come down my mouth,
    the soul of my grandfather's sire
    when he stood harried in slavery.

As I lie beside her in the night I see America's
    birth in death

and tyranny grind its knife to seek my veins,
I see myself in prison camp alone,
hooking the guillotine's eye to my neckflesh when
    morning comes,
and she weeping and engrieved within my breast.

What more marrowed sorrow could there be
when tear large as blackness' pyramid will lodge my eye
    and drop, when my blood prepares to sink beneath
    the soil?

But Trellie's kin
    will run the reindeer down from frozen North
and bring her love to me within my grave,
to all my whiter crimes and grudging heart,
to all my assasination of myself, and all my unyielding
    hatred of tyranny.
All my children's New World conquering will grow like
    elephant tusks from earth I drench in blood:
ten thousand children will redwood from my genes
    to mount the earth in my black people's time!

ON LISTENING TO THE SPIRITUALS

When the master lived a king and I a starving hutted slave
    beneath the lash, and

when my five-year-old son was driven at dawn to cottonfield
    to pick until he could no longer see the sun, and

when master called my wife to the big house when mistress
    was gone,
took her against her will and gave her a dollar to be still, and
when she turned upon her pride and cleavered it, cursed
    her dignity
and stamped on it, came back to me with his evil on her
    thighs,
hung her head when I condemned her with my eyes,

what broken mettle of my soul wept steel, cracked teeth in
self-contempt upon my flesh, crept underground to seek
new roots and secret breathing place?

When all the hatred of my bones was buried in a forgotten
    county of my soul,
then from beauty muscled from the degradation of my
    oaken bread,
I stroked on slavery soil the mighty colors of my song:
    a passionate heaven rose no God in heaven could create!

O AFRICA, WHERE I BAKED MY BREAD

O Africa, where I baked my bread
        in the streets at 15 through
        the San Francisco midnights . . .
O Africa, whose San Francisco shouting-church
        on Geary Street and Webster saw a candle
        burning in the middle of my madness . . .
O Africa, whose Fatha Hines and Teddy Wilson
        I took to my piano . . .
O Africa within every brown breast that's
                    suckled me,
        Africa's thousand calmings of my mother-
                    hunger
        across the North American continent . . .
O Africa, within the black folk who've loved me
        in this prelude to the sip-blood time . . .
Africa, I lay my hand upon your swarthy belly—
        and keep it there till death stubs his toe
        against my manhood in the night!

BUT I KNOW THAT UNSEEN
ANGER RUNS A RAFT

But I know that he runs a raft
on an unseen river somewhere
and shakes his beard at the sky.

I know this greyhaired man, old and iron-muscled
            and iron in his eye.

I see him stand upon his raft and never sing
    or speak but sink his thought in the sweet
    blue river and stare at the purple hills.

214

Unwashed, greyhairchested, resolute, immortal,
   Anger wipes the sweat from his forehead
   and sits to sharpen his knife.

SELF-DOUBT

Is the fire out? Is the fire out?
Slash your breast open, remove the doubt.
If where the heart was known to beat
you hear the sound of boneless feet
shuffling through watery blood and bloodless gristle,
then scratch your brain with a thornless thistle
and bow your head, let it fall
like a fuseless sun in God's coffin hall.

Mari Evans
(1923–)

I AM A BLACK WOMAN

I am a black woman
the music of my song
some sweet arpeggio of tears
is written in a minor key
and I
can be heard humming in the night
Can be heard
                humming
in the night

I saw my mate leap screaming to the sea
and I/with these hands/cupped the lifebreath
from my issue in the canebrake
I lost Nat's swinging body in a rain of tears
and heard my son scream all the way from Anzio
for Peace he never knew. . . . I
learned Da Nang and Pork Chop Hill
in anguish
Now my nostrils know the gas
and these trigger tire/d fingers
seek the softness in my warrior's beard

I
am a black woman
tall as a cypress
strong
beyond all definition still
defying place
and time
and circumstance
    assailed

    impervious
        indestructible
Look
    on me and be
renewed

WHERE HAVE YOU GONE

Where have you gone

with your confident
walk with
your crooked smile

why did you leave
me
when you took your
laughter
and departed

are you aware that
with you
went the sun
all light
and what few stars
there were?

where have you gone
with your confident
walk your
crooked smile the
rent money
in one pocket and
my heart
in another . . .

SPEAK THE TRUTH TO THE PEOPLE

Speak the truth to the people
Talk sense to the people
Free them with reason

217

Free them with honesty
Free the people with Love and Courage and Care for
        their Being
Spare them the fantasy
Fantasy enslaves
A slave is enslaved
Can be enslaved by unwisdom
Can be enslaved by black unwisdom
Can be re-enslaved while in flight from the enemy
Can be enslaved by his brother whom he loves
His brother whom he trusts
His brother with the loud voice
And the unwisdom
Speak the truth to the people
It is not necessary to green the heart
Only to identify the enemy
It is not necessary to blow the mind
Only to free the mind
To identify the enemy is to free the mind
A free mind has no need to scream
A free mind is ready for other things

To BUILD black schools
To BUILD black children
To BUILD black minds
To BUILD black love
To BUILD black impregnability
To BUILD a strong black nation
To BUILD.

Speak the truth to the people.
Spare them the opium of devil-hate.
They need no trips on honky-chants.
Move them instead to a BLACK ONENESS.
A black strength which will defend its own
Needing no cacophony of screams for activation
A black strength which attacks the laws
exposes the lies disassembles the structure
and ravages the very foundation of evil.

Speak the truth to the people
To identify the enemy is to free the mind
Free the mind of the people

Speak to the mind of the people
Speak Truth.

THE WRITERS

Where did they go
the Writers?

> chests pulsing under kente cloth The
> Word clenched in sweaty fists
> Strength so awesome none approached
> without a questioning, a quickening
> "Am I incorrect?" "O tell me, brother!
> Am I incorrect?"

Where did they go
the Writers?

> With the wisdoms learned from bluesteel
> butts from cement crypts and
> With their ancient sealed potential

They have gone to whiteland, sister
                        There they lie

healed by white lips
    soothed by white hands
        stoned in white beds
            bound again in silken chains
whispering in an alien tongue
                        litanies

    None but me/Miss Annie
    None but me/pale comrade

                        with the quick tongue
                        with the rockblue eyes

Where did they go
the Writers?
                Beautiful
                    Black
    chests pulsing under kente cloth The
    Word clenched in sweaty fists

They have gone to whiteland, sister

Am I incorrect?

O tell me, brother

Am I incorrect?

WHO CAN BE BORN BLACK

Who
can be born black
and not
sing
the wonder of it
the joy
the
challenge

And/to come together
in a coming togetherness
vibrating with the fires of pure knowing
reeling with power
ringing with the sound above sound above sound
to explode/in the majesty of our oneness
our comingtogether
in a comingtogetherness

Who
can be born
black
and not exult!

Pinkie Gordon Lane
(1923–   )

A QUIET POEM

This is a quiet poem
Black people don't write
many quiet poems
because what we feel
is not a quiet hurt.
And a not-quiet hurt
does not call
for muted tones.

But I will write a poem
about this evening
full of the sounds
of small animals, some fluttering
in thick leaves, a smear
of color here and there—
about the whisper of darkness
a gray wilderness of light
descending, touching
breathing.

I will write a quiet poem
immersed in shadows
and mauve colors
and spots of white
fading into deep tones
of blue.

This is a quiet evening
full of hushed singing
and light that has no
ends, no breaking
of the planes, or brambles
thrusting out.

MIDNIGHT SONG

If I were sitting
on the banks of the river
I would write poems
about seaweed or flotsam
making their way
to the end of the sea
or the expanse of the bridge
that falls into the sky

If a flight to nowhere
curled waves of air
beneath my feet
or framed my vision, a poem
would draw images
from wings of the jet
filling corners of clouds

But my blue room—
where I die each night—
frames this poem
The curtain is striped
blue on white
the walls the color
of twilight just before death
of the sun
and the doors pale
as the morning sky

And so I write
a blue-room poem
My mind penetrates walls
and hangs like mist
on the wake of trees
swaying low over the town

Only the crickets know
I am there, and they
sing songs
to the low-touching
wind   Only they
will know

I have passed over the earth
gathering periwinkles
and ivy
to take to the hills

This poem plants itself
and grows like the jasmine
coating my fence
It creeps over the page
like holly fern
and bores into the depths
of my mind like the wild palm
that sentinels my yard's
center, spreading fanlike
at all points
caught up in a web
of light—
a ring of gold
painting the earth

TO A WOMAN POET THAT I KNOW

1

When you lie again
in the street of forgetfulness
smashed beyond recognition
courting the dark avenue,
when you wake to the alien
walls that do not touch
your battered flesh,

    your other self
    will fall into the locket
    of your mind and wait
    for truth

A creature without roots
standing on the brink
of private ruin
your voice will not save you
for you have found the power
of destruction

I weep for your lost
self that stands on the edge
of the terrible wood
whose darkness draws

2

If I could I would make
a gift: the magic of souls
spinning in the great center
that place where love meets
merged in the light

I would dispel your personal
and private hell
you, woman: black, lovely,
and lost
you, poet
whose voice cries out
to the silent air
that dissolves you

This elegy, this inscription
becomes the dichotomy,
the oxymoron, the paradox,
the beauty, the strength
of your existence
the destiny of this earth

ELEGY FOR ETHERIDGE

"what now
what now dumb nigger damn near dead
what now
now that you won't dance
behind the pale white doors of death. . . .
your mama sitting in a quiet corner
praying to a white/jesus to save her black boy"
        from "Another Poem for Me (after Recovering
    from an O.D.)" by Etheridge Knight

who knew the knight
of prison, whose poems

from that unholy place made
Hard Rock immortal—

who sang his songs of ancestry
who was linked to the clan, and yet
had "no sons to float
in the space between"—

who rode the trestle
till the end of his days,
whose songs were a spirit,
a "high," a *raison d'être* that
"literally saved my life," he said,
whose "soul [wanted to] sing"—

> Etheridge, like **Pooky Dee** who rode
> that trestle above his head
> daring death with each breath
> he took,
>
> *your* silence now "rolls like oil
> across the wide green water,"
> and you *now* "dance behind the pale
> white doors of death." Your mother
> need no longer pray to a "white/
> jesus to save her black boy."
>
> You left us your songs
>
> > to mourn your death,
> > to mourn your life,
> > to say the prayer that
> > > could not stop your headlong
> > > final plunge.

Etheridge, you dreamer and creator
of lines, you told us that
"Black Poets should live . . ."
are
> ". . . The Flutes of Black Lovers
> . . . The organs of Black Sorrows
> . . . The dust of marching feet."

Why did you leave us this space,
this emptiness, this **BELLY SONG**,
this prayer, this grave stone,
this chant of death for the dead?

Now, all we can say is:

Etheridge, we loved you.
Good-bye, good-bye, good-
bye. . . .

Bob Kaufman
(1925–1986)

BIRD WITH PAINTED WINGS

Monet whispered softly,
Drowned love
In pools of light.

Picasso shouted nightmares,
Screaming: Climb inside yourself,
There is a madness there.

Braque gave the echo, precisely.

Mondrian exposed squares.

As the Mexicans roared
In the star-torn Indian night,
Fire lifted Paricutin,
Springing red from black earth.

Modigliani, naked, exposed sadness.

Degas exposed angels in ballet skins,
Smoked behind walls of Marseilles' absinthe dens.

Kollwitz served tears in wooden spoons,
Under dark moons, forever sorrowed.

Rousseau shouted poetry
From his window on that mad world.

A burning bird whistled on high:
Eat it all,
Die!

WOULD YOU WEAR MY EYES?

My body is a torn mattress,
Disheveled throbbing place
For the comings and goings
Of loveless transients.
The whole of me
Is an unfurnished room
Filled with dank breath
Escaping in gasps to nowhere.
Before completely objective mirrors
I have shot myself with my eyes,
But death refused my advances.
I have walked on my walls each night
Through strange landscapes in my head.
I have brushed my teeth with orange peel,
Iced with cold blood from the dripping faucets.
My face is covered with maps of dead nations;
My hair is littered with drying ragweed.
Bitter raisins drip haphazardly from my nostrils
While schools of glowing minnows swim from my mouth.
The nipples of my breasts are sun-browned cockleburrs;
Long-forgotten Indian tribes fight battles on my chest
Unaware of the sunken ships rotting in my stomach.
My legs are charred remains of burned cypress trees;
My feet are covered with moss from bayous, flowing
   across my floor.
I can't go out anymore.
I shall sit on my ceiling.
Would you wear my eyes?

TO MY SON PARKER, ASLEEP
IN THE NEXT ROOM

On ochre walls in ice-formed caves shaggy Neanderthals
   marked their place in time.
On germinal trees in equatorial stands embryonic giants
   carved beginnings.
On Tasmanian flatlands mud-clothed first men hacked rock,
   still soft.
On Melanesian mountain peaks barked heads were reared
   in pride and beauty.

228

On steamy Java's cooling lava stooped humans raised stones
    to altar height.
On newborn China's plain mythless sons of Han acquired
    peaked gods with teak faces.
On holy India's sacred soil future gods carved worshipped
    reflections.
On Coptic Ethiopia's pimple rock pyramid builders tore
    volcanoes from earth.
On death-loving Egypt's godly sands living sacrifices carved
    naked power.
On Sumeria's cliffs speechless artists gouged messages
    to men yet uncreated.
On glorious Assyria's earthen dens art priests chipped
    figures of awe and hidden dimensions.
On splendored Peru's gold-stained body filigreed temples
    were torn from severed hands.
On perfect Greece's bloody sites marble stirred
    under hands of men.
On degenerate Rome's trembling sod imitators sculpted lies
    into beauty.
On slave Europe's prostrate form chained souls shaped free
    men.
On wild America's green torso original men painted
    glacial languages.
On cold Arctica's snowy surface leathery men raised totems
    in frozen air.
On this shore, you are all men, before, forever, eternally
    free in all things.
On this shore, we shall raise our monuments of stones,
      of wood, of mud, of color, of labor, of belief, of being,
      of life, of love, of self, of man expressed
      in self-determined compliance, or willful revolt,
      secure in this avowed truth, that no man is our master,
      nor can any ever be, at any time in time to come.

[THE NIGHT THAT LORCA COMES]

THE NIGHT THAT LORCA COMES
SHALL BE A STRANGE NIGHT IN THE
SOUTH, IT SHALL BE THE TIME WHEN NEGROES LEAVE
    THE SOUTH FOREVER,
GREEN TRAINS SHALL ARRIVE

FROM RED PLANET MARS
CRACKLING BLUENESS SHALL SEND TOOTH-COVERED CARS
  FOR THEM
TO LEAVE IN, TO GO INTO
THE NORTH FOREVER, AND I SEE MY LITTLE GIRL MOTHER
AGAIN WITH HER CROSS THAT
IS NOT BURNING, HER SKIRTS
OF BLACK, OF ALL COLORS, HER AURA
OF FAMILIARITY. THE SOUTH SHALL WEEP
BITTER TEARS TO NO AVAIL,
THE NEGROES HAVE GONE
INTO CRACKLING BLUENESS.
CRISPUS ATTUCKS SHALL ARRIVE WITH THE BOSTON
COMMONS, TO TAKE ELISSI LANDI
NORTH, CRISPUS ATTUCKS SHALL
BE LAYING ON BOSTON COMMONS,
ELISSI LANDI SHALL FEEL ALIVE
AGAIN. I SHALL CALL HER NAME
AS SHE STEPS ON TO THE BOSTON
COMMONS, AND FLIES NORTH FOREVER,
LINCOLN SHALL BE THERE,
TO SEE THEM LEAVE THE
SOUTH FOREVER, ELISSI LANDI, SHE WILL BE
GREEN.
THE WHITE SOUTH SHALL GATHER AT
PRESERVATION HALL.

230

Maya Angelou
(1928–)

NO LOSER, NO WEEPER

"I hate to lose something,"
    then she bent her head
"even a dime, I wish I was dead.
I can't explain it. No more to be said.
Cept I hate to lose something."

"I lost a doll once and cried for a week.
She could open her eyes, and do all but speak.
I believe she was took, by some doll-snatching-sneak
I tell you, I hate to lose something."

"A watch of mine once, got up and walked away.
It had twelve numbers on it and for the time of day.
I'll never forget it and all I can say
Is I really hate to lose something."

"Now if I felt that way bout a watch and a toy,
What you think I feel about my lover-boy?
I ain't threatening you madam, but he is my evening's joy.
And I mean I really hate to lose something."

WHEN I THINK ABOUT MYSELF

When I think about myself,
I almost laugh myself to death,
My life has been one great big joke,
A dance that's walked
A song that's spoke,
I laugh so hard I almost choke
When I think about myself.

Sixty years in these folks' world
The child I works for calls me girl
I say "Yes ma'am" for working's sake.
Too proud to bend
Too poor to break,
I laugh until my stomach ache,
When I think about myself.

My folks can make me split my side,
I laughed so hard I nearly died,
The tales they tell, sound just like lying,
They grow the fruit,
But eat the rind,
I laugh until I start to crying,
When I think about my folks.

TIMES-SQUARE-SHOESHINE-COMPOSITION

I'm the best that ever done it
(pow pow)
    that's my title and I won it
    (pow pow)
I ain't lying, I'm the best
(pow pow)
    Come and put me to the test
    (pow pow)

I'll clean 'em til they squeak
(pow pow)
    In the middle of next week,
    (pow pow)
I'll shine 'em til they whine
(pow pow)
    Till they call me master mine
    (pow pow)

For a quarter and a dime
(pow pow)
      You can get the dee luxe shine
    (pow pow)
Say you wanta pay a quarter?
(pow pow)

Then you give that to your daughter
(pow pow)

I ain't playing dozens mister
(pow pow)
You can give it to your sister
(pow pow)
Any way you want to read it
(pow pow)
Maybe it's your momma need it.
(pow pow)

Say I'm like a greedy bigot,
(pow pow)
I'm a cap'tilist, can you dig it?
(pow pow)

Ted Joans
(1928–   )

JAZZ IS MY RELIGION

JAZZ is my religion   and it alone do I dig   the jazz
    clubs are
my houses of worship   and sometimes the concert halls
    but some
holy places are too commercial (like churches)   so I
    don't dig the
sermons there   I buy jazz sides to dig in solitude   Like
    man/ Harlem,
Harlem U.S.A. used to be a jazz heaven where most of
    the jazz
sermons were preached   but now-a-days due to chacha
    cha and
rotten rock'n'roll alotta good jazzmen have sold their
    souls   but jazz
is still my religion   because I know and feel the message
    it brings
like Reverend Dizzy Gillespie/ Brother   Bird and
    Basie/ Uncle
Armstrong/ Minster Monk/ Deacon Miles Davis/ Rector
    Rollins/
Priest Ellington/ His Funkness Horace Silver/ and the great
    Pope
John, John COLTRANE   and Cecil Taylor   They
    Preach A Sermon
That Always Swings!!   Yeah jazz is MY religion   Jazz
    is my story
it was my mom's and pop's   and their moms and pops
    from the
days of Buddy Bolden who swung them blues to Charlie
    Parker and

Ornette Coleman's extension of Bebop   Yeah jazz is my
   religion
Jazz is a unique musical religion   the sermons spread
   happiness and
joy   to be able to dig and swing inside   what a
   wonderful feeling
jazz is/ YEAH BOY!!   JAZZ is my religion and dig this:
   it wasnt for
us to choose because they created it for a damn good
   reason   as   a
weapon to battle our blues!JAZZ is my religion   and its
international   all the   way   JAZZ is just an Afroamerican
   music
and like us its here to stay   So remember that JAZZ is
   my religion
but it can be your religion too but JAZZ is a truth that   is
   always
black and blue   Hallelujah I love JAZZ so   Hallelujah I
   dig JAZZ so
Yeah JAZZ   IS   MY   RELIGION

CUSTOMS & CULTURE?

perhaps what beans & potatos
mean to me is what
cornflakes and yoghurt mean to you
maybe the machines tell your insides
something similar to what the
drums inspire in me
do you really believe cold weather is
invigorating as the sunshine
is fine everyday everyway for me all the time
if you really think your way is right and fine
then why do you pass laws against mine?

Sarah Webster Fabio
(1928–1979)

OF PUDDLES, WORMS, SLIMY THINGS
(A Hoodoo Nature Poem)

For Ishmael Reed, Joe Overstreet

1 version

Hv merci on d po wrm who dares go it alone
fr luv of d rest left b' hind 'm
lest d movng shd b mistak'n
as d step brkng chains that bind 'm;

digng d feelng of t'gethrness
puddled tite wid d green 'n slimy things
wid a Jones for beng down wid yr sef
which trpng out brngs . . .

As d tide gos, so d soul gos out t d sea
at dawn; at nite washng bck t d shore;
brngng shells, stones, drift, weed
n puddls in d sand one mor time.

Worms gotta hv d lodestar
pulling 'm frm puddled despair
conning 'm t' split frm d wrm cocoon
n b butterfly n take d air.

GOD'S TROMBONE

*For James Weldon Johnson
creator of the "Negro National Anthem"*

Yesterday,
I heard a blind man
sound a new note

in a hot blast
on an old theme—
that of God's Trombone
which you defined so well
in idiom, form, texture,
harmony.

"Lift every voice
and sing/ till earth
and heaven ring," you
urged on the strength
of spirit that comes
with voices raised in
unison and affirmation
of the God-in-man.

A thing of beauty
your people gave to
the world, those lost
souls who were newly
awakening to the glory
and the mystique of
their ways and to the
prismatic splendor of
their blues-tinged days.

I WOULD BE FOR YOU RAIN

I would be for you rain,
yet, might bring into your
life, again, the storm;
summer days exact their dues:
troubled skies bring earth greener
hues. Lightning flashes through
the heavy air, rending it with
blinding light and thunderous
swells which press against the
inner drums of my still ears.

Have you forgotten
the grace of having wetness
rain about your face, of
watching greeness sprout,

bursting through the earth
beneath your mudcaked feet?

And for as far as the eye
can see lush fields abound,
and rainbows span the distant
hills.

I would be for you rain;
insistent, persistent, yet
intermittent. Too much
would swell the nearby waters,
flood your fruitladen fields,
laying them to waste, And,
drought has kinder hands.

Life stirs to be born again.
The waters usher in flowers
and grain. I would be for you
rain.

A TREE IS A LANDSCAPE: A LANDSCAPE
IS A POINT OF VIEW

1.

A tree
is a tree, is
a tree. A tree
is not
a tree; is a thing—
a physical object
in all its thingyness;
is an aesthetic abstraction—
a beauty; is functional—
a shaded place; is a psychic
balm—an umbrella to ward
off the intensity of the
natural elements; is a
security blanket; is
sometimes, a nuisance,
is an intrusion,
is an irrelevancy.

Have you ever seen
a concrete trunk reaching
skyward for grace, belching
soot and smog and obscene
shouts from its brick-tombed
arbor in some industrial park?

Have you ever seen erect
but charred-limb poles
sprout hot lines of
steel wire, fruiting the
high charged power to feed
a robot world while it
sputters, buzzes, is bugged and
chaos-infested from so many
lifetimes of frantic, futile
attempts at communication?

Nesting together at times,
they are like honeycombs of
alienation which turn a
world into a hornet's nest;
here, there are no willows
to bridge sky and uppointed
grass and the abounding
surrounding vineyards are
riddled with grapes of
wrath.

2.

Another world there is,
another world haunted
by spectral trees, not
of life but of death; or
even when most alive they are charged
with live death. And who
could love such a tree
in such a world?
Barkless, rootless,
leafless, fruitless—
these monsters are sentries
in a tenamented, wartorn

239

jungled world—shadeless,
rubbled, cold.

3.

There is a tree, is a tree,
is a tree manured in
the scum of man-made
city slum that is not
a tree, is not beauty,
is an enemy of beauty;
is an occupational force
and not a security factor;
is a red-lighted nightmare,
and not a shaded picnic spot;

is not a natural wonder,
is an unnatural horror;
is an intrusion;
is an irrelevancy in
the lives of the people
it would thwart in their
human need to seek out
the treeness of trees.

A tree is not a tree.
A tree is a landscape.
A landscape is a point of view.

Sure I trip
on natural things.
But, listen, My Man,
once your firm
limbs flex,
your plum-ripe face,
leaflined, crowned
with the wicked grace
of your curls and kinks,
JJJAAAAAAMMMMMMSSSSS
my mind with the sounds/
scents/feel/of you,
I say to hell with that
lush green tree,

240

the garden-of-eve vision
I contemplated in reverie.

It don't take a thing
but my mother wit, son,
to let this Mama know
you really turn me on.

Don't get me wrong.
Now, I love trees,
Well rooted ones
in fertile ground;
myriad leaves reaching
skyward; branches
offering shade in the
heat of the day.

Nuts, Baby,
What I mean is
that it's not the same thing.
Not the way I go for you,
growing wild,
when you
lumber up, unannounced,
proffering
your weather beaten
restless trunk—
cursed/blessed
with rootlessness.

Spooked, you're still
my ace, and I know you
never spend much time
in the same place.
But, remember,
it only takes a
moment.
And it ain't the deal
but the way it feels
that make me say,
"Whatever, you
sho nuff
come on
REAL."

241

TO TURN FROM LOVE

For Cyril

No,
I cannot
turn from love,
in affirmation,
with measured
finesse, like some
dull fuzzed cocoon
moltering into a
bright-winged butterfly,
a tight-brown bud
metamorphosing, with
sunburst halo, into
a chrysanthemum,
a five-o'clock
blossoming, with
daily gusto, into
full bloom.

No.
If I must
turn from love,
it will be with
the cadence of an
addict flinging poppy
from tremorous grasp
while retched with
the effort of breaking
the habit, or, a
gravedigger turning
daisy-filled clods
on a fresh made
bed.

EVIL IS NO BLACK THING

1.

Ahab's gaily clad fisherfriends,
questing under the blue skies after
the albino prize find the green sea

cold and dark at its deep center,
but calm—unperturbed by the fates
of men and whales.

Rowing shoreward, with wet and empty
hands, their sun-rich smiles fuzz
with bafflement as the frothing
surf buckles underneath and their
sea-scarred craft is dashed to pieces
near the shore: glancing backward,
the spiralling waves are white-capped.

2.

Evil is no black thing: black
the rain clouds attending a storm
but the fury of it neither begins
nor ends there. Weeping tear-clear
rain, trying to contain the hoarse
blue-throated thunder and the fierce
quick-silver tongue of lightning, bands
of clouds wring their hands.

Once I saw dark clouds in Texas
stand by idly while a Northeaster
screamed its icy puffs, ringtailing
raindrops, rolling them into baseballs
of hail, then descending upon the
tin-roofed houses, unrelentingly
battering them down.

3.

And the night is blackest where
gay throated cuckoos sing among the
dense firs of the Black Forest, where
terrible flurries of snow are blinding
bright: somewhere, concealed here deeply,
lies a high-walled town, whitewashed.

Seen at sunset, only the gaping ditch
and overhanging, crooked tree are painted
pitch to match the night: but I've seen

a dying beam of light reach through
the barred windows of a shower chamber,
illuminating its blood-scratched walls.

4.

Evil is no black thing: black
may be the undertaker's hearse
and so many of the civil trappings
of death, but not its essence:
the riderless horse, the armbands
and veils of mourning, the grave shine
darkly; but these are the rituals
of the living.

One day I found its meaning as I
rushed breathless through a wind-parched
field, stumbling unaware: suddenly there
it was, laying at my feet, hidden
beneath towering golden rods,
a criss-crossed pile of
sun-bleached bones.

THE HURT OF IT ALL

Ain't
nobody
heard me
singing
sweet songs
lately;
my sweet notes
soured
some time
ago—
raped,
robbed,
abandoned,
left rotting
in some
Southern
swill

which
stayed
too long
in the
Heart-of-
America
still,
turning
bad.

Ain't
nobody
heard me
singing
sweet songs
lately.
Where have
life's
sweet things
gone?
Flowers,
friends,
love and
tokens of love,
security,
beauty,
hope?
Nope,
nobody
seems to
know
where or
even when
all those
things,
those dreams,
those sentiments
we cherished
perished.

Ain't
nobody
heard me

singing
sweet songs
lately;
they turned
to ashes
in the
flashing
waste of
our great
hate.
Coltrane
couldn't
make it
either;
he knew
Sam Cooke
lied when
he said
"a change's
going to
come;" and
I watched
them
both die
before it
did.

Otis Redding
had an
inkling of
this truth
while sitting
on the dock of
the bay, both
of us swaying
while Aretha
plumbed the
depths of
the black
race's soul,
voicing a
juju of our
visions;

shaking her
head sadly,
she said,
"ain't
no way."

Martin
tried to love,
tried to be
a drum major
for peace,
but juxtaposed
on his deep,
resonant sound
of rolling drums
was the U.S.A.'s
shotgun blast of
apartheid, shattering,
blood splattering
his dreams, our
dreams and those
of his strong
black, stoic
mother, prophet
father, four
brave and beautiful
youth and the
bronzed wonder
of his too-soon
widowed devoted
wife—and all
of us blacks
poor in the
riches of
the world and
spirit.

Mahalia heaved
her deep bosom
and dropped a
tear on his
rough hewn
wooden bier;

crying a cop-out
plea, straining
beyond the trials
of the earth
and the veils of
hate and scorn;
reaching toward
other worldness
from a soul weary
voice, gutted with
despair, "Precious
Lord, take my hand,
lead me on."
Where we
gonna go, Mahalia?
Don't toll the bell
heralding for our
folk an eternity of
hell in the beast's
Walhalla.

Where we
gonna go, Mahalia?
Back to Mother
Africa or just
back to Mother Earth?
to dust as all
living things
must? For not
here or any other
place is there
a chance for black
people to live in
peace, and in
harmony with their
own soulful selves.

Where we gonna
go, Mahalia?
You tell us and
don't just put us on
with notes, not of
murderous discord,

but, with the sweet
submissive sound
of suicide.

If my life must
be a sacrifice,
let it be in the
name of my own
self interests
and those of
my strong black
sons and daughters.

Ain't
nobody
heard me
singing
sweet songs
lately;
but, maybe,
I will find
as a last
word, some sweet
note to leave
behind
when it's said,
"that all
she wrote."

Raymond R. Patterson
(1929–   )

AT THAT MOMENT

When they shot Malcolm Little down
On the stage of the Audubon Ballroom,
When his life ran out through bullet holes
(Like the people running out when the murder began)
His blood soaked the floor
One drop found a crack through the stark
Pounding thunder—slipped under the stage and began
Its journey: burrowed through concrete into the cellar,
Dropped down darkness, exploding like quicksilver
Pellets of light, panicking rats, paralyzing cockroaches—
Tunneled through rubble and wrecks of foundations,
The rocks that buttress the bowels of the city, flowed
Into pipes and powerlines, the mains and cables of the
    city:
A thousand fiery seeds.
At that moment,
Those who drank water where he entered . . .
Those who cooked food where he passed . . .
Those who burned light while he listened . . .
Those who were talking as he went, knew he was water
Running out of faucets, gas running out of jets, power
Running out of sockets, meaning running along taut
    wires—
To the hungers of their living. It is said
Whole slums of clotted Harlem plumbing groaned
And sundered free that day, and disconnected gas and
    light
Went on and on and on. . . .
They rushed his riddled body on a stretcher
To the hospital. But the police were too late.
It had already happened.

BIRMINGHAM 1963

Sunday morning and her mother's hands
Weaving the two thick braids of her springing hair,
Pulling her sharply by one bell-rope when she would
Not sit still, setting her ringing,
While the radio church choir prophesied the hour
With theme and commercials, while the whole house
    tingled;
And she could not stand still in that awkward air;
Her dark face shining, her mother now moving the tiny
    buttons,
Blue against blue, the dress which took all night making,
That refused to stay fastened;
There was some pull which hurried her out to Sunday
    School
Toward the lesson and the parable's good news,
The quiet escape from the warring country of her
    feelings,
The confused landscape of grave issues and people.

But now we see
Now we see through the glass of her mother's wide
    screaming
Eyes into the room where the homemade bomb
Blew the room down where her daughter had gone:
Under the leaves of hymnals, the plaster and stone,
The blue dress, all undone—
The day undone to the bone—
Her still, dull face, her quiet hair;
Alone amid the rubble, amid the people
Who perish, being innocent.

A SONG WAITING FOR MUSIC
(to a strong hand-clapping, foot-stamping rhythm)

A river of tears is my story
A river of pain in this land
A river of angry fire
Will I burn and never tire
Until I am treated like a man
Until I am treated like a man.

A mountain of injustice is my story
A mountain of good men murdered in this land
But like a mountain I'll stand my ground
And I'll never be turned around
For I mean to be treated like a man
Yes, I mean to be treated like a man.

A valley of sorrow is my story
A valley of heartache in this land
Though this valley is dark right now
I'll keep moving anyhow
Toward the day that I'm treated like a man
Toward the day that I'm treated like a man.

A plain of broken promise is my story
A plain of desolation in this land
Like a great plain blowing sand
I'll be restless in this land
Until I am treated like a man
Until I am treated like a man.

In cities unfriendly is my story
And countries against me in this land
Though outlaw sheriffs treat me wrong
I'll still march and sing my song
For I'm bound to be treated like a man
For I'm bound to be treated like a man.

Broad rivers bearing freedom is my story
Deep valleys green with faith in this land
Strong mountains high above
And the great plains rich with love
For the cities, for the counties of this land
Oh, the day that I'm treated like a man
Oh, the day that I'm treated like a man.

TO A WEATHERCOCK

I too am moved by passing winds,
Spun mockingly upon one stand
Where all flight ends where it begins.

Strange breezes from a distant land
Have called me, too, and I have turned
And turned and could not understand.

Beneath each season's sun I've burned
With you, and watched freed wings depart
For dreamed-of-places where I've yearned

To go. Do these things touch your heart?
I've seen you fret on windless days,
Felt more than metal in your art.

And I have pondered on the ways
Of wind and God that so confound,
And I have heard your turning round
Sounding the grief I could not phrase.

Alvin Aubert
(1930–)

ALL SINGING IN A PIE

What is this thing, this elusive conceit,
'brotherhood of poets'? even if such were
possible what would it be? i've lavished
the idea with the tenderest of care. more
than two poets at a time in a room? gives
me the jitters makes me think of blackberries
looking for them on the margins of a south
louisiana swamp. one shoves a branch of
overgrowth aside and presto! there they are
opening like a giant pomegranate revealing
its luscious secret. one charges in, only
to discover the pail brought along is much
too small. you fill your inadequate pail,
each breath, each berry picked a silent
pledge to return to this very spot tomorrow.
you'll not reveal your secret to anyone
not even your brother. this is your scoop.
you'll reap reap reap the secret like pirates
hoard. the long walk home no measure
of your dwindling resolve it pours down
yours legs like sweat on a humid louisiana
afternoon. night comes dreams of berries
lusciously black and hidden except from
the sky and blackbirds blackbirds blackbirds
dying and drying into sparrows in the
midmorning sun.

•

THE REVOLUTIONARY

he is bound to make something happen
he's not quite sure what but
he is determined he flits from flower
to flower he has more legs than a hive
of bees he takes everything out of them
leaving them for dead. it will be a long
time before anything happen. in the
meantime he plies his adversary's craft
on whomever is at hand and is useful
to him in that way, being bound as he is
to making something happen something
worthy of himself almost anything.

SPRING 1937/ FOR HONORÉ ROUSSELL

the fullmoon night hog maws fell
from heaven and pigs knuckles exploded
like bombed crackers in the bloom
of our prized magnolia

the night you lay waked all resplendent
in smooth depression serge
and pennypinch satin
your cold horizontalism
fronting the fireplace plugged
against troublesome swifts
paralleling the closed ragtime piano
locked and draped
as though it might otherwise play
insolently of its own accord

that fateful night of the evergreen sprig
in the sprinkling holywater clutches
of the mournful faithful
and their cascading hail marys

was the night of the mysterious maws
come rain and thunder tumbling
from an invisible sky
spangling a multivoiced presence

in the crest of our featured magnolia
that sang you to an explosive levitation
shattering the plugged fireplace
unmasking the hooded piano
scattering mourners like sootwinged swifts
like rag feathered notes
through all the corridors rooms and chinks
of your wintered house.

ONE MORE TIME

Within this black hive to-night
There swarm a million bees
                    —Jean Toomer, Cane

you should have, jean, stopped them.
those strange bees you saw going
in and out the moon. you lying flat
on your back, spine sucked by old bitch earth.
you should have plucked their looney wings
from space. fell them from that fantastic
height. nipped that mysterious drill.
still, i wonder, whatever harsh master
they danced to—what might he have done
taking me through them by surprise
a raw handed strappling twelve in the raspish
milk-sticky shade leaves of a neighbor's
fig tree. in heat for the cool interior
of the fig. soft seed succulent and
sacramental on the young tongue. jean,
you should have iced them jazzy bees.

NAT TURNER IN THE CLEARING

                              Ashes, Lord—
But warm still from the fire that cheered us,
Lighted us in this clearing where it seems
Scarcely an hour ago we feasted on
Burnt pig from our tormentor's unwilling
Bounty and charted the high purpose your
Word had launched us on. And now, my comrades

Dead, or taken; your servant, pressed by the
Blood-drenched yelps of hounds, forsaken, save for
The stillness of the word that persists quivering
And breath-moist on his tongue; and these faint coals
Soon to be rushed to dying flow by the
Indifferent winds of miscarriage—What now,
My Lord? A priestess once, they say, could write
On leaves, unlock the time-bound spell of deeds
Undone. I let fall upon these pale remains
Your breath-moist word, preempt the winds, and give
Them now their one last glow, that some dark child
In time to come might pass this way and, in
This clearing, read and know.

Etheridge Knight
(1931–1991)

THE IDEA OF ANCESTRY

1

Taped to the wall of my cell are 47 pictures: 47 black
faces: my father, mother, grandmothers (1 dead), grand-
fathers (both dead), brothers, sisters, uncles, aunts,
cousins (1st & 2nd), nieces, and nephews. They stare
across the space at me sprawling on my bunk. I know
their dark eyes, they know mine. I know their style,
they know mine. I am all of them, they are all of me;
they are farmers, I am a thief, I am me, they are thee.

I have at one time or another been in love with my mother,
1 grandmother, 2 sisters, 2 aunts (1 went to the asylum),
and 5 cousins. I am now in love with a 7-yr-old niece
(she sends me letters written in large block print, and
her picture is the only one that smiles at me).

I have the same name as 1 grandfather, 3 cousins, 3 nephews,
and 1 uncle. The uncle disappeared when he was 15, just took
off and caught a freight (they say). He's discussed each year
when the family has a reunion, he causes uneasiness in
the clan, he is an empty space. My father's mother, who is 93
and who keeps the Family Bible with everybody's birth dates
(and death dates) in it, always mentions him. There is no
place in her Bible for "whereabouts unknown."

2

Each fall the graves of my grandfathers call me, the brown
hills and red gullies of mississippi send out their electric
messages, galvanizing my genes. Last yr/like a salmon
    quitting

258

the cold ocean-leaping and bucking up his birthstream/I
hitchhiked my way from LA with 16 caps in my pocket and a
monkey on my back. And I almost kicked it with the kinfolks.
I walked barefooted in my grandmother's backyard/I
    smelled the old
land and the woods/I sipped cornwhiskey from fruit jars
    with the men/
I flirted with the women/I had a ball till the caps ran out
and my habit came down. That night I looked at my
    grandmother
and split/my guts were screaming for junk/ but I was almost
contented/I had almost caught up with me.
(The next day in Memphis I cracked a croaker's crib for a fix.)

This yr there is a gray stone wall damming my stream,
    and when
the falling leaves stir my genes, I pace my cell or flop on
    my bunk
and stare at 47 black faces across the space. I am all of them,
they are all of me, I am me, they are thee, and I have no
    children
to float in the space between.

HARD ROCK RETURNS TO PRISON FROM
THE HOSPITAL FOR THE CRIMINAL INSANE

Hard Rock / was / "known not to take no shit
From nobody," and he had the scars to prove it:
Split purple lips, lumbed ears, welts above
His yellow eyes, and one long scar that cut
Across his temple and plowed through a thick
Canopy of kinky hair.

The WORD / was / that Hard Rock wasn't a mean nigger
Anymore, that the doctors had bored a hole in his head,
Cut out part of his brain, and shot electricity
Through the rest. When they brought Hard Rock back,
Handcuffed and chained, he was turned loose,
Like a freshly gelded stallion, to try his new status.
And we all waited and watched, like a herd of sheep,
To see if the WORD was true.

As we waited we wrapped ourselves in the cloak
Of his exploits: "Man, the last time, it took eight
Screws to put him in the Hole." "Yeah, remember when he
Smacked the captain with his dinner tray?" "He set
The record for time in the Hole—67 straight days!"
"Ol Hard Rock! man, that's one crazy nigger."
And then the jewel of a myth that Hard Rock had once bit
A screw on the thumb and poisoned him with syphilitic spit.

The testing came, to see if Hard Rock was really tame.
A hillbilly called him a black son of a bitch
An didn't lose his teeth, a screw who knew Hard Rock
From before shook him down and barked in his face.
And Hard Rock did *nothing.* Just grinned and looked silly,
His eyes empty like knot holes in a fence.

And even after we discovered that it took Hard Rock
Exactly 3 minutes to tell you his first name,
We told ourselves that he had just wised up,
Was being cool; but we could not fool ourselves for long,
And we turned away, our eyes on the ground. Crushed.
He had been our Destroyer, the doer of things
We dreamed of doing but could not bring ourselves to do,
The fears of years, like a biting whip,
Had cut deep bloody grooves
Across our backs.

BELLY SONG

—for the Daytop Family

*"You have made something
Out of the sea that blew
And rolled you on its salt bitter lips.
It nearly swallowed you.
But I hear
You are tough and harder to swallow than most . . ."*
                                        —S. Mansfield

1

And I   and I / must admit
that the sea in you

          has sung / to the sea / in me
and I   and I / must admit
that the sea in me
          has fallen / in love
     with the sea in you
because you have made something
out of the sea
     that nearly swallowed you

And this poem
This poem
This poem / I give / to you.
This poem is a song / I sing / I sing / to you
from the bottom
     of the sea
          in my belly

This poem / is a song / about FEELINGS
about the Bone of feeling
about the Stone of feeling
     And the Feather of feeling

                    2

This poem
This poem
This poem / is /
a death / chant
and a grave / stone
and a prayer for the dead:
     for young Jackie Robinson.
a moving Blk / warrior who walked
among us
     with a wide / stride—and heavy heels
moving   moving   moving
thru the blood and mud and shit of Vietnam
moving   moving   moving
thru the blood and mud and dope of America
     for Jackie / who was /

a song
and a stone
and a Feather of feeling

now dead
and / gone / in this month of love

This poem
This poem / is / a silver feather
and the sun-gold / glinting / green hills breathing
river flowing . . .

3

This poem
This poem
This poem / is / for ME—for me
and the days / that lay / in the back / of my mind
when the sea / rose up /
    to swallow me
and the streets I walked
    were lonely streets
    were stone / cold streets

This poem
This poem / is /
for me / and the nights
    when I
wrapped my feelings
    in a sheet of ice
and stared
    at the stars
        thru iron bars
           and cried
in the middle of my eyes . . .

This poem
This poem
This poem / is / for me
    and my woman
    and the yesterdays
when she opened
    to me like a flower
    But I fell on her
    like a stone
I fell on her like a stone . . .

And now—in my 40th year
    I have come here
to this House of Feelings
to this Singing Sea
and I   and I / must admit
that the sea in me
    has fallen / in love
with the sea in you
because the sea
that now sings / in you
    is the same sea
that nearly swallowed you—
    and me too.

Seymour, Connecticut
June 1971

A POEM OF ATTRITION

I do not know if the color of the day
Was blue, pink, green, or August red.
I only know it was summer, a Thursday,
And the trestle above our heads
Sliced the sun into black and gold bars
That fell across our shiny backs
And shimmered like flat snakes on the water,
Worried by the swans, shrieks, jackknives,
And timid gainers—made bolder
As the day grew older.
Then Pooky Dee, naked chieftain, poised,
Feet gripping the black ribs of wood,
Knees bent, butt out, long arms
Looping the air, challenged
The great "two 'n' a half" gainer . . .
I have forgotten the sound of his capped
Skull as it struck the block . . .
The plop of a book dropped? The tear of a sheer blouse?
I do not know if the color of the day
Was blue, pink, green, or August red.
I only know the blood slithered, and

Our silence rolled like oil
Across the wide green water.

HAIKU

1

Eastern guard tower
glints in sunset; convicts rest
like lizards on rocks.

2

The piano man
is stingy at 3 A.M.
his songs drop like plum.

3

Morning sun slants cell.
Drunks stagger like cripple flies
On jailhouse floor.

4

To write a blues song
is to regiment riots
and pluck gems from graves.

5

A bare pecan tree
slips a pencil shadow down
a moonlit snow slope.

6

The falling snow flakes
Cannot blunt the hard aches nor
Match the steel stillness.

7

Under moon shadows
A tall boy flashes knife and
Slices star bright ice.

8

In the August grass
Struck by the last rays of sun
The cracked teacup screams.

9

Making jazz swing in
Seventeen syllables AIN'T
No square poet's job.

Tom Dent
(1932–)

NIGHTDREAMS (BLACK)

Being beat down,
I would fly away on the wings of a hawk
    to Burma
    or Peru
    or 141st Street where black memories lie
    or float ascendingly like soft cigarette
smoke—
    memories float: their persistence
terrorizes me like awakening tigers clawing
at the cage of my mask—
    were I a tiger
    were I ever a tiger!
    were I reject tigerness
    were I cry a tiger roar
    were I tiger roar a cry against my cage
    caged were my tiger:

Gloria was my son!
Would I forget that? Was my child in growing . . .

    You tell me that my Harlem is jazz . . . Black
zoot-suited women with longer dangling dicks
that eat barbecue and talk rhythm.
    You tell me that black shines in the silly
masturbating dream of some wet-sheeted night . . .

    Oh, turn away, I see the narcotic weave—
the estranged float on a thousand street corners
of my generation—and now the weave is descending
into a trickling, lazy fall—to the cold pavement
where leaping roaches and muffled cries lie!

your nakedness
is my beauty
cat me in
wiggle me out
my apple of love
too tough to mount—

trees blown away
tears wished away
dreams,
terrorized away—

Then my child is the youness of me and you
which adds to nothing and nothing and equals
hot nights freezing colder . . .

And still the girl, her head shoved into a
toilet bowl remains silently fixed in the picture
of our love moments, central to our love moments,
inextricable. Was her scream drowned by our
loving? Perhaps. Perhaps she was already cold . . .

Sweet murder, Harlem lover, sweet murder,
knifing the heart of her loved ones, knifing the
heart of her chosen, as always!

I would blackness, and love, and life go on
forgetting, like an ant who eats only for today . . .

Were I that simple: shoot me!
Were I that white: color me!

Were I nowhere near heaven, being beat down,
but nearer Paris, or Venus, or second base,
or even the silly think five-yard line of my dream,
I would float through the skin of my torture like
smoke rising, like clouds sliding, like bones
becoming dust, life becoming death. . . .

TIME IS A MOTOR

Time is a motor, you know
that never unwinds
never unwinds
and we who worship Time
never unwind
never unwind
driving, slashing, cutting, severing, beheading our way
    through
a daily mass of time-stoppers
and time-slowers
and time-disobeyers
until we become automatic
and sure
and certain
and has-to-be
and a little perfect
absolute
like a motor, you know
like a motor.

ST. HELENA ISLAND

slaves are said to have worked
hard & long
on this island
sunup to sundown & beyond
sundays and christmas off
two clothes a year
are memories bestowed
to old Penn School.

nearby expressionless summer homes
of early plantation owners sit observing the bay
the stately museums of Beaufort
the arsenals and ports of the english
built above Native remains:
the romance of american history.

sand blows across the island
from ocean beaches.
palmettoes & dark green foliage
                hover menacingly

this land has been stolen and stolen
again . . .
made into cotton & rice riches
off strong brown backs . . .
the blowing sand and the palmettoes
                  know much of these things
but speak only at night
speak their silent mysterious language
only to themselves.

today black bodies frisk
about the beaches
listening to soul radio
thinking of what?
when night becomes shimmering black
the small cabins of the blacks
grow silent
while voices of the land rise
to a feverish pitch.
voices
of endless
memory.

TEN YEARS AFTER UMBRA

(for David & Calvin)

We had seen
      our minds reach out
      touch fingertips
      musics crawl in like
      lazy smoke on Friday nights
      taste the wind &
      leave us a whiff of real road
we had seen
      our fingertips recoil
      our minds reel
      from the impact
of our tongued knives
          but then
we were naked then
and we stripped our souls
easy as the sun rose
and what went on
in that tenement prison

was something in us
bursting free like
a flash fire.

do you too now feel
the drag of too many jammed years?
Stanley's fades into dreams
and so with our touching
our hurting . . .
as for me
the dirt roads of Mississippi
are a long way
from anywhere.

but then the sun will rise
just as easy tomorrow
over this black earth

join me there.

SECRET MESSAGES

(for Danny Barker)

rain
rain drenches the city
as we move past
stuffed black mammies
chained to Royal St. praline shops
check it out

past Bourbon St. beer cans
shadowed moorish cottages
ships slipping down the riversnake past
images of the bullet-riddled bodies of
Mark Essex & Bras Coupe
buried in the beckoning of the blk
shoeshine boy
when it rains it pours
check it out

pass blk tap-dancers of the shit-eating grin
the nickle & dime shake-a-leg
shades of weaving flambeau carriers
of the dripping oil & the grease-head

"we *are* mardi gras" one said
check it out

past that to where you play yr banjo
"it's plantation time again" you say to us
& we laugh . . .
outside a blk cabdriver helps crippled
Sweet Emma into the front seat
she done boogied the piano another night
for maybe the 250th year
she laughs loudly to herself as tourists
watch
there is an Ashanti saying
when one hears something but does not understand, they say:
        "like singing to the white man"
check it out

tripping past raindrops with the ancient slick-haired
Jelly Roll piano player
to listen to some "modern musicians"
at Lu & Charlie's
& the old piano player saying
"they can play a little bit can't they"
teasing our god of fallen masks
check it out . . .

& maybe someday when nobody is
checking it out the drummers will come to life in
St. Louis No. 1 at midnight
beating out the secret messages
& all the masks will drop.
jest like we said they would.
secret messages
secret messages of the gods.

rain
rain drenches the city
as we move past grinning stuffed black mammies
the god of fallen masks offstage
waiting, waiting . . .

Calvin Hernton
(1932–)

THE DISTANT DRUM

I am not a metaphor or symbol.
This you hear is not the wind in the trees.
Nor a cat being maimed in the street.
I am being maimed in the street
It is I who weep, laugh, feel pain or joy.
Speak this because I exist.
This is my voice
These words are my words, my mouth
Speaks them, my hand writes.
I am a poet.
It is my fist you hear beating
Against your ear.

MEDICINE MAN

North of Dark
North from Shango
In kangaroo jungle of West Lost
Dressed in hide of fox
Dressed at last to kill
Thirteen grains of sand
Seven memories
And Ten voices whispering in a rock

Time medicine riddle
Time rock disguised in evil bite
In devil flight
Time encloses cycles
Voice memory
Revolve

Age leaps upon the lips
Hawk! Kiss of hatred
Is turtle blood
Is love's hair buried in an old tin can

Then I said to my knee bones
Teach me how to bend
My knee bones hardening seven memories
Recalled what I fail to know
In an estranged familiar tongue
Said:
    If you must go
    Go by the abandoned railroad yard

The muddy ditch
The lizard infested by-pass
Flank to the left where an old black woman
With prayers for you in her wrinkled hands
Cupped in an old-fashioned apron lap
Rocks eternally
Eternal rock
Rocking chair
Pause, leave a tear
Beneath the fallen viaduct
But do not linger
For the road back is never
Home is never where you were born
Oh Grandmother, figurine gris gris Goddess
Do I
Should I
Can I live so that I may die easily

Thirty years wrinkle
My belly folds
When I sit
When I stand
My belly spreads

Thirty red years contending with Satan
The backbones breaking pain
Thirty times ten removed from gods
My fathers knew

Oh, Shango, man of mothers
Will you join us in trance

In eating of the bowels of black man
Who is our victim
Who no longer is father of his man

And do I approve
If I do not approve
I have done somebody wrong
If I do approve
Why should I approve
Thirty times ten removed from voices
Ancestral

Birth is April fish belly.
Love is love going the wrong way.
And if I weep
I weep for my twin rising out of
The marriage womb leaping upon me mid-years

Hence I put away old handed-down ailments
Put away hence common motives that drive men
To conventional madness
And weep for the mother of my twin
And conjure Dance on pages of medicine book
      of white hands
And by ceaseless slapping on genital organ
And by eating of embryo taken from ovaries
      of the dead infant boy
Leaping to meet me death
If I weep at all

We may not live until love
Until moon
And if I approve
Eating entrails of multitude of living victims
It will not resurrect those already dead
It will not heal ear and tongue of betrayal
April is a time of betrayal
And I do not approve
I do not approve

And if I pray
I pray not to God nor Shango
I pray to bellies of deep sea sharks
And pray for us survived west lost
North of dark in chains

After the present pain is gone.
The hate who roars in the brain.
The one who sucks my breath like an evil cigarette
The one who crushes the young men and smashes them
Who will be left to care

So shameless black men speak blood of their sisters!
And will it if I weep
Drive away juju of the fox
And if I pray
I have done somebody wrong

And if I do not pray
I pray for those who will live until moon
And to those residing in evil bite
And to the old black woman living in my wounds
And for the twin of the father who falters

I pray because I was born
And have sinned my birth to clay.

Wherefore I said to my knee bones
Instruct me how to stand
Teach me how to love and how to die
And my bones wherein the hot oil
Of the sun is contained
Said:
  Go by the abandoned railroad yard
  Flank to the left your black mamma
  Is rocking
  Seven memories recall what
You know
North of the dark path in juju jungle
Age leaps upon the lips and caresses
The kiss of wisdom is love
Hold thirteen grains of sand
Look at the sun until it three-times
Blinds you, and listen
Listen to ten voices
Singing in that rocking chair

Singing in that rock!
Singing in that rock!

Gerald Barrax
(1933–)

FOR A BLACK POET

BLAM! BLAM! BLAM! POW! BLAM! POW!
RATTTTTTTAT! BLACK IS BEAUTIFUL, WHI
TY! RAATTTTTTTAT! POW! THERE GO A HON
KIE! GIT'M, POEM! POW! BLAM! BANG!
BANG! RATATAT! BLAM! COME ON, POEM! GET
THAT WHI-TE BEAST! BLAM! BLAM! POW!
ZAP! BANG! RAAATTTTTTTATAT! BLAM! BLAM!

How many fell for you, Brother?
How many did you leave
in the alley ballsmashed
headkicked in by your heavy feet?

The things we make as men
are guns triggered more efficiently than poems
and knives / and targets for the fires.

Men make revolutions
Poems will brings us to resurrection

There is prophecy in fire
and a beauty you can not see
    a sound you cannot hear
    below the exploding level of your poems
                          dress to kill
                          shoot to kill
                          love to kill
                          if you will
                          but write to bring back
                              the dead

And you are beautiful, Brother
not because you say so but because

276

black is the beauty of night a Black woman
the way a woman knows her beauty
   whose blackness falls
   softly from the spaces between stars
    who confirms our terror at her beauty in silence
and whose deepest blackness is the matrix
for the pendant worlds that hang
                     spinning from her ears.

And Black, like the swan
the shadow of itself who knows the secret
in the middle of its beauty is doubled silence
rarer than the white rush of lust
that led Leda's swan children
slouching thru their cycles of destruction.

The black panther.
His soft walk of lithe strong paces
a way of knowing   the hunter
                       the hunted

the beautiful) (silent (terrible beauty) quiet (terror
from   fear) the
panicked   (fear
beast / 's   (fear
crash / ing   (fear
bel / low   (fear and
ug / ly   fear

Beautiful as
a Black poempoetperson should be who
   knows what beauty lurks in the lives of men who
   know what Shadow falls between promise and praise.

The things that make us men.
Your child's questioning black fingers
touching you
is the poem
and more terror and beauty
because of the Shadow between you
than all your words.

   The way blackness absorbs   swallows everything
   and you Brother bring back up only upper cases

undigested at that

> while beaten far below
> the level of your voice
> your life's deepest mean-
> ings lie fallow.

What I mean is the way some things scream
at you   when synesthesia destroys   sometimes the be-
                                            holder and the
                                            beauty
and the sense of beauty is not truth
and no longer hurts
and frightens instead of making us
feel its terror.

GREENHOUSE

First a fable, and then the truth. We sensed
The execution of the plants at their stands
As they guarded us at the door and frozen window
From the light's surprise entrance to the darkest room
We'd known—as if an evening star had collapsed
Into the house's basement room where we
lay dazed in the singularity of a black
Hole in time; our bodies' gravity twisting
Space into the bed's depression, we cancelled
Natural laws, displaced all other matter
And light into the opposite system, beyond
Our control and caring. But when that light
Exploded past our plants faster than its
Own limit, we turned from each other's arms to the sounds
We imagined: ghosts of footsteps overhead,
And Venus's plant, the sundew, pitcher plant,
Cobra lily, sidesaddle flower and butter-
Wort shrieking warning silences and dying for us.

First the fable, and now a truth. But one
Is as strange, has as much charm, color, and beauty
As the other. What matters is the energy of
Its telling, else why do the heathen rage,
The godly rant? In truth, they are the same
If based on what we see (even through our

Instruments) and most of all, feel, or expect
One day to prove on the senses. It does matter
That matter is, and that what matter isn't
(except energy and the unified field) is not.
This is truth: an elegy for whatever died
From neglect while we made love. That night "the music
Of the spheres" was organ music, and when the pipes
Burst, the poor devils froze to death in their places.

We were in the darkest room we'd ever
Known, a true house, a real room, and even
Though half buried in a hillside, was neither
A Swelling in the Ground, nor monarch Thought's
Dominion—not those symbols. It was our darkest
Room because when I put the light out (an
Ordinary light) we had only each
Other, nothing but the comfort and solace
Of our bodies, bodies no denser than all
Ordinary matter and would rot in graves
Less intensely dark than that room where we
Could have stared openeyed forever, forever
Blind waiting for something to emerge,
Reveal itself, take shape. It was that absolute.
The desperate hunger of our bodies, the need
For simple touch, for light, for dark in which
To find the truth about our need—that's what
Devoured the light and left the moon hollow.
That's why the dark was so real: we discovered
That deprivation in love is hunger, is pain
Too common, too necessary to sublimate in fables.
That was truth's light and dark: the necessity
Of pain in our world to make the joy of its
Complete reversal in each other's love with
Even the most primitive harmony that sets
Us apart from the ghostly lives upstairs:
The smooth surprise of tongues in our mouths; our hands
And backs shaping themselves to their own curves and
Hollows from their instant recall of absence.
And it was we and not the spider, coffee,
Coleus, philodendron, African violet,
English and devil's ivy who sang God God
I love you in that dark, because in none
Of the perfect days of unvarying gold had we
Seen so much. That was the truth. Now the fable again.

279

WHOSE CHILDREN ARE THESE?

1

Whose children are these?
Who do these children belong to?
With no power to watch over,
He looks at them, sleeping,
Exhaustion overwhelming hunger, barely
Protected with burlap from the cold
Cabin. Fear and rage make him tremble
For them; for himself, shame
That he can do no more
Than die for them,
For no certain purpose. He heard
About the woman, Margaret Garner,
In spite of the white folks' silence.
How she killed two
Of hers to keep them from being taken
Back; killed herself
After the others were taken back
Anyway. So she saved
Two. He couldn't save
His Ellen and Henry.
Who do these belong to?
He doesn't dare kiss them
Now, but stands dreaming,
Willing these five back
To a place or forward to a time
He can't remember or imagine.
All he can do is find the place
He knows about. Leave now
Before dawn sets the white fields glowing
And murders the North Star.

2

I have them all, all the five you sent
That night, all of them, Brother, and safe.
I have stood over them, warm in their beds,
Stood over each one and choked on your rage
Trying to imagine that our children belonged
To someone who could take them as he pleased.
Like you I have revered that fierce woman,

Envied her courage, looked at our children
Unable to imagine either their
Enslavement or her solution. The Greeks
Named it Tyche and made a goddess of chance
That put you there rather than me, than us.
Others call it their god's mysterious will.
The children are safe. But I am unable to forgive.

Audre Lorde
(1934–1992)

SAHARA

High
above this desert
I am
becoming
absorbed.

Plateaus of sand
dendrites of sand
continents and islands and waddys
of sand
tongue sand
wrinkle sand
mountain sand
coasts of sand
pimples and pustules and macula of sand
snot all over your face from sneezing sand
dry lakes of sand
buried pools of sand
moon craters of sand
Get your "I've had too much of people"
out of here sand.

My own place sand
never another place sand
punishments of sand
hosannahs of sand
Epiphanies of sand
crevasses of sand
mother of sand
I've been here a long time sand
string sand

spaghetti sand
cat's cradle ring-a-levio sand
army of trees sand
jungle of sand
grief of sand
subterranean treasure sand
moonglade sand
male sand
terrifying sand

Will I never get out of here sand
open and closed sand
curvatures of sand
nipples of sand
hard erected bosoms of sand
clouds quick and heavy and
desperate sand
thick veil over my face sand
sun is my lover sand
footprints of the time on sand
navel sand
elbow sand
play hopscotch through the labyrinth sand
I have spread myself sand
I have grown harsh and flat
against you sand
glass sand
fire sand
malachite and gold diamond sand
cloisonné coal sand
filagree silver sand
granite and marble and ivory sand

Hey you come here and she came sand
I will endure sand
I will resist sand
I am tired of no
all the time sand
I too will unmask my dark
hard rock sand.

POWER

The difference between poetry and rhetoric
is being
ready to kill
yourself
instead of your children.

I am trapped on a desert of raw gunshot wounds
and a dead child dragging his shattered black
face off the edge of my sleep
blood from his punctured cheeks and shoulders
is the only liquid for miles and my stomach
churns at the imagined taste while
my mouth splits into dry lips
without loyalty or reason
thirsting for the wetness of his blood
as it sinks into the whiteness
of the desert where I am lost
without imagery or magic
trying to make power out of hatred and destruction
trying to heal my dying son with kisses
only the sun will bleach his bones quicker.

The policeman who shot down a 10-year-old in Queens
stood over the boy with his cop shoes in childish blood
and a voice said "Die you little motherfucker" and
there are tapes to prove that. At his trial
this policeman said in his own defense
"I didn't notice the size or nothing else
only the color." and
there are tapes to prove that, too.

Today that 37-year-old white man with 13 years of police
    forcing
has been set free
by 11 white men who said they were satisfied
justice had been done
and one black woman who said
"They convinced me" meaning
they had dragged her 4'10" black woman's frame
over the hot coals of four centuries of white male approval
until she let go the first real power she ever had

and lined her own womb with cement
to make a graveyard for our children.

I have not been able to touch the destruction within me.
But unless I learn to use
the difference between poetry and rhetoric
my power too will run corrupt as poisonous mold
or lie limp and useless as an unconnected wire
and one day I will take my teenaged plug
and connect it to the nearest socket
raping an 85-year-old white woman
who is somebody's mother
and as I beat her senseless and set a torch to her bed
a greek chorus will be singing in 3/4 time
"Poor thing. She never hurt a soul. What beasts they are."

Sonia Sanchez
(1934–)

POEM NO. 10

you keep saying you were always there
waiting for me to see you.
                    you said that once
on the wings of a pale green butterfly
you rode across san francisco's hills
and touched my hair as i caressed
a child called militancy
you keep saying you were always there

holding my small hand
                as i walked
unbending indiana streets i could not see around
and you grew a black mountain
of curves and i turned
and became soft again
you keep saying you were always there

repeating my name softly
                as i slept in
slow pittsburgh blues and you made me
sweat nite dreams that danced
and danced until the morning
rained yo/red delirium

you keep saying you were always there
you keep saying you were always there
                will you stay love
                  now that i am here?

YOUNG WOMANHOOD

And i entered into young
  womanhood. you asked.
  who goes there?

who calls out
  to this perennial
  Black man of ruin?

and time on her annual
  pilgrimage squatted and
  watched as i called
  out to love from my door.

what a lovely smell love
was. like a stream of
violets that warmed your face.

and i was found at the four
  corners of love. a Black
  man and I imprisoned
  with laughter at himself.

a man made sterile
by hatred
a famine man
starved and starving
those around him
in this plentiful country.

as i entered into my
young womanhood i became
  a budding of laughter. i
  moved in liquid dreams
  wrapped myself in a
  furious circuit of love
  gave out quick words
  and violent tremblings
  and kisses that bit
  and drew blood
  and the seasons fell
  like waterfalls on my thighs

287

and i dressed myself
in foreign words
    became a proper painted
    european Black faced american
    going to theatre parties and bars
    and cocktail parties and bars
    and downtown village apartments
    and bars and ate good cheese
    and caviar with wine that
    made my stomach stretch for artificial warmth.
    danced with white friends who
    included me because that was
    the nice thing to do in the late
    fifties and early sixties

and i lost myself
down roads
i had never walked.

and my name was
without honor
and i became a
stranger at my birthright.

        *   *   *

who is that
making noise on this earth
while good people sleep
i wondered, as i turned
in our three year old bed of love.

in the morning
i reminded you of the noise
and you said,
just some niggers pretending
    to be the wind.

the nite brought more noise
    like a swift courier
    and i leaped from our bed
    and followed the sound.

    and visions came from the wall.
    bodies without heads, laughter without mouths.

then faces crawling on the walls
like giant spiders,
came toward me
and my legs buckled and
    i cried out.

one face touched mine and said:

"you are a singer of songs
    but you do not listen to what men have said
    therefore you cannot sing."

a second face murmured:

"you are a reader of books
    but books that do not teach you truth
    are false messiahs."

a third face smiled as i closed my eyes:

"you move as a free woman,
    but your body is a monument to slavery
    and is dead."

When morning came
you took me to one
inebriated with freud.

massaging his palms
he called out to me
a child of the south,
and i listened to
european words
that rushed out to
me and handcuffed
me.

And for awhile i rode
on horseback
among my youth
remembered southern days
and nites
remembered a beginning new york

girlhood where tall buildings looked
like aqueducts.
remembered stutters
i could not silence.

at the end of a month
when he couldn't explain
away continued acts that
killed.
at the end of a month
of stumbling alibis,
after my ancestral voices
called out to me against
past and future murders,
i moved away from reconciling myself to
murderers
and gave myself up to
the temper of the times.

stood against discrimination
in housing.
jobs.
picketed. sat in. sang about
overcoming that which would
never come.
closed woolworths. marched
against T.V. stations while
ducking horseriding cops
advancing like funeral hawks.

was knocked to the ground
while my child screamed
at the cannibals on horseback.

and i screeeamed.
calling out to those who
would listen.

called out from carolinian
slave markets, mississippi
schools, harlem streets that
beasts populated us.
beasts with no human heartbeats
when they came among BLACKNESS.

and i vomited up the past.
the frivolous years and i
threw up the smiles and bowings
and nods that had made
me smile so many smiles.

and i vomited up the stench
of the good ship *Jesus*
sailing to the new world
with Black gold
i vomited up the cries of
newborn babies thrown
overboard

i vomited up the waters
that had separated me
from Dahomey and Arabia
and Timbuktoo and Muhammad
and Asia and Allah.

i vomited up denmarkvesey
and nat turner and rebellious
slave women
their big stomachs split open
in the sun.

i vomited up white robed choirs
and preachers hawking their sermons
to an unseeing God.

and i vomited out names like beasts.
and death. and pigs and death.
and devil and death
and the vomiting ceased.
and i was alone.

                    *   *   *
wokc up alone
to the middle sixties
full of the rising wind of history

alive in a country of echoes
convulsive with gods

291

alone with the
apocalypse of beasts,
in america. The repository
of european promise.
rabid america.
   where death is
   gay and obscene
   and legal in the sight
   of an unseeing God.

I HAVE WALKED A LONG TIME

i have walked a long time
much longer than death that splinters
wid her innuendos.
my life, ah my alien life,
is like an echo of nostalgia
bringen blue screens to bury clouds
rinsen wite stones stretched among the sea.

> *you, man, will you remember me when i die?*
> *will you stare and stain my death and say*
> *i saw her dancen among swallows*
> *far from the world's obscenities?*
> *you, man, will you remember and cry?*

and i have not loved.
always
while the body prowls
the soul catalogues each step;
while the unconscious unbridles feasts
the flesh knots toward the shore.
ah, i have not loved
wid legs stretched like stalks against sheets
wid stomachs drainen the piracy of oceans
wid mouths discarden the gelatin
to shake the sharp self.
i have walked by memory of others
between the blood night
and twilights
i have lived in tunnels
and fed the bloodless fish;

between the yellow rain
and ash,
i have heard the rattle
of my seed,
so time, like some pearl necklace embracen
a superior whore, converges
and the swift spider binds my breast.

>   *you, man, will you remember me when i die?*
>   *will you stare and stain my death and say*
>   *i saw her applauden suns*
>   *far from the grandiose audience?*
>   *you, man, will you remember and cry?*

TOWHOMITMAYCONCERN

watch out fo the full moon of sonia
shinin down on ya.
git yo/self fattened up man
you gon be doing battle with me
ima gonna stake you out
grind you down
leave greasy spots all over yo/soul
till you bone dry. man.
you gon know you done been touched by me
this time.
ima gonna tatoo me on you fo ever
leave my creases all inside yo creases
i done warned ya boy
watch out
for the full moon of sonia
shinin down on ya.

ELEGY

(for MOVE* and Philadelphia)

1.

philadelphia
   a disguised southern city
squatting in the eastern pass of
colleges cathedrals and cowboys.
philadelphia. a phalanx of parsons
and auctioneers
   modern gladiators
erasing the delirium of death from their shields
while houses burn out of control.

2.

c'mon girl hurry on down to osage st
they're roasting in the fire
smell the dreadlocks and blk/skins
roasting in the fire.

c'mon newsmen and tvmen
hurryondown to osage st and
when you have chloroformed the city
and after you have stitched up your words
hurry on downtown for sanctuary
in taverns and corporations

and the blood is not yet dry.

3.

how does one scream in thunder?

4.

they are combing the morning for shadows
and screams tongue-tied without faces

*MOVE: a philadelphia based back to nature group
whose headquarters was bombed by the police on May
13, 1985, killing men, women and children. An entire
city block was destroyed by fire.

look. over there. one eye
escaping from its skin
and our heartbeats slowdown to a drawl
and the kingfisher calls out from his downtown capital
And the pinstriped general reenlists
his tongue for combat
and the police come like twin seasons of drought and flood.
they're combing the city for lifeliberty and
the pursuit of happiness.

5.

how does one city scream in thunder?

6.

hide us O lord
deliver us from our nakedness.
exile us from our laughter
give us this day our rest from seduction
peeling us down to our veins.

and the tower was like no other.   amen.
and the streets escaped under the
cover of darkness   amen.
and the voices called out from
their wounds   amen.
and the fire circumsized the city   amen.

7.

who anointeth this city with napalm?   (i say)
who giveth this city in holy infanticide?

8.

beyond the mornings and afternoons
and deaths detonating the city.
beyond the tourist roadhouses
trading in lobotomies
there is a glimpse of earth
this prodigal earth.
beyond edicts and commandments

commissioned by puritans
there are people
navigating the breath of hurricanes.
beyond concerts and football
and mummers strutting their
sequined processionals.
there is this earth. this country. this city.
this people.
collecting skeletons from waiting rooms
lying in wait. for honor and peace.
one day.

Amiri Baraka
(1934–   )

THE END OF MAN IS HIS BEAUTY

And silence
which proves but
a referent
to my disorder.
            Your world shakes

cities die
beneath your shape.
            The single shadow

at noon
like a live tree
whose leaves
are like clouds

weightless soul
at whose love faith moves
as a dark and
withered day.

They speak of singing who
have never heard song; of living
whose deaths are legends
for their kind.

PREFACE TO A TWENTY
VOLUME SUICIDE NOTE
(For Kellie Jones, born 16 May 1959)

Lately, I've become accustomed to the way
The ground opens up and envelops me

Each time I go out to walk the dog.
Or the broad-edged silly music the wind
Makes when I run for a bus . . .

Things have come to that.

And now, each night I count the stars,
And each night I get the same number.
And when they will not come to be counted,
I count the holes they leave.

Nobody sings anymore.

And then last night, I tiptoed up
To my daughter's room and heard her
Talking to someone, and when I opened

The door, there was no one there . . .
Only she on her knees, peeking into

Her own clasped hands.

AS A POSSIBLE LOVER

Practices
silence, the way of wind
bursting
its early lull. Cold morning
to night, we go so
slowly, without
thought
to ourselves. (Enough
to have thought
tonight, nothing
finishes it. What
you are, will have
no certainty, or
end. That you will
stay, where you are,
a human gentle wisp
of life. Ah . . .)
              practices

loneliness,
as a virtue. A single
specious need
to keep
what you have
never really
had.

BLACK DADA NIHILISMUS

. Against what light

is false what breath
sucked, for deadness.
Murder, the cleansed

purpose, frail, against
God, if they bring him
bleeding, I would not

forgive, or even call him
black dada nihilismus.

The protestant love, wide windows,
color blocked to Mondrian, and the
ugly silent deaths of jews under
the surgeon's knife. (To awake on
69th street with money and a hip
nose. Black dada nihilismus, for

the umbrella'd jesus. Trilby intrigue
movie house presidents sticky the floor.
B.D.N., for the secret men, Hermes, the

blacker art. Thievery (ahh, they return
those secret gold killers. Inquisitors
of the cocktail hour. Trismegistus, have

them, in their transmutation, from stone
to bleeding pearl, from lead to burning
looting, dead Moctezuma, find the West

a grey hideous space.

2.

From Sartre, a white man, it gave
the last breath. And we beg him die,
before he is killed. Plastique, we

do not have, only thin heroic blades.
The razor. Our flail against them, why
you carry knives? Or brutaled lumps of

heart? Why you stay, where they can
reach? Why you sit, or stand, or walk
in this place, a window on a dark

warehouse. Where the minds packed in
straw. New homes, these towers, for those
lacking money or art. A cult of death,

need of the simple striking arm under
the streetlamp. The cutters, from under
their rented earth. Come up, black dada

nihilismus. Rape the white girls. Rape
their fathers. Cut the mothers' throats.
Black dada nihilismus, choke my friends

in their bedrooms with their drinks spilling
and restless for tilting hips or dark liver
lips sucking splinters from the master's thigh.

Black scream
and chant, scream,
and dull, un
earthly
hollering. Dada, bilious
what ugliness, learned
in the dome, colored holy
shit (i call them sinned

or lost
          burned masters
                        of the lost
                                   nihil German killers
                                        all our learned

art, 'member
what you said

money, God, power,
a moral code, so cruel
it destroyed Byzantium, Tenochtitlan, Commanch
                                    (got it, *Baby*!

For tambo, willie best, dubois, patrice, mantan, the
bronze buckaroos.

                    For Jack Johnson, asbestos, tonto, buckwheat,
                    billie holiday.

                    For tom russ, l'overture, vesey, beau jack,

(may a lost god damballah, rest or save us
against the murders we intend
against his lost white children
black dada nihilismus

BLACK PEOPLE: THIS IS OUR DESTINY

The road runs straight with no turning, the circle
runs complete as it is in the storm of peace, the all
embraced embracing in the circle complete turning road
straight like a burning straight with the circle complete
as in a peaceful storm, the elements, the niggers' voices
harmonized with creation on a peak in the holy black man's
eyes that we rise, whose race is only direction up, where
we go to meet the realization of makers knowing who we are
and the war in our hearts but the purity of the holy world
that we long for, knowing how to live, and what life is, and
who God is, and the many revolutions we must spin through
    in our
seven adventures in the endlessness of all existing feeling, all
existing forms of life, the gases, the plants, the ghost minerals
the spirits the souls the light in the stillness where the storm
the glow the nothing in God is complete except there is
    nothing
to be incomplete the pulse and change of rhythm, blown flight
to be anything at all . . . vibration holy nuance beating against
itself, a rhythm a playing re-understood now by one of
    the 1st race
the primitives the first men who evolve again to civilize the
world

301

Henry L. Dumas
(1935–1968)

SON OF MSIPPI

Up
from Msippi I grew.
(Bare walk and cane stalk
make a hungry belly talk.)
Up
from the river of death.
(Walk bare and stalk cane
make a hungry belly talk.)

Up
from Msippi I grew.
Up
from the river of pain.

Out of the long red earth dipping, rising,
spreading out in deltas and plains,
out of the strong black earth turning
over by the iron plough,

out of the swamp green earth dripping
with moss and snakes,

out of the loins of the leveed lands
muscling its American vein:
the great Father of Waters,
I grew
up,
beside the prickly boll of white,
beside the bone-filled Mississippi
rolling on and on,
breaking over,

cutting off,
ignoring my bleeding fingers.

Bare stalk and sun walk
I hear a boll-weevil talk
cause I grew
up
beside the ox and the bow,
beside the rock church and the shack row,
beside the fox and the crow,
beside the melons and maize,
beside the hound dog,
beside the pink hog,
flea-hunting,
mud-grunting,
cat-fishing,
dog pissing
in the Mississippi
rolling on and on,
ignoring the colored coat I spun
of cotton fibers.

Cane-sweat river-boat
nigger-bone floating.

Up from Msippi
I grew,
wailing a song with every strain.

Woman gone woe man too
baby cry rent-pause daddy flew.

TIS OF THEE

1.

You are oversized, you are overrated, you are overblown,
fat and filled with hardened rocks.
You are sick and stumbling like an old man without
a stick in the mud.
You make me sick to my stomach, and I am sad
that I have to look at you.
You have eaten too much garlic

303

and drunk too much beer,
and built too many empty churches.
You are fat with starch and lies.

2.

Your steeled cities range like malignant cancers across
the belly of your land.
Your sons race death in metal machines that
defecate poison into the air.
Your ideas are machine made,
your values operated by machines
your truths nourished by machines,
your history written by machines,
your language sounds like millions of coins jingling
into an empty barrel.
Your heroes are dead.
Your wars are massacres.
You are an overkiller,
oversexed, overripe, overrotten.

3.

You are a sinful old man who has no repentance
in his heart,
a lecherous old winebelly vomiting blood.
You are a murderer of your sons
and a raper of your daughters.
You are cold and filled with death.
Few flowers grow from your gardens
and the snow and the ice shall be your grave.

4.

You are a despiser of black and misunderstander of white.
You are a mystery of yourself and a hater of that.
You once were a star that blazed,
but now you are overcivilized, oversterilized, oversated.
If you were a barren tree in my garden
I would come and cut you down.

Ahmos Zu-Bolton II
(1935–)

SUNSET BEACH

She sang me the churchsong
of the southern ghetto, there
by the pacific,
                    there where
the great waves tongued soul
and blackverse was quicktalk.

She sang me the melody of gospel
till late-late afternoon,
till the waves
lent themselves to rebirth,
and as babytides
tip-toed against our legs
I gave her horizontal
to the sea.

Her body was the rhyme of ju-ju
all of deep-rich-beautiful black,
all of chaos and nonsense,
all of seventeen years
of prehistoric craving;
but I was the warrior
                    who knew no past:

I was born that day, born of
imperfections, word formulas,
nicklebags of poetry,
an image of love
yet a greenthumb for hate

For I am he they fed
to the sugarcane crop,

& he they slaved
on the 4th.

THE SEEKER

blackjack moses
returning from the war,
returned to seek the fugitive freedom
which hides in bright & open light,

talks
with tangents
tied to his tongue:

nothing is believable, the light
lies, at least in this reality,
for the same old songs
are sung.

blackjack hates
the fact that he cannot completely hate
& in this there is rage.

he cannot face
the night   the moon   the stars
seem to plot against him,
there are very few shadows
to hide in, & all the faces
frown.

but for blackjack
there is no fear here,
& sleep is possible.

the dawn approaches
& he prepares himself
as best he can:

he has no weapon
(he threw away his gun
when he threw away
his bible).

SISTER BLUES WITH LIVEWIRE DAVIS

She couldnot make him over.
Or silence him.

She measured him
and he failed her so.
She couldnot kill the mirror
of her mother's eyes.

Her mother: the sad Negrolady
who could rule with a glance.
A properwoman of the blues.
He failed her mother
and didnot know his place:
much too loud in a prayerful
kingdom, too uncontrollable
in a world of controls.

This tore at her as if to cripple,
this loss of face.

So she made him babies
in the image of other men.
And spent her days in sturdy dream.
And spent her nights as
the darkmistress
of wounded love.

STRUGGLE-ROAD DANCE

> *"when freedom comes
> there'll be no more blues*
>   (repeat)
> *but lawd lawd
> it ain't here yet"*
>   —Adesanya Alakoye

This is the camping ground
the waterhole
the rest area

this is the tree
under which I will lay
this poem
       plant it here
       to see if there is growth:

Come to the campfire with me,
make peace with your brothers
love for the sisters,

we make this
a dance celebration:

       circle the flames
       warm yourself
       and rest . . .

We only wait here
till it dawns on us:

       what is the nature
       of this distance
       How hard was
       that last mile . . .

Count our numbers
(we have never been all present
and accounted for:

       we lost Blackjack
       back at the creek
       bloodriver and some mean nigger
       shooting him down

       last we saw of him
       he was tiptoeing off into
       the white world

       at least we think
       that's where he
       was going . . .

But Livewire Davis
made it, and Sister Blues
survived—

this place
must be a workshop
for our people

make a home
and build a family

study
the growth
of our tribe

we know how far off
is morning

      when freedom comes
      there'll be no more blues

(this dance
will not be sung
when sweet freedom dawns on us
but
      sing it now
      sing it now
      sing it now

INTRO TO MY FINAL BOOK OF POEMS

this is to say that i am
coming round the bend. the darkness
inside your flashes of light know me.
i throw yu curves cause I wanted to be
a pitcher. a sidearming hero
    you could turn to
in the late innings   (i would
    save the game
before my wounded brother got to
the shower.

but this ain't no playground
they told me. that & the fact
that i never mastered

the screw-
ball
is the reason i am here.

AIN'T NO SPRING CHICKEN

1

I am as old as sin
quiet as it's kept

As ancient as an exorcism
from paradise

I used to swing by my feet,
make a dance out of trees catching me,
I used to stand on my hands and throw huge rocks
with the bow of my legs

I used to outrun daylight
home to a woman dressed in nightfall
older than the blues,
older than the grace of sitting years later
on the porch of a rockingchair poem

I used to turn my eyes insideout
and cure a headache,
in a time before color 3D TV
in a time before footprints on the moon
in a time before the wheel

2

Let me tell you
of a time long before Lucifer:
when the sky and the sea were the same,
when we could swim to the stars

I am slowdragging against the walls of a cave
combing the wind with my hair,
I wear a rainbow as my diaper
and a feather in my ear,
I am tapdancing majestic waves

310

surfing for the rocky ground
where the tribe waits

They throw chains out to fetch me,
pulling me in like old age
with open arms,
they bite and growl a song
which welcomes me.

Even then there was more to the world
than meets the eye

Lucille Clifton
(1936–)

in the inner city
or
like we call it
home
we think a lot about uptown
and the silent nights
and the houses straight as
dead men
and the pastel lights
and we hang on to our no place
happy to be alive
and in the inner city
or
like we call it
home

HARRIET

if i be you
let me not forget
to be the pistol
pointed
to be the madwoman
at the rivers edge
warning
be free or die
and isabell
if i be you
let me in my
sojourning
not forget
to ask my brothers

ain't i a woman too
and
grandmother
if i be you
let me not forget to
work hard
trust the Gods
love my children and
wait.

LAST NOTE TO MY GIRLS

for sid, rica, gilly and neen

my girls
my girls
my almost me
mellowed in a brown bag
held tight and straining
at the top
like a good lunch
until the bag turned weak and wet
and burst in our honeymoon rooms.
we wiped the mess and
dressed you in our name and
here you are
my girls
my girls
forty quick fingers
reaching for the door.

i command you to be
good runners
to go with grace
go well in the dark and
make for high ground
my dearest girls
my girls
my more than me.

313

I ONCE KNEW A MAN

i once knew a man who had wild horses killed.
when he told about it
the words came galloping out of his mouth
and shook themselves and headed off in
every damn direction. his tongue
was wild and wide and spinning when he talked
and the people he looked at closed their eyes
and tore the skins off their backs as they walked away
and stopped eating meat.
there was no holding him once he got started;
he had had wild horses killed one time and
they rode him to his grave.

CONFESSION

father
i am not equal to the faith required.
i doubt.
i have a woman's certainties;
bodies pulled from me,
pushed into me.
bone flesh is what i know.

father
the angels say they have no wings.
i woke one morning
feeling how to see them.
i could discern their shadows
in the shadow. i am not
equal to the faith required.

father
i see your mother standing now
shoulderless and shoeless by your side.
i hear her whisper truths i cannot know.
father i doubt.

father
what are the actual certainties?
your mother speaks of love.

the angels say they have no wings.
i am not equal to the faith required.
i try to run from such surprising presence;
the angels stream before me
like a torch.
in populated air
our ancestors continue.
i have seen them.
i have heard
their shimmering voices
singing.

Clarence Major
(1936–)

THE COTTON CLUB

duke look at you.
hay. look how duke
stays & stays UP
all night, how the music
reaches through. the
waves. he got waves slicked
back, too. duke been
staying up all night all
his. time, the afternoon
in his eyes. yellow sun-
light, going down. honor
the institutions, the
idea of duke. tho a person,
human through his own
nights. sleeping late,
being slow at home. knew
& remember jungle nights.
recorded harlem on
the open wings of a
bluebird. electric economy,
& somebody already always
ready to say hold still
let me take your
picture. and they can't
even see him. no lie

IN THE INTEREST OF
PERSONAL APPEARANCE

i wait on your carved ugly stool.
while you cut heads to the bone.
slice the skin off
under the hair. you all
right, tho. see you, i can't
always speak. not even
to you at these crazy
parties. don't go often where
the terra cotta skulls deck.

and the bronze plaques the
ekpo society masks and the
ceremonial objects decorate the
*in*direct-lit D I N S of very
smooth, people. i burn
the invitations and stay into
my. own touch.

always a lot to do besides i
got a way to get inside. our
emotional folklore right. here
, an even space behind your eye-
balls. all through me.

when i sit i set straight, you
know. that but baby i need
an edge, you clip close. even
use a razor on the neck, leave
circles around the ears, clean.
ostensive, dainty hands.

but i keep coming. to you,
straight, cause tho your mouth
might your fingers don't lie
, they sure

Jayne Cortez
(1936–   )

DO YOU THINK

Do you think this is a sad day
   a sad night
full of tequila   full of el dorado
   full of banana solitudes

And my chorizo face a holiday for knives
   and my arching lips   a savannah for cuchifritos
and my spit curls a symbol for you
   to overcharge   overbill   oversell me
these saints   these candles
   these dented cars   loud pipes
no insurance and no place to park
   because my last name is Cortez

Do you think this is a sad night
   a sad day

And on this elevator
   between my rubber shoes
in the creme de menthe of my youth
   the silver tooth of my age
the gullah speech of my one trembling tit
full of tequila   full of el dorado
   full of banana solitudes you tell me
i use more lights   more gas
   more telephones   more sequins   more feathers
more iridescent headstones
   you think i accept this pentecostal church
in exchange for the lands you stole

And because my name is Cortez
   do you think this is a revision

of flesh studded with rivets
   my wardrobe clean
the pick in my hair
   the pomegranate in my hand
14th street   delancey street   103rd street
   reservation where i lay my skull
the barrio of need
   the police state in ashes
drums full of tequila   full of el dorado
   full of banana solitudes say:

Do you really think time speaks english
   in the men's room

ROSE SOLITUDE

(For Duke Ellington)

I am essence of Rose Solitude
my cheeks are laced with cognac
my hips sealed with five satin nails
i carry dreams and romance of new fools and old
flames
between the musk of fat
and the side pocket of my mink tongue

Listen to champagne bubble from this solo

Essence of Rose Solitude
veteran from texas   tiger from chicago   that's me
i cover the shrine of Duke
who like Satchmo   like Nat (King) Cole
will never die because love they say
never dies

I tell you from stair steps of these navy blue nights
these metallic snakes
these flashing fish skins
and the melodious cry of Shango
surrounded by sorrow
by purple velvet tears
by cockhounds limping from crosses
from turtle skinned shoes

from diamond shaped skulls and canes
made from dead gazelles
wearing a face of wilting potato plants
of grey and black scissors
of bee bee shots and fifty red boils
yes the whole world loved him

I tell you from suspenders of two-timing dog odors
from inca frosted lips
nonchalant legs
i tell you from howling chant of sister Erzulie
and the exaggerated hearts of a hundred pretty
women
they loved him
this world sliding from a single flower
into a caravan of heads made into ten thousand
flowers

Ask me
Essence of Rose Solitude
chickadee from arkansas that's me
i sleep on cotton bones
cotton tails
and mellow myself in empty ballrooms
i'm no fly by night
look at my resume
i walk through the eyes of staring lizards
i throw my neck back to floorshow on bumping goat
skins
in front of my stage fright
i cover the hands of Duke who like Satchmo
like Nat (King) Cole will never die
because love they say
never dies

IF THE DRUM IS A WOMAN

If the drum is a woman
why are you pounding your drum into an insane
babble
why are you pistol whipping your drum at dawn
why are you shooting through the head of your drum

and making a drum tragedy of drums
if the drum is a woman
don't abuse your drum   don't abuse your drum
                don't abuse your drum
I know the night is full of displaced persons
I see skins striped with flames
I know the ugly disposition of underpaid clerks
they constantly menstruate through the eyes
I know bitterness embedded in flesh
the itching alone can drive you crazy
I know that this is America
and chickens are coming home to roost
on the MX missile
But if the drum is a woman
why are you choking your drum
why are you raping your drum
why are you saying disrespectful things
to your mother drum   your sister drum
your wife drum and your infant daughter drum
If the drum is a woman
then understand your drum
your drum is not docile
your drum is not invisible
your drum is not inferior to you
your drum is a woman
so don't reject your drum
don't try to dominate your drum
don't become weak and cold and desert your drum
don't be forced into the position
as an oppressor of drums
and make a drum tragedy of drums
if the drum is a woman
don't abuse your drum   don't abuse your drum
                don't abuse your drum

June Jordan
(1936–)

POEM ABOUT THE HEAD OF A NEGRO
Painted by Peter Paul Rubens, 1577–1640

Up the shaken stairway
Back four hundred years
Before the meaningless emancipation
In an arbitrary corner
Of an old room
I find the face a tender contradiction
To the not entirely invisible bullet
Hole
The circling blush macabre as its history
Told into the left temple of the humbling skull

I find a man
the mother of mysterious crime
I find a man
the mother of me

The sweet the burden of the air around the head
that must look down
down
down into the flesh
down
down
down into the muscle of the flesh
down
down
down into the bleeding of the muscle
down
down
down into the candle of the blood

322

A SONG OF SOJOURNER TRUTH

Dedicated to Bernice Reagon

The trolley cars was rollin and the passengers all white
when Sojourner just decided it was time to take a seat
The trolley cars was rollin and the passengers all white
When Sojourner decided it was time to take a seat
It was time she felt to rest a while and ease up
on her feet
So Sojourner put her hand out
tried to flag the trolley down
So Sojourner put her hand out
for the trolley crossin town
And the driver did not see her
the conductor would not stop
But Sojourner yelled, "It's me!"
And put her body on the track
"It's me!" she yelled, "And yes,
I walked here but I ain walkin back!"
The trolley car conductor and the driver was afraid
to roll right over her and leave her lying dead
So they opened up the car and Sojourner took a seat
So Sojourner sat to rest a while and eased up on her feet

Refrain:
Sojourner had to be just crazy
tellin all that kinda truth
I say she musta been plain crazy
plus they say she was uncouth
talkin loud to any crowd
talkin bad insteada sad
She just had to be plain crazy
talkin all that kinda truth

If she had somewhere to go she said
I'll ride
If she had somewhere to go she said
I'll ride
jim crow or no
she said *I'll go*
just like the lady
that she was in all the knowing darkness
of her pride
she said *I'll ride*

she said *I'll talk*
she said *A Righteous Mouth*
ain nothin you should hide
she said she'd ride
just like the lady
that she was in all the knowing darkness
of her pride
she said *I'll ride*

They said she's Black and ugly and they said she's
really rough
They said if you treat her like a dog
well that'll be plenty good enough
And Sojourner said
I'll ride
And Sojourner said
I'll go
I'm a woman and this hell has made me tough
(Thank God!)
This hell has made me tough
I'm a strong Black woman
and Thank God!

Refrain:
Sojourner had to be just crazy
tellin all that kinda truth
I say she musta been plain crazy
plus they say she was uncouth
talkin loud to any crowd
talkin bad insteada sad
She just had to be plain crazy
talkin all that kinda truth

SUNFLOWER SONNET NUMBER ONE

But if I tell you how my heart swings wide
enough to motivate flirtations with the trees
or how the happiness of passion freaks inside
me, will you then believe the faithful, yearning freeze
on random, fast explosions that I place
upon my lust? Or must I say the streets are bare
unless it is your door I face

unless they are your eyes that, rare
as tulips on a cold night, trick my mind
to oranges and yellow flames around a seed
as deep as anyone may find
in magic? What do you need?

I'll give you that, I hope, and more
But don't you be the one to choose me: poor.

SUNFLOWER SONNET NUMBER TWO

Supposing we could just go on and on as two
voracious in the days apart as well as when
we side by side (the many ways we do
that) well! I would consider then
perfection possible, or else worthwhile
to think about. Which is to say
I guess the costs of long term tend to pile
up, block and complicate, erase away
the accidental, temporary, near
thing/pulsebeat promises one makes
because the chance, the easy new, is there
in front of you. But still, perfection takes
some sacrifice of falling stars for rare.
And there are stars, but none of you, to spare.

I MUST BECOME A MENACE TO MY ENEMIES

*Dedicated to the Poet Agostinho Neto, President of
The People's Republic of Angola: 1976*

I

I will no longer lightly walk behind
a one of you who fear me:
                              Be afraid.
I plan to give you reasons for your jumpy fits
and facial tics
I will not walk politely on the pavements anymore
and this is dedicated in particular
to those who hear my footsteps
or the insubstantial rattling of my grocery
cart

then turn around
see me
and hurry on
away from this impressive terror I must be:
I plan to blossom bloody on an afternoon
surrounded by my comrades singing
terrible revenge in merciless
accelerating
rhythms
But
I have watched a blind man studying his face.
I have set the table in the evening and sat down
to eat the news.
Regularly
I have gone to sleep.
There is no one to forgive me.
The dead do not give a damn.
I live like a lover
who drops her dime into the phone
just as the subway shakes into the station
wasting her message
cancelling the question of her call:

fulminating or forgetful but late
and always after the fact that could save or
condemn me

I must become the action of my fate.

II

How many of my brothers and my sisters
will they kill
before I teach myself
retaliation?
Shall we pick a number?
South Africa for instance:
do we agree that more than ten thousand
in less than a year but that less than
five thousand slaughtered in more than six
months will
WHAT IS THE MATTER WITH ME?

I must become a menace to my enemies.

III

And if I
if I ever let you slide
who should be extirpated from my universe
who should be cauterized from earth
completely
(lawandorder jerkoffs of the first the
terrorist degree)
then let my body fail my soul
in its bedevilled lecheries

And if I
if I ever let love go
because the hatred and the whisperings
become a phantom dictate I o-
bey in lieu of impulse and realities
(the blossoming flamingos of my
wild mimosa trees)
then let love freeze me
out.

I must become
I must become a menace to my enemies.

Eugene Redmond
(1937–)

PARAPOETICS

*(For my former students and writing friends
in East St. Louis, Illinois*

Poetry is an *applied science:*
Re-wrapped corner rap;
  Rootly-eloquented cellular, soulular sermons.

Grit reincarnations of
Lady Day
Bird
& Otis;
Silk songs pitched on 'round and rhythmic rumps;
Carved haloes (for heroes) and asserted maleness:
Sounds and sights of fire-tongues
Leaping from lips of flame-stricken buildings in the night.

Directions: apply poetry as needed.
Envision.
Visualize.
Violate!
Wring minds.
Shout!
Right words.
Rite!!
Cohabitate.
Gestate.
Inpregnate your vocabulary.
Dig, a parapoet!

Parenthesis: Replace winter with spring, move Mississippi
  to New York, Oberlin (Ohio) to East St. Louis, Harlem
  to the summer whitehouse. Carve candles and flintstones
  for flashlights.

Carry your poems.
Grit teeth. Bear labor-love pains.
Have twins and triplets.
Furtilize poem-farms with after-birth,
Before birth and dung (rearrange old words);
Study/strike tradition.

Caution to parapoets.
Carry the weight of your own poem.
. . . it's a *heavy lode.*

CANE-BRAKE-BLUES

Remembering Jean Toomer's Cane

Got me some canebrake blues / baby / this sugarpain sho
    is bad;
Got me some canebrake blues / baby / this sugarpain sho
    is bad;
This sweet/sweet sore /man / just keeps me happy-sad.

Cane blade cuts my mind / make my thoughts runred;
Cane blade cuts my mind / make my thoughts runred;
Cane dagger in my brain / knife-sweetenin' my head.

Cane crams wind down my throat / I'm hollerin from
    earth's hole;
Cane crams wind down my throat / I'm hollerin from
    earth's hole;
Sounds just symphonizing / resurrecting my old, old soul.

Got some canebrake blues, sweet / mama,
Got some canbrake blues
Got some canbrake blues, sweet / mama,
     / got some canebrake blues /
But with this sugarpain power
How can I lose
How can I lose
How can I lose . . . .

AUTUMN GOD

On an autumn day
I took a leaf,
Yellowing in its
Tenuous attachment
To the tree.

There were others,
But of no interest to me,
Since the one I held
Held itself a worm
Rushing to be free.

And cruelly,
With each attempt to flee,
I brought it back
To the center of the dead leaf.

Until at last, in seeming glee,
The worm struggled
To one corner
And in a jump
Was rid of me.

Undaunted, I stopped
To see
Where it dragged slowly
Along leaf after leaf;
'Til it reached the trunk
Of the tree
And turned.
Then again it was worm
And me.

Under my heel
I crushed the vicious thing!

HIS EMINENCE PLAYS THE SOULAR SYSTEM

(Following recording session: Hammett Bluiett with cameo
appearances by LadySmith Black Mambazo, Hugh Masekela
and Quincy Troupe—NYC 7/7/87)

kora kora hear the strings attached
whining wires across holy-whittled wood
choral whistles warbling through soulular valves:
CPR for the communiversal flock

i hear hyena hearts
shrieking in innercantations:

humming umbilical hook-ups
intimations & extensions
soular connectives: sonic blooms.

percussive divinations!
diasporan indentations!
bluesplendent scarifications!

hammet i hear you hammett

gutbucketeer:
tonguing the riversax:
inverting the tribal viscera
evoking the metaphysical funk
coaxing the metaphorical flame
bluesplendent: extempore extempore

continuum: connectives:
   archives streams bridges linkages
     retentions survivals ditties
rattle slap roll suck the scrumptious drum
explore implore empower our antiphonal pertinence

soweto kingston harlem
soweto kingston harlem
hear the rooty contrapuntalisman:
masekela mojo masekela
hugh and cry
hugh and sky
hear in the wry where riffs writhe i
hear sojourner conching thru
umoja caverns of escape

(lovejoy/brooklyn/madison/east saint love/north
saint luck/the island/fireworks station/kinloch)

331

kingdoms of escape to holy-roller relief
and from passages low way-weigh low
come the lumbrous/labyrinthine tropes
    of troupe:
bluescandescent rite-tales reptilic scats

hammett hugh quincy
zulu xhosa yoruba
highlife reggae gospel

gourds trilling gluttonous memories
lush descendent-gifts of groove-art:
hallelujahs hainted by field hollers

ogun
odetta
ogloom
o/moms
obatala
o/bessie
obeah
hound-dog-woman
hoochie koochie washboard
john o john yo henry

"can't you hear me . . .
can't you hear me when i call."

Larry Neal
(1937–1981)

POPPA STOPPA SPEAKS FROM HIS GRAVE

Remember me baby in my best light,
lovely hip style and all;
all laid out in my green velour
stashing on corners
in my boxcar coat—
so sure of myself, too cool for words,
and running down a beautiful game.

It would be super righteous
if you would think of me that way sometimes;
and since it can't be that way,
just the thought of you digging on me that way
would be hip and lovely even from here.

Yeah, you got a sweet body, baby,
but out this way, I won't be needing it;
but remember me and think of me
that way sometimes.

But don't make it no big thing though;
don't jump jive and blow your real romance.
but in a word, while you high-steppin and finger-poppin
tell your lovin' man that I was a bad
motherfucker till the Butcher cut me down.

DON'T SAY GOODBYE TO THE PORKPIE HAT

Mingus, Bird, Prez, Langston, and them

Don't say goodbye to the Porkpie Hat that rolled
along on nodded shoulders
> that swang bebop phrases
> in Minton's jelly roll dreams

Don't say goodbye to hip hats tilted in the style of a
soulful era;
the Porkpie Hat that Lester dug
swirling in the sound of sax blown suns
> phrase on phrase, repeating bluely
> tripping in and under crashing
> hi-hat cymbals, a fickle girl
> getting sassy on the rhythms.

Musicians heavy with memories
move in and out of this gloom;
the Porkpie Hat reigns supreme
smell of collard greens
and cotton madness
commingled in the nigger elegance of the style.
> The Porkpie Hat sees tonal memories
> of salt peanuts and hot house birds
> the Porkpie Hat sees . . .

Cross riffing square kingdoms, riding midnight Scottsboro
trains. We are haunted by the lynched limbs.
On the road:
It would be some hoodoo town
It would be some cracker place
you might meet redneck lynchers
face to face
but mostly you meet mean horn blowers
running obscene riffs
Jelly Roll spoke of such places:
the man with the mojo hand
the dyke with the .38
the yaller girls
and the knifings.

Stop-time Buddy and Creole Sydney
wailed in here. Stop time.
chorus repeats, stop and shuffle.
stop and stomp.

listen to the horns, ain't they mean?
now ain't they mean
in blue
in blue
in blue streaks of mellow wisdom
blue notes
coiling around
the Porkpie Hat
and ghosts of dead musicians drifting through
here on riffs that smack
of one-leg trumpet players
and daddy glory piano ticklers
who
twisted arpeggios
with diamond-flashed fingers.
There was Jelly Roll Morton, the sweet mackdaddy,
hollering Waller, and Willie The Lion Smith—
some mean showstoppers.

Ghosts of dead holy rollers ricocheted in the air funky
with white lightnin' and sweat.
Emerald bitches shot shit in a kitchen smelling
of funerals and fried chicken.
Each city had a different sound:
there was Mambo, Rheba, Jeanne;
holy the voice of these righteous sisters.

Shape to shape, horn to horn
the Porkpie Hat resurrected himself
night to night, from note to note
skimming the horizons, flashing bluegreenyellow lights
and blowing black stars
and weird looneymoon changes; chords coiled about him
and he was flying
fast
zipping
past
sound
into cosmic silences.
And yes
and caresses flowed from the voice in the horn in the blue
of the yellow whiskey room where bad hustlers with big
coats moved, digging the fly sister, fingerpopping while
tearing at chicken and waffles.

335

The Porkpie Hat loomed specter like, a vision for the world;
shiny, the knob toe shoes,
sporting hip camel coats
and righteous pin stripes—
pants pressed razor shape;
and caressing his horn, baby like.

So we pick up our axes and prepare
to blast the white dream;
we pick up our axes
re-create ourselves and the universe,
sounds splintering the deepest regions
of spiritual space
crisp and moaning voices
leaping in the horns of destruction,
blowing death and doom to all who have no use for the spirit.

So we cook out of sight
into cascading motions of joy delight
shooflies the Bird lollygagging
and laughing for days,
and the rhythms way up in there
wailing, sending scarlet rays, luminescent,
spattering bone and lie.
we go on cool lords
wailing on into star nights,
rocking whole worlds, unfurling song on song
into long stretches of green spectral shimmerings,
blasting on, fucking the moon with the blunt edge
of a lover's tune, out there now, joy riffing
for days and do
railriding and do
talking some lovely shit and do
to the Blues God who blesses us.

No, don't say goodbye to the Porkpie Hat—
he lives, oh yes.

Lester lives and leaps
Delancey's dilemma is over
Bird lives
Lady lives
Eric stands next to me

while I finger the Afro-horn
Bird lives
Lady lives
Lester leaps in every night
Tad's delight
is mine now
Dinah knows
Richie knows
that Bud is Buddha
that Jelly Roll dug juju
and Lester lives
in Ornette's leapings
the Blues God lives
we live
live
spirit lives
and sound lives
bluebird lives
lives and leaps
dig the mellow voices
dig the Porkpie Hat
dig the spirit in Sun Ra's sound
dig the cosmic Trane
dig be
dig be
dig be
spirit lives in sound
dig be
sound lives in spirit
dig be
yeah ! ! !
spirit lives
spirit lives
spirit lives
SPIRIT ! ! !

SWHEEEEEEEEEEEEEEEETT ! ! !

take it again
this time from the top

I am the Seventh Son of the son
who was also the seventh.
I have drunk deep of the waters of my ancestors,
have traveled the soul's journey toward cosmic harmony—
the Seventh Son.

Have walked slick avenues
and seen grown men, fall, to die in a blue doom
of death and ancestral agony;
have seen old men glide, shadowless, feet barely
touching the pavements.

I sprang out of the Midwestern plains
the bleak Michigan landscape, the black blues of Kansas
City, these kiss-me-nights;
out of the bleak Michigan landscape wearing the slave name
Malcolm Little.

Saw a brief vision in Lansing when I was seven, and in
my momma's womb heard the beast cry death;
a landscape on which white robed figures ride, and my
Garvey father silhouetted against the night-fire
gun in hand,
form outlined against a panorama of violence.

Out of the Midwestern bleakness, I sprang, pushed eastward,
past shack on country nigger shack, across the wilderness
of North America.
I hustler. I pimp. I unfulfilled black man
bursting with destiny.
New York City Slim called me Big Red,
and there was no escape, close nights of the smell of death.
Pimp. Hustler. The day fills these rooms.
I'm talking about New York, Harlem.
Talking about the neon madness.
Talking about ghetto eyes and nights
Talking about death protruding across the room
Talking about Small's Paradise.
Talking about cigarette butts, and rooms smelly with white
sex-flesh, and dank sheets, and being on the run.
Talking about cocaine illusions.
Talking about stealing and selling.

Talking about these New York cops who smell
of blood and money.
I am Big Red, tiger, vicious, Big Red, bad nigger, will kill.

But there is rhythm here
Its own special substance:
I hear Billie sing, no Good Man, and dig Prez, wearing
the Zoot suit of life, the Porkpie hat tilted at the
correct angle; through the Harlem smoke of beer and
whiskey, I understand the mystery of the Signifying
Monkey;
in a blue haze of inspiration
I reach for the totality of being.
I am at the center of a swirl of events.
War and death.
Rhythm.
Hot women.
I think life a commodity bargained
for across the bar in Small's.
I perceive the echoes of Bird
and there is a gnawing the maw
of my emotions.

And then there is jail.
America is the world's greatest jailer,
and we are all in jails
Holy spirits contained like magnificent
birds of wonder.
I now understand my father urged on by the ghost of Garvey,
and see a small brown man standing in a corner.
The cell. Cold. Dank.
The light around him vibrates.
(Am I crazy?)
But to understand is to submit to a more perfect will,
a more perfect order.
To understand is to surrender the imperfect self
for a more perfect self.

Allah formed man, I follow
and shake within the very depth of my most interesting being;
and I bear witness to the Message of Allah
and I bear witness; all praise is due Allah.

Spring 1967

Ishmael Reed
(1938–   )

I AM A COWBOY IN THE BOAT OF RA

*'The devil must be forced to reveal any such physical evil
(potions, charms, fetishes, etc.) still outside the body
and these must be burned.'* (Ritual Romanum, *published
1947, endorsed by the coat-of-arms and introductory
letter from Francis cardinal Spellman*)

I am a cowboy in the boat of Ra,
sidewinders in the saloons of fools
bit my forehead   like   O
the untrustworthiness of Egyptologists
who do not know their trips. Who was that
dog-faced man? they asked, the day I rode
from town.

School marms with halitosis cannot see
the Nefertiti fake chipped on the run by slick
germans, the hawk behind Sonny Rollins' head or
the ritual beard of his axe; a longhorn winding
its bells thru the Field of Reeds.

I am a cowboy in the boat of Ra. I bedded
down with Isis, Lady of the Boogaloo, dove
down deep in her horny, stuck up her Wells-Far-ago
in daring midday getaway. 'Start grabbing the
blue,' I said from top of my double crown.

I am a cowboy in the boat of Ra. Ezzard Charles
of the Chisholm Trail. Took up the bass but they
blew off my thumb. Alchemist in ringmanship but a
sucker for the right cross.

340

I am a cowboy in the boat of Ra. Vamoosed from
the temple i bide my time. The price on the wanted
poster was a-going down, outlaw alias copped my stance
and moody greenhorns were making me dance;
    while my mouth's
shooting iron got its chambers jammed.

I am a cowboy in the boat of Ra. Boning-up in
the ol West i bide my time. You should see
me pick off these tin cans whippersnappers. I
write the motown long plays for the comeback of
Osiris. Make them up when stars stare at sleeping
steer out here near the campfire. Women arrive
on the backs of goats and throw themselves on
my Bowie.

I am a cowboy in the boat of Ra. Lord of the lash,
the Loup Garou Kid. Half breed son of Pisces and
Aquarius. I hold the souls of men in my pot. I do
the dirty boogie with scorpions. I make the bulls
keep still and was the first swinger to grape the taste.

I am a cowboy in his boat. Pope Joan of the
Ptah Ra. C/mere a minute willya doll?
Be a good girl and
bring me my Buffalo horn of black powder
bring me my headdress of black feathers
bring me my bones of Ju-Ju snake
go get my eyelids of red paint.
Hand me my shadow

I'm going into town after Set

I am a cowboy in the boat of Ra

look out Set   here i come Set
to get Set   to sunset Set
to unseat Set   to Set down Set

              usurper of the Royal couch
              —imposter RAdio of Moses' bush
              party pooper O hater of dance
              vampire outlaw of the milky way

341

DUALISM
In Ralph Ellison's Invisible Man

I am outside of
history. i wish
i had some peanuts, it
looks hungry there in
its cage

i am inside of
history. its
hungrier than i
thot

SKY DIVING

"It's a good way to live and
A good way to die"
From a Frankenheimer video about
Sky diving
The hero telling why he liked to

The following noon he leaped
But his parachute wasn't with him
He spread out on the field like
Scrambled eggs

Life is not always
Hi-lifing inside
Archibald Motley's
"Chicken Shack"
You in your derby
Your honey in her beret
Styling before a small vintage
Car

Like too many of us
I am a man who never had much
Use for a real father
And so when I'm heading
For a crash
No one will catch me but
Me

The year is only five days old
Already a comet has glittered out
Its glow sandbagged by
The jealous sun

Happens to the best of us
Our brilliance falling off
Like hair from Berkeley's roving
Dogs

Even on Rose Bowl day
An otherwise joyous occasion
A float veered into the crowd
Somebody got bruised over the incident
Like a love affair on second ave.

It's a good lesson to us all
In these downhill days of a
Hard-hearted decade
Jetting through the world
Our tails on fire

You can't always count
On things opening up for you
Know when to let go
Learn how to fall

THE REACTIONARY POET

If you are a revolutionary
Then I must be a reactionary
For if you stand for the future
I have no choice but to
Be with the past

Bring back suspenders!
Bring back Mom!
Homemade ice cream
Picnics in the park
Flagpole sitting
Straw hats

343

Rent parties
Corn liquor
The banjo
Georgia quilts
Krazy Kat
Restock

The syncopation of
Fletcher Henderson
The Kiplingesque lines
of James Weldon Johnson
Black Eagle
Mickey Mouse
The Bach Family
Sunday School
Even Mayor La Guardia
Who read the comics
Is more appealing than
Your version of
What Lies Ahead

In your world of
Tomorrow Humor
Will be locked up and
The key thrown away
The public address system
Will pound out headaches
All day
Everybody will wear the same
Funny caps
And the same funny jackets
Enchantment will be found
Expendable, charm, a
Luxury
Love and kisses
A crime against the state
Duke Ellington will be
Ordered to write more marches
"For the people," naturally

If you are what's coming
It must be what's going

Make it by steamboat
I likes to take it real slow

POINTS OF VIEW

I

The pioneer stands in front of the
Old pioneer's home with his back-pack
walking stick and rifle
Wasn't me that Kisadi Frog-Klan
Indian was talking about when he
mentioned the horrors of Alaska
What horrors of Alaska?
Why Baranof was a swell fellow
Generous to the Indians, he was
known as far south as California
for his good deeds
Before we came the Indians were
making love to their children and
sacrificing their slaves, because
the Raven told them so, according
to them
"They couldn't even speak good
English and called the streams and
the mountains funny names
They were giving each other refrigerators
the potlatches had become so bad

We made them stop
They'd build a canoe abandon
it, then build another
We made them stop that, too
Now they have lawyers

They can have anything they want
If they want to go whaling
when we know they don't need to
go whaling
The lawyers see to it that they
go whaling
They're just like us
They buy frozen snow peas

345

just like we do
They're crazy about motorcycles
Just like we are

We brought them civilization
We brought them penicillin
We brought them Johnny Carson
Softball
We brought them trailer camps
They'd get married at fourteen
and die at 24
We brought them longevity

II

They brought us carbon dioxide
They brought us contractors
We told them not to dig there
They were clawed by two eagles
While uncovering the graves of
two medicine men

The white man has the mind of a
walrus's malignant left ball
We don't think the way they do
They arrive at the rate of one
thousand per month in cars
whose license plates read
texas oklahoma and mississippi
They built the Sheffield Hotel on
a herring bed
Everywhere are their dogs
Everywhere are their guns
Everywhere are their salmon-faced
women who get knocked up a lot
and sometimes enter the Chanel
restaurant wearing mysterious black
eyes, socked into their Viking-eyes
by men whose hair is plastered with
seal dung
It all began when
Chief Kowee of the Raven Klan showed
Joe Juneau the location of the gold
Now Mount Juneau is as empty as

346

a box of popcorn on the floor of
a picture show
When our people saw the first
Russian ship, we thought it was
the White Raven's return
Instead it was the Czarina's pirate
Dressed in Russian merchant's clothes
and a peacock's hat.
He shot Katlian in the back

Askia Muhammad Touré
(1938–)

FLOODTIDE

(for the black tenant farmers of the South)

"They carry on.
though sorrows completely
bend them down.
they carry on.
though butchered
and maimed
by nature and whitefolks,
they carry on
and sing their songs."

1

drought,
the river is a tricklin' stream.
drought,
dust on the dry tongues
of livestock.
drought,
tobacco leaves
droopin' in the merciless
sunlight.
clear skies, hot and dry.
haze on green mountains.
dustdevils
scamper on the blazin' wind'
drought.

(lawd,
we pray for warm soft rain;
for moisture in the fields,

for fat cattle,
lawd,
heah our prayer; rid us
of dis dry spell,
dis merciless heatspell,
dis drought.)

2

black clouds on the horizon.
black clouds over green mountains,
lightnin' on the hills.
baaroom, baaroom,
the rumblin' of thunder,
fills the air,
shakes the ground;
it comes:
lightnin' and thunder,
flash and crash;
it comes:
the violent spatter
of burstin'
clouds.

the rain comes
and washes the green mountains;
floods the cotton land.
the rain comes,
ruins the tobacco,
kills the livestock; makin' a mock'ry
of our prayers
for rain.
the killer rain comes:
the river is a ragin' madman
the river breaks our hearts.

the killer rain comes:
the river takes our shack away.
the river breaks our hearts.
the rain;
the drippin', flooded fields.
the rain;
the dead livestock.

the rain;
the rumblin' of thunder,
the green mountains,
the ragin' river,
the shack;
the killer rain,
the rain.
the killer rain,
the rain.
the killer rain.

3

silence;
gray mist and heartaches,
the flooded land.
now, screams; now, crys of rage.
the wails of women
and children,
the cursin' men.
wetsmells, *deathsmells*
of cattle, pigs,
of bloated men,
of hope,
of fallen dreams.

(lawd,
why did yuh cuss us
wit yo' anger?
why did yuh take mah man away?
mah henry,
mah man,
oh lawd!)

churchbells,
the chirpin' of blackbirds,
the sunday air.
sunlight on the flooded fields,
black throngs gathered,
flowers,
tears for brother henry
and others.

monday,
the rooster sounds
his horn:
wake up and live;
cleanup
the flooded land,
the fallen trees, the fields.
rebuild
the shattered homes,
the shattered lives,
the hopes.
rebuild
your shattered dreams.

"though sorrows completely
bend them down.
though butchered and maimed
by nature and whitefolks,
they sing their songs,
they sing their songs,
they sing their songs,
and carry on."

REBELLION SUITE/
Straight. No Chaser.

(for Thelonious Sphere Monk
and the Bebop Rebellion)

No trumpets announce
                              this
Maybe skies   heroe's
              toned   arrival.
                    a deeper
              sapphire.
                                        Intense the days
brimmed with his sacramental hipness. stride.
              elemental
                        vision.
The world we recognize
                        takes on

additional tones. textures. colors.
                    (Language
conveys our usual coded
                sophisticated
                     overtones.
But another dynamic strikes the depths:

           our rhythms lyrics harmonies
           vibrate
               an
                  electricity
adding a charismatic joy
                  which
                    reverberates
                        across
      urban plantations   momentarily
          causing a transcendance
              –Zen-like–
interrupting the mundane schizophrenia
                which
normally smothers bluesy
              shouters,
                screamers.
    finga-poppin'
        on
      the urban
         killing ground.

Oyeah
Oyeah
Oyeah
Oyeah/   scarlet flametones highlight
      the
        satiny
          skintight
            elegant dress
of this gardinia-wearing goddess boppin
        to his
          complexities. (Sweaty
              coon-toned
                pianos
smile their ivory teeth awaiting
        his familiar
            caress.)

Spotlight kissed,
   the
        bronze
            enchantress
                enhances a language
                            rife
                            with
                            polished gestures
motion. silence.   dramatic pauses
round about midnight when the indigo sky
conjures
        a mulatto moon/
                        spotlights pierce
                        the
                            purple haze
                    Dahomey profiles bedazzle
                                    enchant
            elements
            of
                Negritude
                    in patent leather conks
                                –marcels–
                above Benin bronze. Atavistic
                            sweatstains. moans
embrace
    the
        harmony/joys
release the memories
                    of
                    Downsouth dues
                    (lynchrope screams amid
                        terror
                        tar
                            & kerosine).

But/
        O the velvet-toned honey
                            ripe now
in his rippling fingers/
                    arpeggios
                        of
                    interwoven ecstasies
353

Flashpoint
                of
                profound perception/
                vision
                        highlighting
a new language. form. sound.
                        highlighting
                a new
                        humanity!

Rippling keys forsee
                        a Revolution/
                a renaissance
                        of
                        sound/language: forms
                                        heroic;
                at Minton's   a race of giants
"Salt Peanuts!
                Salt Peanuts!
                        Salt Peanuts!"

—New York, N.Y.
February 17, 1981

Julia Fields
(1938–)

HIGH ON THE HOG

Take my share of Soul Food—
I do not wish
To taste of pig
    Of either gut
        or Grunt
          from bowel
            Or jowl
I want caviar
Shrimp scoufflé
Sherry
        Champagne
            And not because
        These are the
        Whites' domain
        But just because
        I'm entitled—

For I've been
          V.d.'d enough
          T.b.'d enough
      and
        Hoe-cake fed Knock-Knee'd enough
        Spindly leg-bloodhound tree'd enough
To eat
High on the Hog
        I've been
          Hircd last
          Fired first enough
      I've sugar-watered my
          Thirst enough—

                    Been lynched enough
                              Slaved enough
                              Cried enough
                              Died enough
                    Been deprived—
                              Have survived enough
                                        To eat
                              High on the Hog

Keep the black-eyed peas
                              And the grits
                              The high blood-pressure chops
                              And gravy sops

I want apertifs supreme
                              Baked Alaska—
                    Something suave, cool
                    For I've been considered faithful fool
                    From 40 acres and a mule . . .

I've been
                              Slighted enough
                              Sever-righted enough
                              And up tighted enough
                    And I want
                    High on the Hog

For dragging the cotton sack
                              On bended knees
                              In burning sun
                              In homage to the
                                        Great-King cotton
                    For priming the money-green tobacco
                                        And earning pocket-change

                    For washing in iron pots
                    For warming by coal and soot
                    For eating the leavings from
                                        Others' tables

I've lived my wretched life
                    Between domestic rats
                                        And foreign wars

Carted to my final rest
             In second-hand cars

But I've been leeched enough
             Dixie-peached enough
             Color bleached enough

             And I want
             High on the Hog!

Oh, I've heard the Mau Mau
             Screaming

             Romanticising Pain
             I hear them think
             They go against the Grain

But I've lived in shacks
                          Long enough
             Had strong black beaten
                          Backs long enough

And I've been
             Urban-planned
                          Been monyihanned
                          Enough
             And I want
             High on the Hog

                    TREES

             Some trees, standing in groves
             have people inside them holding
             meetings,
             some trees have people locked
             and braced in love.
             a pine tree is a gigolo —
             notice the scent—always the best
             mouth wash,
             the best sheen of green shirt,
             the tallest, straightest back,
             the gentlest arms.

                    357

and do not even speak of oaks.
they know the game, get better
and better and better at it.
they are the rugged type, born rough
and with no tender shoots.
they stand alone, majestic, and
are of the order of warriors.

a weeping willow minces.
it draws mantles about itself
and takes small steps, ever
looking into bodies of water
Narcisscus-like, to preen
for itself and no other.
it weeps, droops, wilts, and hangs
with limp branches and
leans over the shoulders of
timid types

birches are adolescent boys,
standing taller than their heights
suggest, in groups, boasting and
leaning from the hips like cowboys.
skin breaking out in spots,
set restlooking on sharp terrain,
not complete in form or
individuality, in mode not plain.

maples are pregnant, the madonna trees
sugary motherhood enough
splash with quick, self-denigrating leaves
which are russet and reticent.
against the enthusiastic and the rough
they stand, making nurturement.
some trees are courtesans, some
whores, some priests and nuns.
but more are men:

          statesmen, sentries, chiefs
          granduncles, foremen and
          lovers. there are people
          in them. from time out of
          record, memory, or mind.

Michael S. Harper
(1938–   )

DEAR JOHN, DEAR COLTRANE

> *a love supreme, a love supreme*
> *a love supreme, a love supreme*

Sex fingers toes
in the marketplace
near your father's church
in Hamlet, North Carolina—
witness to this love
in this calm fallow
of these minds,
there is no substitute for pain:
genitals gone or going,
seed burned out,
you tuck the roots in the earth,
turn back, and move
by river through the swamps,
singing: *a love supreme, a love supreme;*
what does it all mean?
Loss, so great each black
woman expects your failure
in mute change, the seed gone.
You plod up into the electric city—
your song now crystal and
the blues. You pick up the horn
with some will and blow
into the freezing night:
a love supreme, a love supreme—

Dawn comes and you cook
up the thick sin 'tween
impotence and death, fuel

the tenor sax cannibal
heart, genitals and sweat
that makes you clean—
a love supreme, a love supreme—

Why you so black?
cause I am
why you so funky?
cause I am
why you so black?
cause I am
why you so sweet?
cause I am
why you so black?
cause I am
a love supreme, a love supreme:

So sick
you couldn't play *Naima,*
so flat we ached
for song you'd concealed
with your own blood,
your diseased liver gave
out its purity,
the inflated heart
pumps out, the tenor kiss,
tenor love:
a love supreme, a love supreme—
a love supreme, a love supreme—

PRAYER: MT. HOOD AND ENVIRONS

The windows of America
are faceless, incestuous screens
pumiced in pure glass,
triangular, innocent,
wired white hoods
cropped in green grass.

Comatose and armed
explorers brought salt water
from the ocean to boil
in three kettles as an offering;

360

The Indians smoked
on the mountaintrails
in buck heat
high along the Columbia;

Lewis and Clark,
their slave, York,
took their salt up
in their webbings;

the meat now cured,
the lumber stink off
the river,
fertilize no soil
without Indian blood
or red roses.

KIN

When news came that your mother'd
smashed her hip, both feet caught
in rungs of the banquet table,
our wedding rebroken on the memory
of the long lake of silence
when the stones of her body
broke as an Irish fence of stones,
I saw your wet dugs drag
with the weight of our daughter
in the quick of her sleep
to another feeding;
then the shoulders dropped
their broken antenna branches
of fear at the knife
running the scars
which had borne into the colon
for the misspent enema,
the clubbed liver unclean
with the stones of the gall bladder,
and the broken arch of hip
lugging you to the lake,
the dough inner tube of lading
swollen with innerpatching.

I pick you up from the floor
of your ringing fears, the floor
where the photographs you have worked
into the cool sky of the gray you love,
and you are back at the compost pile
where the vegetables burn,
or swim in the storm of your childhood,
when your father egged you on with his
open machinery, the exhaust choking your sisters,
and your sisters choked still.

Now his voice stops you in accusation,
and the years pile up on themselves
in the eggs of your stretched sons,
one born on his birthday, both dead.
I pull you off into the sanctuary
of conciliation, of quiet tactics,
the uttered question, the referral,
which will quiet the condition you have seen
in your mother's shadow, the crutches
inching in the uncut grass,
and the worn body you will carry
as your own birthmark of his scream.

THE MILITANCE OF A
PHOTOGRAPH IN THE PASSBOOK
OF A BANTU UNDER DETENTION

Peace is the active presence of Justice.

The wrinkles on the brown face
of the carrying case
conform to the buttocks,
on which the streaks of water
from a five-gallon can
dribble on the tailfront
of the borrowed shirt
he would wear if he could
drain the pus from his swaddling
bandages, striations of skin
tunneling into the photograph.

This is no simple mug shot
of a runaway boy in a training
film, Soweto's pummeled wire,
though the turrets of light
. glisten in smoke, the soft
coal hooding his platform
entrance, dull and quiet.

His father's miner's shoes
stand in puddles of polish,
the black soot baked
into images of brittle torso,
an inferno of bullets laid
out in a letter bomb,
the frontispiece of one sergeant-
major blackening his mustache.

On the drive to Evaton
a blank pass away from Sharpeville
where the freehold morgans
were brought by a black bishop
from Ontario, Canada, on a trek
northward from the Cape in 1908,
I speak to myself as the woman
riding in the backseat talks
of this day, her husband's
death, twenty-three years ago,
run over by an Afrikaner in the wrong
passing lane; the passbook on the shoulder
of the road leading to Evaton
is not the one I have in my hand,
and the photograph is not of my great-
grandfather, who set sail for Philadelphia
in the war year of 1916.
He did not want a reception, his letters
embarking on a platform at Queenstown
where his eloquence struck two Zulu warriors
pledged to die in the homelands
because they could not spin their own gold.

These threaded heads weigh down the ears
in design of the warrior, Shaka,
indifferent to the ruthless offerings

over the dead bodies of his wives,
childless in his campaigns with the British,
who sit on the ships of the Indian Ocean
each kraal shuddering near the borders;

her lips turn in profile
to the dust rising over a road
where his house once stood;
one could think of the women
carrying firewood as an etching
in remembrance to the silence,
commencing at Sharpeville,
but this is Evaton, where he would come
from across the galleyship of spears
turning in his robes to a bookmark;
it is a good book, the picture of words
in the gloss of a photograph,
the burned image of the man who wears
this image on the tongue of a child,
who might hold my hand
as we walk in late afternoon
into the predestined sun.

The press of wrinkles on the blanketed
voice of the man who took the train
from Johannesburg
is flattened in Cape Town,
and the history of this book
is on a trestle where Gandhi
worshipped in Natal,
and the Zulu lullaby
I cannot sing in Bantu
is this song in the body
of a passbook
and the book passes
into a shirt
and the back that wears it.

Al Young
(1939—)

THE SONG TURNING BACK INTO ITSELF 2
A song for little children

Always it's either
a beginning
or some end:
the baby's being born
or its parents are
dying, fading on
like the rose
of the poem
withers, its light going out
while gardens come in
to bloom

Let us stand on streetcorners
in the desolate era
& propose a new kind
of crazyness

Let us salute one another
one by one
two by two
the soft belly
moving toward
the long sideburns
the adams apple
or no apple at all

Let there be
in this crazyness
a moon

a violin
a drum

Let the beautiful brown girl
join hands with
her black sister
her golden sister
her milkskinned sister
their eternal wombs
turning with the moon

Let there be a flute
to squeal above
the beat & the bowing
to open us up
that the greens
the blues
the yellows
the reds
the silvers &
indescribable rusts
might flow out
amazingly
& blend
with the wind

Let the wobbly spin
of the earth
be a delight
wherein
a caress forms
the most perfect circle

Let the always be love
the beginning be love!
love the only
possible
end

THE BLUES DON'T CHANGE

*"Now I'll tell you about the
Blues. All Negroes like Blues.
Why? Because they was born with
the Blues. And now everybody
have the Blues. Sometimes they
don't know what it is."*

— *Leadbelly*

And I was born with you, wasn't I, Blues?
Wombed with you, wounded, reared and forwarded
from address to address, stamped, stomped
and returned to sender by nobody else but you,
Blue Rider, writing me off every chance you

got, you mean old grudgeful-hearted, table-
turning demon, you, you sexy soul-sucking gem.

Blue diamond in the rough, you *are* forever.
You can't be outfoxed don't care how they cut
and smuggle and shine you on, you're like a
shadow, too dumb and stubborn and necessary
to let them turn you into what you ain't
with color or theory or powder or paint.

That's how you can stay in style without sticking
and not getting stuck. You know how to sting
where I can't scratch, and you move from frying
pan to skillet the same way you move people
to go to wiggling their bodies, juggling their
limbs, loosening that goose, upping their voices,
opening their pores, tolling their hips and lips.

They can shake their boodies but they can't shake *you.*

YES, THE SECRET MIND WHISPERS
for Bob Kaufman
Poetry's a tree
forever at your door
neither scratching nor
knocking but everywhere
eager to force its way

into the soft warm room
of your ornery old heart,
   slipping
    its fat pink tongue
      into sensitive linings
    of your weary young ear

A tree bearing blossoms, a flower
surfacing in a canal of blood,
the dream auto with dream motor
that idles eternally but has
no moving parts, no fumes just
fragrances beneficial to breathe

It breathes mystery this tree
     but no more so
    than moons over midnight seas
    or the breast of a woman/child
       to whom menstruation's happening
       for the first time

It's the practice of yoga
    on rainy nights in cities,
      the sudden thought of death
       halfway thru dessert, a
     magic wafer you take
       into your mouth
        &
    swallow for dear life

Nayo Barbara Malcolm Watkins (1940–)

BLACK WOMAN THROWS A TANTRUM

I want me a home
Man do you hear me
I want me a home
you understand.
You done stood and let that cracker
take my home
Now I want me a home, nigger
I wants a land that's mine.

I hardly remember my home
been so long
you stood idle
Now you git off ya ass
and make me a home
Make me a land that's mine
  so I can set a spell
  and breathe fresh air
  and ease my mind
  live—
  and love—
  and be buried
  in a land that's mine

DO YOU KNOW ME?

you cannot love me
if you do not know me
if you do not know why

my hands are calloused
and my feet are bunioned
and i smell not of rose waters
and oil baths

if you do not know why
my straightened hair
contradicts at the roots
and why my feet do not fit
very well in high heeled shoes
no, you cannot love me

you see, i sweat out
a sunday crepe dress
and my ample rear makes
a hemline lose its level

besides that, i take no pleasure
in sticking my pinkie out
while holding a cup of tea
and if you cannot understand
you cannot love me

i try to deal with certain customs
so as not to seem strange
but i really do prefer socks
over my nylons, multi-colored
wraps around my head, and i'd rather
leave the gap between my teeth
unchanged

it is utterly important
that you know these things
before you dive off
into some fantasy
of what i might be only to be
shocked by what i am

i must tell you i have picked
cotton and chopped wood
i have busted suds in iron wash pots
and i have obeyed masters
i did not want to obey

there are scars upon my mind
and bruises on my soul
mostly i try to forget
but when i remember
i am often bitchy

if you think you want to love me
you must know what turns me on
why i sing stirring grits
in my faded bathrobe
why i need to see you smile
and why sometimes i do not need to see you at all

you must understand that this outer image
is but a proper disguise
while i preserve and conserve
the real me inside

i am an African woman
and in the privacy of the private chambers
of my mind
in the intimacy of the intimate corridors
of my soul
when the doors to western civilization
are shut
i open the doors
to myself
and i am an African woman

MISSIONS AND MAGNOLIAS

would that i could i'd write a poem
for a Black man, a teacher-woman,
5 astronauts, one also female, one somewhat Brown,
and the made-in-america towel of babel

it was hushed in the ole miss union
disbelieving eyes held to the horror
on television as we cremated them
in the sky that fell into the sea

outside magnolias sighed and swished
hooped skirts of evergreen
in the face of the cold clear sky
and we quietly remembered christa
who would have taught lessons from space

56 manned missions with a few women,
Blacks and Browns; america has asked the heavens
for answers we could not find on earth
now we pay a sacrifice of seven
while the media directs our mourning

but my thoughts will not be directed; they
soar thru the space of my mind like unmanned
space ships, reaching for reasoning, racing
to outrun the raw pain, seeking to know why
i am so troubled when magnolias sway undaunted

the teacher . . . this was the one with the teacher . . .
we wanted her to come back . . . and teach . . .
and teach . . . maybe she could've taught
about magnolias . . . we don't know enough
bout magnolias . . . magnolias and mississippi . . .
we don't know . . . we babel our hi-tech talk
but we don't know . . . just be babeling . . . building
towers and babeling . . . in mississippi . . . what's
mississippi and magnolias got to do with . . .
nothing maybe, maybe everything . . . peace on earth . . .

and i just read winnie mandela's book . . .
what's mandela got to do with it . . . nothing
maybe . . . maybe something on that shuttle
came from south africa . . . mined by Black
hands . . . don't reduce everything to color . . .
i was already feeling raw rage for winnie,
now this . . . missions and magnolias and mississippi
and mandela . . . lawd! the colonel hides
under magnolias and waves rebel flags
at Black boys and girls trying to be teachers
and engineers and astronauts . . . there you go
again, it ain't a color matter . . . he went up too,
didn't he . . . he was an american astronaut,
you know . . . guess we're equal now . . .

we die like them . . . not hanging from trees
like before . . .

we don't even know why magnolias
stand eternally green and sigh politely
as we dash foolishly to and fro
searching for answers to questions
we've not yet couraged to ask

they say we'll build another one . . . the goulish
and greedy await the contracts . . . the president
tells the children they too will fly into the sky . . .
the media shows the fireball again . . . and
again . . . will there be no peace on earth

who was mcnair's granddaddy anyhow . . . what
plantation was he from . . . did he know about
magnolias . . . will his grandson's ashes fall
from south carolina to south africa . . . really now,
must you always see everything in blk and wht . . .
my tears are quite colorless . . . i will cry . . .
i will cry but not today . . . today i am
mandela's mississippi cousin . . . and i need
peace on earth . . .

someday i will cry for america: her teachers
and astronauts and farmers and workers and
women and minorities . . . perhaps even her
colonels and presidents, so goulish and greedy . . .
i will cry but not today . . . today there are lessons
to learn . . . missions and magnolias and
mississippi and mandela . . . peace on earth.

Sterling D. Plumpp
(1940–)

BLACK ETHICS

Not a new thing
but an excavated gem
long lost in centuries
of self-separations.

Will make man strong,
ready to die for his
woman/ child/ and country/
which is obscured in doubt.

the priceless dynamo
called human love that
makes a man, a man,
and moves him to self-pride.

HALF BLACK, HALF BLACKER

i went down to malcolmland
me come back a man.

me returned with blackness
drippin from my every breath.
i went down to malcolmland
unprepared
but him gave me a grass sack
him told me
to stuff-in all the blackness
i could
him told me
to run as fast as me could

374

back to blackpeople
back to blackpeople
so me wouldn't lose
all my goodies.

i went down to malcolmland
me come back a man.

me left my knees
& lifted my eyes eastward
& me ran   me ran . . .
malcolm say god black love black
man black heaven black heaven here
me made black
but me hadta run back
thru fire
with a sack of blackness
on my shoulders.
me think i all black, sometimes
me think i half black others
cause me may lose some blackness
tryin to bring it to blackpeople

i go down to malcolmland
me come back a man.

me black when
me think about malcolm, medgar, martin,
fred, bobbies, mark, lumumba . . .
me lose some blackness
when me don't do nothin
ain't me black?
ain't me black?
when
i am in malcolmland
me know me be blacker . . .

ZIMBABWE

(for Freedom Fighters)

Take this
black mother's anguish and wave

breezes of fight
on the hands,
common hands, the true owners of man;
wave fits
of historical necessity, violence cleansing.
Listen
as slave mothers sigh
for children killed to stop blood
from wearing another's name;
listen to their vows
to birth avengers, common hands,
the working integers of order.

Take this black worth
this silent song of black mothers
and throw it out on fields
sprinkle your earth with seeds
those precious fortune peddlers
of tomorrow. Reach past Soweto's screams,
grab the mother's pain
twisted by knowing
each hour
their blood will flow;
each hour their children will call
for parents to bury them;
grab that pain
and paper your chants with it.

You are
makers straining sunshine from darkness.
You, breakers of the demon's hold
                of the imperialists' strangle
                of colonial grip,
portray the future in gladness
because you are the day torn from a cloud
a wrecking crew of time
summoned to cure Rhodesia's existence.
Earth shakers
you wound the tiger
stick openings in his side
so his roar becomes a death cry
and all hands, common hands,
can clap for your victory
because it is also theirs.

Take this,
our mothers' anguish:
widows of lynchees silently praying defiance
runaways' mothers sobbing in uncertainty.
Take it!
It is yours
because you move.
          Because the day you make
is the day of tomorrow.
Because from your hands
come
the common hands' destiny

SANDERS BOTTOM

(For Mattie Emmanuel)

Home/the land the landless
inherited/ Plots of the
future/down behind generations.
Heir property/locked in blood.
Land/nobody wants to know.
Winding acres of unsung blues.
Land/the spirituals come up
in. Pasture of suffering/
home of yearnings. Twisting
miles in my soul. Like rusted
wire/tangled round a sampling.

Plodding for food/like a man;
gallon of blackberries and
a bucket of peas or beans
clutching each hand. Balanced
on my head a basket/of okra
or something to sell or
swap. Reckly after sunrise/
setting out: not coming back
til money   or food is gotten.
Remembering/remembering Auntie
done told me a thousand times;
never come back with nothing.
Remembering/her pushing a

straw hat/down almost over
my eyes/and saying, "Now git."

Places to go/round Sanders
Bottom or Clinton or even Bolton.
Thinking maybe/I'll drop dead
many a day. Tired. Sore.
Sun climbing down; no wind
caring to sail by with a breeze.

Walking and walking;
through woods/down gullies/
on burning dust/and cracking
tracks. Raining/sometimes.
Drenched. But still going
and going. Remembering/Auntie
is big. Will strip me naked,
sit on my head/beating til blood
and whelps/all over me.

A piece of paper on somebody
else's floor/given away.
Stepped on. Chunked outside
in arms of cold wind. Laying
in the outhouse/used
for you know what. Trying to cry/
but eyes run dry. Like ponds
or creeks. Feeling the dust jump
inside my head and play about.

A corner/all I ever got.
Do-mes hanging me out
like clothes on a line.
My days/scattered before me
like wild geese without
a leader. And my prayers
calling them together again.

My life/a string tied
to every need in the house.
Backward I go/for my road
is always up a muddy hill.
I am throwed away/nobody
never gives a child away.

378

Remember Momma/saying
she was marrying. And the man
didn't want me and Riley.
Only wanted his chilluns
by her. Remember how
I looked out and saw a
ought/and the ought was me.

Something cut the rope/pulling
my dreams from a pit. And I
felt waterless tears/falling
into years.

Where you stay/is a kinda
bridge; it link what happened
yesterday with wherever
you at. No matter how mean
times may be; it digs a place
so you kin brace yourself/
not be blown every whichaway.

Like moles/I go unnoticed
til something upset a eye
or hand. Then stares bore
through my soul/and blows
turn my face like strawberries.
Don't know/what I would do
wasn't for the Lord/His Hand
always sewed up torn parts
of my heart/always rubbed
color back in my cheeks.

His Hand is a saving Hand/a
unchanging Hand. But some
don't believe it; His is a
leavening Hand, baking tomorrows.

Been believing/ever since
on a mourners bench/and I asked.
And He done answered my prayers.
Some git they 'ligion with
they tongues and heads/got mine
with my heart believing.

Nine years old/and down on
my knees wanting salvation.
Not knowing what saved was/
but I asked Him; no, I believe,
sweat had bathed me and only
silence come out when I open
my mouth. But I said: "Lord,
I accept You but I need a sign."
Then one night/I went outside.
Saw five stars all hugging and
I asked Him to separate them/as
a sign.

   I shut my eyes/when I
opened them/He done stretched distance
'tween them blinking lights/way up
yonder in the sky.

    I was His/and His presence
reached down and touched me/yes it
did

O remembering/Riley let
nobody put knots on him.
Heard the Leamus boys saying
they gon git him/gon git him
in the woods; kill him. He beat
them up/and Auntie hear it too/
and make Riley/pack up his
sack/ Take him to Old Man
Whitley/a white man/give him
away again. Then Riley/gone
and Mister Whitley say last
time/he seed him/he walking along
banks of the pond.

Then/I felt darkness crowding
my eyes/like they say death
pulls down your eyelids and
you can't see in the broad
daylight. Riley/gone and maybe
I'll be gone soon.

                    But He lifted
the night away and though my body wept/
joy led me through the days.

I grew/like a trim sampling
and kept serving them/

motherless

                though I minded
my aunt. Soon the Leamus boys/start
messing with me. Tell Auntie/Mr. Leamus

say no blood 'tween me and
his boys.

Don't care what happen to me.

The ground moved
from under me/Auntie tell me

stop what you doing
pack your little rags
I'm taking you back
to your momma:

                        don't want no Leamuses
                        in my family.

Sometimes/you wonder. I looked
out/all I seen was wilderness.
Not one ray
was in my life; started going
to Mound Hood. That's how I met
Victor/he was ugly and evil.
But he was good
to me/all forty-two years;
he was good
to me and never let
nobody mistreat me.

When I met him/Momma was glad
she could marry me off. Then a

little clearing appeared out
in the wilderness.

Then/I was big, kinda like one
small vine wanting to climb
a pole/in a big field. Each time
I got big/another vine climb
a pole. On and on/til seven vines
climb up; then it seem like
a whole forest. Mothering them/
through colds, mumps, and measles;
take blood from my heart.

                                   I look
out/and the wilderness is gone.

All seven/my chilluns grow
and Victor make me/stay home.
Clean up
wash and iron
work my flower yard
and plant my garden.

                                Farming/a
see-saw and booweavils and droughts
up
more times than good crops.
We make do, somehow; keep going,
somehow; and going some more.

Afterwhile/grandchilluns come
til seven reached. Victor them
in fields/stay out there; hot sun
boiling down. Stay out there/plowing
and cultivating and
harrying and chopping
and thinning
and weeding
and laying by. They/stay out
there working
from sunup
til sundown/all them years.

When Victor left/for Bolton;
left for the gin/I was on needles.
He'd always come back/late. Come
back with something. Mostly/he
took his first picking
to Jackson
or Flora/ginned it

with somebody else's cotton.

Cause he never got nothing/
where he owed the man.

By and by Momma sick/ask
forgiveness/for putting me

out in the world. Tell me/
the Lord done whipped her/
she ready; go home.

Auntie/say same thing;

way she treated me
was wrong. Each pain

taking her breath/mean
she reaping
what she sowed on me.
I don't hold no grudges;
tell them bygones
is bygones. Ask for His mercy;

He will touch them, too.

My chilluns/move on
                like crowder peas took
from bushes. Bro/overseas
where killings at. Long time
'tween letters/then we hear
nothing/after they drop
that bomb. Then/Bro coming

down road/two sacks; wobbling
like a young duck. Then my life/
a well-cropped field; something

hanging on every stalk
and vine
and 'tached to every root.

Not long/Victor down low;
can't hardly sleep/short
breath and coughs keep
him woke. Then his liver/bad
and he can't eat; start going
down. Tell me: soon be gone
over the river. Then I'm
holding him/
              and he gone.
And I hear a tree fall
in my field. But he come
back

stand over me
a long time/don't say
nothing. Then he/gone.

Remembering/Jackson, John,
and Miss Easter, my bible
and praying. Thanking

the Lord/putting all my burdens

in His Hands.

                    Victor stayed
with me/still resting somewhere
in my heart. Forty-two years
with a man; ain't easy for him
leave/he with me though he gone.
But I keep going/cause I know

the Lord will make a way, somehow.

O remembering/his face
cold and stiff. Fire
in him at last breath/

gone.

His coughs and grunts/gone.

Old winter preach goodbye
with a blizzard/sun bleeding red;

too evil/let its shine come
outside. But life/what

you leave/crisscrossing paths/vines
of your days wrap round. Marrow

in roots of your touches; something

green/and live in your deeds. People
go/but life stays.

Years/long and plenty full:
time quilts with sorrows,
troubles, loneliness, hard times—
patches up from little things/make
up a day; add up to a week;
push into a month;
                        and build
into a year. My life/somewhere
in the basket/made into

patterns by time. Ain't had
much but I lived, we lived;

I live, we live. Each other/

all we ever had/now He calls us
one by one

Knowed Scootie down low/
heard her call Him. Tell
Him take life's suffering
away/ease her on home. But

two long years go by/she

still here. Tell me/her
life was dense woods.

And each day

she done cut down a bush
            pulled up a sprout
            sawed down a tree
            and dug up a stump

til all/clear.

                        Then/she start

fencing in her land;

finding a plank here
and one there. Afterwhile/it

all done. She seen her way

clear; He done touched her.

Seeing her/kinda drifting/made me
feel part of myself sinking.

That thing/sucking her life away;
it start

on one breast
skip over to the other one
run down in her bones
and hop into her lungs.

She/gone and my insides ache.
Worries cloud my mind. Walking
to her grave/meant roots of my harvest
on top of the ground. And grief

can't smell the flowers.

Remembering/my long time;
ninety-four and more. Every
sunrise/a gift. Roses for just
living. Every midday/a hymn
for veins and bones. And evening/

soft music as the moon and
stars sing. All the days/I clap
for more. Our lives/our treasure.
What little we got/from working;
ain't been much.

We done worked/Lord knows
we have. All the rows/our
feet trailed plows down;
all the nights we sot out,
pulled up, and dug. All the
time/we sure worked. But the
land got it all; got my husband,
my third child, and my baby.
Walter/git my breakfast and
talk. Gone/the land got him.
Funeral at Mound Hood/buried
near Sixteen Sections. Ground
got him/my steps the heaviest
yet.

MISSISSIPPI GRIOT

(for Ann Abadie)

He sat there
on the porch of eternity
like a melon on a bed.
Emitting
dark seeds of prophecy
through teeth of storms.
Mississippi griot,
Mississippi son, native of
genocides, emitting
black seeds of prophecy.
He
had the river
inside him.
It was his tale and memory.
Wish I was a mocking bird
Out on a limb to swing.
They done stole all I own
and all I can do is sing.

He had the river in
side him.
Patted his feet and cat
fish fell from his muddy rhythms.
Crying
cause they woman done gone.
Crying
cause the blues from depths
upsetting their veins.
Mississippi griot,
Mississippi son.

He
bent strings and my grandfather's
fields were flooded and I
stood out
on a
red
clay hill/looking at
the pain.
I used to feel. The blues
he played built the levee
as the river with
in him ran down
through my eyes and my pen
trembled like Lucille does
when B.B.'s tender fingers
stroke her hair in tongues.
The
delta rolled out
beneath his shadow
and he sang shacks
along perimeters of debts.
The
crowd, stunned
ran to banks and
his muddy red words
moaned down stream.

He
had the river in
side him and sang it.

It
was his burdened story of time.
It
was his lush epic of ancestry.
It
was his personal chronicle of trials.
It
was his collective psalms of testifying.
It
was his blues.
He
sang for those
who done lived out the dues.

Ain't got nothing, yall,
just my empty broken hand.
Said I'm broke, yall,
All I got is a empty hand.
Would be a rich man
if I could blues you to understand.

He
takes Emmet Till's decomposing body
from the river in
side him. Lifts it
with the fork of his cries
to a corner
in my skull. And I
scream terrors of multitudes.

Every bone
from nameless black victims interred in the
river
recite their identities
in pulses breathing.

Mississippi griot
Mississippi son.

Water rises
to his waist. The river with
in him flows.

The crowd
watches history.
He laughs
the bewildering troubles away.
Calls un
known poets to rituals.
The river is my history.
I was born with
in the mud in
side his lyrics. Snakes,
turtles, and frogs
were my play
mates in the river.
He
has it in
side him.
It
is my history and
it
is my autobiography
when he sings.

SPEECH

1

They
could tell
it was war.
By
the sound
it made.
If you beat out
memory on its
quivering palms.
People
would know
how to move heads,
twist hips
or legislate feet
by
the sound.
The

drum talked:
Language, history,
myth, ritual,
and memory.
The drum talked
if you planted
rhythms on its skin
and caressed it
with moods of
improvisation

2

My grand
mother knew not
drums.
Her
pots and
pans talked.
If
she squeezed the dish
rag like wringing
off
a chicken's head and
pondered the depths of
the image
less water
then
the old rooster
was crowing: a storm
was coming.
If
she held the pot
out
like it was a new
born
baby and screened
its rivers of dark flesh
through nets of her vision
then Poppa
was gon die.
Swooping
wings of the angel

was heard
clapping beneath
the grease.
If
she clenched her fist and
shoved it
under water in silence
then
some angel of
mercy was on
its way
to rain
down a little
ease.

If
she rattled pots and
pans like two cats
fussing and fighting
under the house
then
some
body
was messing with her man.
a
low
down
rat
done brought the blues
in
to her happy home.

Haki R. Madhubuti
(1942–)

THE BLACK CHRIST

without a doubt
rome did the whi
te thing when it
killed

               christ

it has been proven
that j. c. was non-whi
te in the darkest
way possible

               black ink on whi
               te paper

contradictions
from the west
ern cowBoys

               with two guns & music
               written on paper with
               black lines

it makes mary in—
too a first class
whore
john the bas
tard on
ly got people
wet
the cat
holic church cried
all the way to the
bank

               most of the priests
               are still in the
               ghettos—pimping

left the pope in
a soup line on st.
paul's day sold his
gold filled teeth
to a smiling jew
riding on a black
jackass

moses was hanged
in effigy by
smiling negroes
tearing up the
first commandment
judas became the
hero of the west
ern world & nick
named it lady bird

she got it from
a cat named parker

she ain't been
right sense

all the negro
preachers are driv
ing volkswagens & back
in night high school

taking black speech
& black history

off one god
can't get hooked
on another elijah

negro & whi
te cops riding
each other in
dark ghettos

negro cops with
naturals & whi
te minded negroes
with naturals wigs

more whi
te people read
ing fanon than
blacks

they know
all in sun try

ing to get black

> man tan ain't
> gone ta get it
> you can't hide
> tomorrow is here

history repeats
itself   ask
st. malcom
all because j. c.
was a nigger

> the only things
> that didn't change
> were his
> words

the world's best
seller
had sold out

> (to bible reading eskimos).

IN A PERIOD OF GROWTH

like,
if he had da called me
black seven years ago,
i wd've—

> broke his right eye out,
> jumped into his chest,
> talked about his momma,
> lied on his sister
> & dared him to say it again

all in one breath—

seven years ago.

BIG MOMMA

finally retired   pensionless
from cleaning somebody else's house
she remained home to clean
the one she didn't own.

in her kitchen where we often talked
the *chicago tribune* served as a tablecloth
for the two cups of tomato soup that went
along with my weekly visit & talkingto.

she was in a seriously-funny mood
& from the get-go she was down, realdown:

>roaches around here are like
>letters on a newspaper
>or
>u gonta be a writer, hunh
>when u gone write me some writen
>or
>the way niggers act around here
>if talk cd kill we'd all be dead.

she's somewhat confused about all this *blackness*
but said that it's good when negroes start putting themselves
first and added: we've always shopped at the colored stores,
>& the way niggers cut each other up round
>here every weekend that whiteman don't
>>haveta
>worry bout no revolution specially when he's
>gonta haveta pay for it too, anyhow all he's
>gotta do is drop a truck load of *dope* out
>>there
>on 43rd st. & all the niggers & yr
>>revolutionaries
>be too busy getten high & then they'll turn
>>round
>and fight each other over who got the
>>mostest.

we finished our soup and i moved to excuse myself,
as we walked to the front door she made a last comment:
>now *luther* i knows you done changed a lots but if
>you can think back, we never did eat too much pork
>round here anyways, it was bad for the belly.
i shared her smile and agreed.

touching the snow lightly i headed for 43rd st.
at the corner i saw a brother crying   while

trying to hold up a lamp post,
thru his watery eyes i cd see big momma's words.

at sixty-eight
she moves freely, is often right
and when there is food
eats   joyously with her own
real teeth.

WE WALK THE WAY OF THE NEW WORLD

1.

we run the dangercourse.
the way of the stocking caps & murray's grease.
(if u is modern u used duke greaseless hair pomade)
jo jo was modern/ an international nigger
                    born: jan. 1, 1863 in new york, mississippi.
his momma was mo militant than he was/is
jo jo bes no instant negro
his development took all of 106 years
& he was the first to be stamped "made in USA"
where he arrived bow-legged a curve ahead of the 20th
        century's new weapon: television.
which invented, "how to win and influence people"
& gave jo jo his how/ever look: however u want me.

we discovered that with the right brand of cigarettes
that one, with his best girl,
cd skip thru grassy fields in living color
& in slow-motion: Caution: niggers, cigarette smoking
                    will kill u & yr/health.
& that the breakfast of champions is: blackeyed peas & rice.
& that God is dead & Jesus is black and last seen on 63rd
        street in a gold & black dashiki, sitting in a pink
        hog speaking swahili with a pig-latin accent.
& that integration and coalition are synonymous,
& that the only thing that really mattered was:
    who could get the highest on the least or how to expand
    & break one's mind.

in the coming world
new prizes are
to be given

we *ran* the dangercourse.
now, it's a silent walk/ a careful eye
jo jo is there
to his mother he is unknown
(she accepted with a newlook: what wd u do if someone
      loved u?)
jo jo is back
& he will catch all the new jo jo's as they wander in & out
and with a fan-like whisper say: you ain't no
                                    tourist
                                    and Harlem ain't for
                                    sight-seeing, brother.

2.

Start with the itch and there will be no scratch. Study
      yourself.
Watch yr/every movement as u skip thru-out the southside of
      chicago.
be hip to yr/actions.

our dreams are realities
traveling the nature-way.
we meet them
at the apex of their utmost
meanings/means;
we walk in cleanliness
down state st/or Fifth Ave.
& wicked apartment buildings shake
as their windows announce our presence
as we jump into the interior
& cut the day's evil away.

We walk in cleanliness
the newness of it all
becomes us
our women listen to us
and learn.
We teach our children thru
our actions.

We'll become owners of the   New World
the New World.

will run it as unowners
for
we will live in it too
& will want to be remembered
as   realpeople.

A POEM TO COMPLEMENT OTHER POEMS

change.
life if u were a match i wd light u into something beauti-
    ful. change.
change.
for the better into a realreal together thing. change, from
    a make believe
nothing on corn meal and water. change.
change. from the last drop to the first, maxwellhouse
    did. change.
change was a programmer for IBM, thought him was a
    brown computer. change.
colored is something written on southern out-
    houses. change.
greyhound did, i mean they got rest rooms on buses.
    change.
change.
change nigger.
saw a nigger hippy, him wanted to be different. changed.
saw a nigger liberal, him wanted to be different.
    changed.
saw a nigger conservative, him wanted to be different.
    changed.
niggers don't u know that niggers are different. change.
a doublechange. nigger wanted a double zero in front of
    his name; a license to kill,
niggers are licensed to be killed. change. a negro: some-
    thing pigs eat.
change. i say change into a realblack righteous aim. like
    i don't play
saxophone but that doesn't mean i don't dig 'trane.'
    change.
change.
hear u coming but yr/steps are too loud. change. even a
    lamp post changes nigger.
change, stop being an instant yes machine. change.

niggers don't change they just grow. that's a change;
    bigger & better niggers.
change, into a necessary blackself.
change, like a gas meter gets higher.
change, like a blues song talking about a righteous to-
    morrow.
change, like a tax bill getting higher.
change, like a good sister getting better.
change, like knowing wood will burn. change.
know the realenemy.
change,
change nigger: standing on the corner, thought him was
                cool. him still
                    standing there. it's winter time, him cool.
change,
know the realenemy.
change: him wanted to be a TV star. him is. ten o'clock
                news.
            wanted, wanted. nigger stole some lemon & lime
                popsicles,
            thought them were diamonds.
change nigger change.
know the realenemy.
change: is u is or is u aint. change. now now change. for
            the better change.
        read a change. live a change. read a blackpoem.
            change. be the realpeople.
        change. blackpoems
will change:
know the realenemy. change. know the realenemy. change
    yr/enemy change know the real
change know the realenemy change, change, know the
    realenemy, the realenemy, the real
realenemy change your the enemies/change your change
    your change your enemy change
your enemy. know the realenemy, the world's enemy.
    know them know them know them the
realenemy change your enemy change your change
    change change your enemy change change
change change your change change change.
your
mind nigger.

KILLING MEMORY

For Nelson and Winnie Mandela

the soul and fire of windsongs must not be neutral
cannot be void of birth and dying
wasted life
locked
in the path of vicious horrors
masquerading
as progress and spheres of influence

what of mothers
without milk of willing love,
of fathers
whose eyes and vision
have been separated from feelings of earth and growth,
of children
whose thoughts dwell
on rest and food and
human kindness?

Tomorrow's future rains in
atrocious mediocrity and suffering deaths.

in america's america the excitement is over
a rock singer's glove and burning hair
as serious combat rages over
prayer in schools,
the best diet plan,
and women
learning how to lift weights
to the rhythms of
"what's love got to do with it?"

ask the children,
always the children caught in the
absent spaces of adult juvenility
all
brake dancing and singing to
"everything is everything" while
noise occupies the mind as
garbage feeds the brain.

in el salvador mothers search for their sons
and teach their daughters the way of the knife.

in south afrika mothers bury hearts without bodies
while pursuing the secrets of forgotten foreparents.

in afghanistan mothers claim bones and teeth from
mass graves and curse the silent world.

in lebanon the sons and daughters receive horror hourly
sacrificing childhood for the promise of land.

in ethiopia mothers separate wheat from the desert's dust
while the bones of their children cut through dried skin.

tomorrow's future
may not belong to the people,
may not belong to dance or music
where
getting physical is not an exercise but
simply translates into people working,
people fighting,
people enduring insults and smiles,
enduring crippling histories and black pocket politics
wrapped in diseased blankets
bearing AIDS markings in white,
destined for victims that do not question
gifts from strangers
do not question
love of enemy.

who owns the earth?
most certainly not the people,
not the hands that work the waterways,
nor the backs bending in the sun,
or the boned fingers soldering transistors,
not the legs walking the massive fields,
or the knees glued to pews of storefront or granite churches
or the eyes blinded by computer terminals,
not the bloated bellies on toothpick legs
all victims of decisions
made at the washington monument and lenin's tomb
by aged actors viewing
red dawn and the *return of rambo part IX.*

tomorrow
may not belong to the
women and men laboring,
hustling,
determined to avoid contributing
to the wealth
of gravediggers from foreign soil
& soul.
determined to stop the erosion
of indigenous music
of building values
of traditions.

memory is only precious if
you have it.

memory is only functional
if it works for you.

people
of colors and voices
are locked in multi-basement state buildings
stealing memories
more efficient
than vultures tearing flesh
from
decaying bodies.

the order is that the people are to
believe and believe
questioning or contemplating
the direction of the weather is
unpatriotic.

it is not that we distrust poets and politicians.

we fear the disintegration of thought,
we fear the cheapening of language,
we fear the history of victims and the loss of vision,
we fear writers whose answer to
maggots drinking from the open
wounds of babies

is
to cry genocide while demanding
ten cents per word and
university chairs.
we fear politicians
that sell coffins at a discount
and consider ideas blasphemy
as young people world over bleed from the teeth while
aligning themselves with whoever
brings the food.
whoever brings love.

who speaks the language of
bright memory?

who speaks the language of
necessary memory?

the face of poetry must be fire erupting volcanoes,
hot silk forging new histories,
poetry delivering light greater than barricades of silence,
poetry dancing, preparing seers, warriors, healers
and parents beyond the age of babies,
poetry delivering melodies that cure dumbness & stupidity
yes, poets uttering to the intellect and spirit,
screaming to the genes and environments,
revitalizing the primacy of the word and world.
poets must speak the language of the rain,
    decipher the message of the sun,
    play the rhythms of the earth,
    demand the cleaning of the atmosphere,
    carry the will and way of the word,
    feel the heart and questions of the people
    and be conditioned and ready
    to move.

to come
at midnight or noon

to run
against the monied hurricane in this
the hour of forgotten selves,
forgiven promises

404

and
frightening whispers
of rulers in heat.

FIRST WORLD

For Cheikh Anta Diop

We were raised on the lower eastside of detroit,
close to harlem, new york, around the block from watts,
next to the mississippi delta in north america.
unaware of source or history, unaware of reasons,
whys, or beginnings. accepting tarzan and she woman,
accepting kong as king, accepting stanley—livingstone and
europecentric afrika, accepting british novels, french language
and portuguese folktales that devastated afrika's music &
    magic,
values and vision, people.

you helped restore memories,
gave us place and time,
positioned us within content and warnings,
centered us for the fire from the
first world:
original at dawn, founder of knowledge, inception. definer.
center of life, initial thinker, earliest, earliest order.
primary and wise, foremost, predominantly black, explainer,
mature pioneer, seer, roundrooted, earthlike, beginning tree,
cultivator, sourcegiver, genesis, entrance, tomorrow's light.
vision, unarguably afrikan.

David Henderson
(1942–)

DO NOTHING TILL YOU HEAR FROM ME

For Langston Hughes

i arrive   / Langston
the new york times told me when to come
but i attended your funeral
late
by habit of colored folk
and didnt miss a thing

you lie on saint nicholas avenue
between the black ghetto & sugar hill
where slick black limousines await yr body
for the final haul
from neutral santa claus avenue
harlem usa

you are dressed sharp & dark as death
yr cowlick is smooth
like the negro gentleman
in the ebony whiskey ads /
gone is yr puff of face
yr paunch of chest
tho   yr lips are fuller now
especially
on the side
where hazard had you
                              a cigarette /

two sisters
            felines of egypt
vigil yr dead body
one is dressed in a bean picker's brown

406

the other is an erstwhile gown
of the harlem renaissance /
they chatter
like all the sapphires
of Kingfish's harem /
                old sisters
                      old relations

in writing the fine details
of yr last production
you would have the black sapphires / there
guardians of yr coffin
                yr argosy
                     in life & death
the last time blues /
              with no hesitations . . .

                    day of the vernal winds / 1967

BURGUNDY STREET

four stories high
i viz both waterways of new o
the mississippi crescents devil horns
as lake ponchartrain shimmies to the ancient fires along
   her shores
both bring the breezes
from the gulf of mexico or usa proper
to this point
where all
            empties out

a bourbon street jiggle
by sundown or sunrise
will uncover legions of white women
shouting   arms high
bellyrollin   and   ahumpin   to public climax
amid the consumption of light

walk the track
step back
emperors line motel balconies

toasting the din
toasting the death

round the corner
the old black jassmen are preserved in a hall
waiting for the saints
to come amarching in
& riot

i live in *vieux carré*
the old quarter of the french
where the blacks line the narrow arcades
drinking regal beer /
    they await the late
             marie   laveau   the vodun queen
                     to come on in
but the train from congo square
                is lost.

EGYPTIAN BOOK OF THE DEAD

pharisees come bloom
water eddys the twilight air
blue for music
red for fire
look out along the rooftops
ancient cities pop up
old testaments
tribes muster at grey street corners
sparks of cigarettes gleam the glass arcades
wine bottles libate the sidewalk
no more
the wine from palms
no more
the beer from bananas
but
easy now
easy
this night will turn you on /

where
death is a beautiful thing

408

done in the right way
and to die
tonight
in the street
on the radio
in the fire
will fare us well

we who are nothing
to the incarnate computers
save factors on a graph
we who are nothing
rescued by love
we cannot fathom
walk jaded neon jewelry
twinkling
twinkling
so delicate to the touch
to fall down
in a blaze of trumpets
in a blossom of fire
we
are from a place far off

de bar room was full of black men
coo cooing in each others ears
some sapphire
was screaming some shit
all de way from detroit
torpedo heads
lips as lank
as the flap of an arm
in gesture
the flow of upturned glasses
flashing white gin
into de basket

trance oriental
horace silver
song for my father
in a pyramid set
master
of de temple

in a pyramid set
cairo stockholm hong kong
philadelphia paris morocco
harlem jass
charka drums
sticks beat concrete
brass screams crack the walls /

the black boy
was ragged in white
his sky
all upside his head
bopping
into the garden of music
looking for isis /

tenor roars
obbligato
laughin like a drunken woman
walk up the stairs
scream
and then fall back   down
again

chant chant sheet glass windows
glaciers of upper kingdom
stark screams shatter glass
runs the tracks under trees of lightning
hung out over red trailers
diminishing
into civilization
ciditty

sax man
of the baronette
he relax
in the blue contours
of your soul

amber glows
golden wheels of fire
yellow vapor rises in the room
and slips thru the door

the sequined man shimmers across the floor
holding an ax between his teeth
he's fucking with the walls of the void
mama said
the crowd responded:
YOU AINT NOTHING BUT THE OLD TESTAMENT!

city of the people
leaves of the grass
e-lectronic shimmy sounds
move red decked legs quick and lean
step the step
slake the wine
blow de boo
canary yellow shades
valley of the yams
shake it up
ball de jack
do the thing
its your thing
cakewalking
into plumes of power

poem
tone place poem
about that blues bip bop
upside my head
happening
when i was least ready
and most open to

in the mist of bessie smith
i saw an old time movie
a man in a yam colored suit
black and happy
white buck shoes
white buck teeth
walking down that yellow dog road
a model t yellow cab blinking on and off
rolling sand vapor down the wooden road

and mamie
talkin   about that pot of cabbage

411

a boiling   overflowing
when the stick of bacon
came inside
almost overflowed the top
that salty dog
come on in

a marching band
over the delta land
thru time
thru space
thru thin dollar bills
thru death

reach thru space
thru a giant vaseline jar
come and get that memory

Quincy Troupe
(1943–)

THE SYNTAX OF THE MIND GRIPS

the syntax of the mind grips
the geography of letters
the symbol burns, leaves, black
ocean bleeds pearls/washing the shore
darkness crawls in alone like a panther
all luminous eyes watching us make
love, under trees the beautiful
woman in the grass curls
her pulling legs
around my shoulders
the old maid weeps in the window
covers her face with blue veined white hands,
her fingernails painted red
gouges out her love-shattered eyes
while the mirror breaks in the bathroom
falls like razors to the floor
where a junkie is sprawled
with a death needle in his arm
a child cuts his feet in the streets
screams for the old maid
who makes the flags
who is weeping in the window
because the stars have fallen from the flags
she does not hear anything
but her own weeping
hanging, the flag has become a garrote
choking the breath/love of a people
whose hero is the armless/legless brainless
vegetable who sits upon his bandaged stump
in a wheel/chair, in a veteran's
hospital in washington;
he cannot speak-tell the blood

413

he has swallowed;
he cannot see for the death
his eyes have seen;
he cannot hear for the screams
his ears have heard; but he feels
the sorrow of the old maid
who is weeping because the stars
have fallen from the flag
and because of the love scene
in wet grass beneath her window

IT IS NOT

it is not who or what
you see
but how you see
it. the night.

the woman. the rhythm
of night lights going on.
off. in her face.
the smile of neon.
jewels on fingers.

the sound of ash
colliding with cotton.
the sound tears make falling
through blues. the voices.
guitar strings strummed
by silence. echoes.

echoes. gold-capped
dues of a mississippi black
man's grin. is. not who or what.
you see. but how.
you see it. thin.
or otherwise. deep.

this life is.
what you make it. not
what you hope it to be. but
what it is. right or wrong.

what it is what you make it
to be it is right
or wrong. thin.
or otherwise. deep.
a blues. or its absence.
it is. a lyrical
rhythm. dissonant.
painting the night. the sound
of ashes. colliding with cotton.
is. how you hear it. feel it.
is. not what or who.
you either hear. or. you do
not hear. but how you hear
is the question here.

this poem. that gold-
capped blues. of that. black
man's grin. mississippi. is.
the sound tears make falling
through guitar strings.
colliding with cotton.

echoing bones
that lay screaming under-
water. under earth. is
the feeling you hear. chains.
is not what you see
but how you see it. death.
this life. is how you
make it. see it.

feeling. see it. hear
this life wedded to death.
see it. feeling. see it.

feeling. see it.
see. it.
hear. it.

MY POEMS HAVE HOLES SEWN INTO THEM

my poems have holes sewn into them
& they run searching for light
at the end of tunnels they become trains
or at the bottom of pits they become blackness
or in the broad winging daylight
they are the words that fly

& the holes are these words
letters or syllables with feathered wings
that leave their marks on white pages
then fly off like footprints tracked in snow
& only God knows where they go

this poem has holes stitched into it
as our speech which created poetry in the first place
lacerated wounded words that strike out original
meaning bleeding into language
hemorrhaging out of thick or thin mouths
has empty spaces & silences sewn into it.

so my poems have holes sewn into them
& their voices are like different keyholes
through which dumb men search for speech blind
men search for sight
words like drills penetrating sleep
keys turning in the keyholes of language
like knives of sunrays stabbing blind eyes

my poems have holes sewn into them
& they are the spaces between words
are the words themselves
falling off into one another/ colliding
like people gone mad they space out
fall into bottomless pits
which are the words
like silent space between chords of a piano
or black eyes of a figure in any painting
they fall back into themselves
into time/ sleep
bottom out on the far side of consciousness
where words of all the worlds poets go
& whisper in absolute silence

this poem has deep holes stitched into it
& their meanings have the deadly suck of quicksand
the irreversible pull of earth to any skydiver
the tortured pus-holes in arms of junkies

my poems have holes sewn into them
& they run searching for light at the end
of tunnels or at the bottom of yawning pits
or in the broad daylight where
the words flapping like wings of birds
fly whispering in absolute silence

Nikki Giovanni
(1943–   )

FOR SAUNDRA

i wanted to write
a poem
that rhymes
but revolution doesn't lend
itself to be-bopping

then my neighbor
who thinks i hate
asked—do you ever write
tree poems—i like trees
so i thought
i'll write a beautiful green tree poem
peeked from my window
to check the image
noticed the school yard was covered
with asphalt
no green—no trees grow
in manhattan

then, well, i thought the sky
i'll do a big blue sky poem
but all the clouds have winged
low since no-Dick was elected

so i thought again
and it occurred to me

maybe i shouldn't write
at all
but clean my gun
and check my kerosene supply

perhaps these are not poetic
times
at all

NIKKI-ROSA

childhood remembrances are always a drag
if you're Black
you always remember things like living in Woodlawn
with no inside toilet
and if you become famous or something
they never talk about how happy you were to have
your mother
all to yourself and
how good the water felt when you got your bath
from one of those
big tubs that folk in chicago barbecue in
and somehow when you talk about home
it never gets across how much you
understood their feelings
as the whole family attended meetings about Hollydale
and even though you remember
your biographers never understand
your father's pain as he sells his stock
and another dream goes
And though you're poor it isn't poverty that
concerns you
and though they fought a lot
it isn't your father's drinking that makes any difference
but only that everybody is together and you
and your sister have happy birthdays and very good
Christmasses
and I really hope no white person ever has cause
to write about me
because they never understand
Black love is Black wealth and they'll
probably talk about my hard childhood
and never understand that
all the while I was quite happy

419

MY POEM

i am 25 years old
black female poet
wrote a poem asking
nigger can you kill
if they kill me
it won't stop
the revolution

i have been robbed
it looked like they knew
that i was to be hit
they took my tv
my two rings
my piece of african print
and my two guns
if they take my life
it won't stop
the revolution

my phone is tapped
my mail is opened
they've caused me to turn
on all my old friends
and all my new lovers

if i hate all black
people
and all negroes
it won't stop
the revolution

i'm afraid to tell
my roommate where i'm going
and scared to tell
people if i'm coming
if i sit here
for the rest
of my life
it won't stop
the revolution

if i never write
another poem
or short story
if i flunk out
of grad school
if my car is reclaimed
and my record player
won't play
and if i never see
a peaceful day
or do a meaningful
black thing
it won't stop
the revolution

the revolution
is in the streets
and if i stay on
the 5th floor
it will go on
if i never do
anything
it will go on

Alice Walker
(1944–)

WOMEN

They were women then
My mama's generation
Husky of voice—Stout of
Step
With fists as well as
Hands
How they battered down
Doors
And ironed
Starched white
Shirts
How they led
Armies
Headragged Generals
Across mined
Fields
Booby-trapped
Ditches
To discover books
Desks
A place for us
How they knew what we
Must know
Without knowing a page
Of it
Themselves.

FOR MY SISTER MOLLY
WHO IN THE FIFTIES

Once made a fairy rooster from
Mashed potatoes
Whose eyes I forget
But green onions were his tail
And his two legs were carrot sticks
A tomato slice his crown.
Who came home on vacation
When the sun was hot
and cooked
and cleaned
And minded least of all
Th children's questions
A million or more
Pouring in on her
Who had been to school
And knew (and told us too) that certain
Words were no longer good
And taught me not to say us for we
No matter what "Sonny said" up the
road.

FOR MY SISTER MOLLY WHO IN THE FIFTIES
Knew Hamlet well and read into the night
And coached me in my songs of Africa
A continent I never knew
But learned to love
Because "they" she said could carry
A tune
And spoke in accents never heard
In Eatonton.
Who read from *Prose and Poetry*
And loved to read "Sam McGee from Tennessee"
On nights the fire was burning low
And Christmas wrapped in angel hair
And I for one prayed for snow.

WHO IN THE FIFTIES
Knew all the written things that made
Us laugh and stories by
The hour   Waking up the story buds

Like fruit. Who walked among the flowers
And brought them inside the house
And smelled as good as they
And looked as bright.
Who made dresses, braided
Hair. Moved chairs about
Hung things from walls
Ordered baths
Frowned on wasp bites
And seemed to know the endings
Of all the tales
I had forgot.

WHO OFF INTO THE UNIVERSITY
Went exploring   To London and
To Rotterdam
Prague and to Liberia
Bringing back the news to us
Who knew none of it
But followed
crops and weather
funerals and
Methodist Homecoming;
easter speeches,
groaning church.

WHO FOUND ANOTHER WORLD
Another life   With gentlefolk
Far less trusting
And moved and moved and changed
Her name
And sounded precise
When she spoke   And frowned away
Our sloppishness.

WHO SAW US SILENT
Cursed with fear   A love burning
Inexpressible
And sent me money not for me
But for "College."
Who saw me grow through letters
The words misspelled   But not
The longing   Stretching

Growth
The tied and twisting
Tongue
Feet no longer bare
Skin no longer burnt against
The cotton.

WHO BECAME SOMEONE OVERHEAD
A light   A thousand watts
Bright and also blinding
And saw my brothers cloddish
And me destined to be
Wayward
My mother remote   My father
A wearisome farmer
With heartbreaking
Nails.

FOR MY SISTER MOLLY WHO IN THE FIFTIES
Found much
Unbearable
Who walked where few had
Understood   And sensed our
Groping after light
And saw some extinguished
And no doubt mourned.

FOR MY SISTER MOLLY WHO IN THE FIFTIES
Left us.

BE NOBODY'S DARLING

for Julius Lester

Be nobody's darling;
Be an outcast.
Take the contradictions
Of your life
And wrap around
You like a shawl,
To parry stones
To keep you warm.

425

Watch the people succumb
To madness
With ample cheer;
Let them look askance at you
And you askance reply.

Be an outcast;
Be pleased to walk alone
(Uncool)
Or line the crowded
River beds
With other impetuous
Fools.

Make a merry gathering
On the bank
Where thousands perished
For brave hurt words
They said.

Be nobody's darling;
Be an outcast.
Qualified to live
Among your dead.

Lorenzo Thomas
(1944–)

RHUMBA NEGRO

This I have told you before

Downtown east your own sky
Green as the oceans you came from
The rhumba negroes are
Hypnotizing the pigeons

Messenger messenger
  Wash their eyes
Flash like snow in the eyes
  Of the deep witness
New year we have made
  Our keepsake fearing
Its impression it make
  On our souls,

We are bad men on the street
                           inside

Your mother and invisible sisters
Static from your radio thought
It was very late in the evening

Kerchief in my hand heart on my sleeve

Europe snows where my arms
Lift without muscles

I wear a blunt white village
Talents on my wrist
When it hears the orisa
It cannot keep the time

1965

ONION BUCKET

All silence says music will follow
No one acts under any compulsion
Your story so striking and remain unspoken
Floods in the mind. Each one trying now
To instigate the flutter of light in your
Ear. The voice needling the flashy token
Your presence in some room disguised
As the summer of the leaves. Hilltops
Held by the soft words of the running
Wind. What lie do you need more than this
The normal passion. And each thing says
Destroy one another or die. Like a natural
Introducing here on this plant to Europe
The natural. A piece of furniture, smell
Taste some connection to your earth and
"Realize" nothing more than you need
Another view nothing more than you need yourself
Or that is beautiful. Or your luck that speaks.
Lifting its shoulders out the language
Of the streets. Above. The sky worried
Into its own song. Solid rhythm. She stays
Too close for a letter, scared of a telegram
The finger drum express. Impatient blues.
Anxious blues. Her chemical song loud and
Bright in his dimension. This is the world.
The vegetables are walking

HISTORIOGRAPHY

Bird is a god of good graciousness.
                                    —Ted Joans

1

The junkies loved Charles Parker and the sports
And the high living down looking ones
Those who loved music and terror and lames
Who in Bird's end would someday do better

As the Bird spiralled down in disaster
Before the TV set some would come to prefer

428

Out of the sadness of Mr Parker's absence
Never again hearing the strings of Longines

Symphonette

Without hearing the keening cry of the Bird
Nailed to the wax they adored. In the memories
And warmth of their bodies where our Bird
Stays chilly and gone. Every cat caught with

A while girl wailed Bird Lives! And the dopies
Who loved Charlie Parker made his memory live
Those who loved music made his memory live
And made the young ones never forget Bird

Was a junkie

2

We lost others to pain stardom and
Some starved at vicious banquets
Where they played until the victuals
Was gone. Pretty music. For all that

Pain. Who made the young ones remember the pain
And almost forget the dances? Who did that?
Steal the prints and the master and burn down
The hope of his rage when he raged? It was

Not only pain

There was beauty and longing. And Love run
Down like the cooling waters from heaven
And sweat off the shining black brow. Bird
Was thinking and singing. His only thought

Was a song. He saw the truth. And shout the Truth
Where Indiana was more than the dim streets of Gary
A hothouse of allegedly fruitful plain America
Some will never forgive the brother for that. Bird

Was a junkie

3

According to my records, there was something
More. There was space. Seeking. And mind
Bringing African control on the corny times
Of the tunes he would play. There was Space

And the Sun and the Stars he saw in his head
In the sky on the street and the ceilings
Of nightclubs and Lounges as we sought to
Actually lounge trapped in the dull asylum

Of our own enslavements. But Bird *was* a junkie!

MY OFFICE

I've spent the last 10 years
In other people's offices
Learning the alphabet of nods and eyebrows
And pursed lips, straining for the purse
Legs crossed in easy confidence
Confident nervous gestures of assurance
Approved blue suits
And sudden dreamed-up lies to be delivered

A net of thirty days and sixty days and ninety
Insanely stretched past promise into years
Next week, for certain
Floated haphazardly on possibles
As slight as handshakes,
Firm as agreements of subjective verbs

And got nowhere.

This happy corner, sucking up hard-boiled eggs
And polish hots
The seidel sliding down the polished bar
Clatter of friendly pool balls in the margin
Not exactly somewhere, but a certain place.

A regular's dark hair and polished eyes
Glow in the glasses lined before her face

Smoking and berating the muzak
"Jack, when you gonna get some country music?"

"Country Charlie Pride?"

Outside, it's as bright as the important phone call
I always pretend to await
Setting up the lunch meeting at Stouffer's
Linen napkins and hope's frozen green peas

Set up another round of handshake laughter for the
    pictures

"Hey sweet thing, when we gonna have that date?"
The barmaid pouts a 1940s frown—
It's Arnie (reaching now to slap me on the back)
A gleaming brazen polyester clown,
Tuesday seems longer than the day before
Since I began to organize my life around My Office
I stay a little later every day.
A little rain hangs fire in the clouds

Next trip, I think I'll bring the wife

THEY NEVER LOSE
after Cranach

A woman's sense is not her education
But what escapes from Logic,
Literature, and fads of aim
For security's sake, "set your cap for a doctor"
A dentist. At least, a real estate man.

So girls go daft
With or without education
Thinking up men as special Bargain prizes
That only need a little polishing,

A little work. So, they get married
Then, to sanctify the fact, they must buy *something*.
Whatever. A major purchase.
In the final showroom, tired of dallying,

"Jew him down" floods to her mind
In half-whispers. Theatrical for days.

You go for that?

Well, Rubens ate it up

Thought he was smart, too
Meddling mythology. I tried to tell him
Cranach tried to complain
About the silly hat, but who
Can tell a real or would-be goddess?

Chattlesome morons call it "human nature"
Popping their eyes at any lisp of news.
But, then again, what else is human nature?

Yeah?
How about him, who sees his dreams
Feel too large for the golden ring
A woman with or without education
Sees him performing in?
His purse knows better even if his heart
Is pumping bleeds of Red Grooms
Lithographs from the spring
Trip to New York City. For the foyer.

II

> *Take this badge off of me*
> *I can't use it anymore.*
> *It's getting dark,*
> *Too dark to see;*
> *I feel like I'm knocking on Heaven's door*
> > *—Bob Dylan*

He sees himself an exile in his flesh
Flitting from place to place to relocate
And earn promotions. Finally to some nondescript Chicago,
An overdone but prim Lake Forest home,
Working till nine to pay the premium on his estate.

Be careful, daughter . . .

432

When the everyday commuter's
Train of thought
Stops short approaching minute stations
Along the pilgrimage to or from toil
And modest dreams of freedom
Ranking somewhere below wealth
But near to comfort
Where no known drug's peace
Is more inebriating
Than the tiresome but firmly-held belief
That pain will vanish in the afternoon,
When thought and music masters noise
As effortless as you please,
Umm hmmm. That's when it crashes!

*

*Ok, I'd classify that one as a dream
—or a disaster.*

*Lucky we live down South
Everything is flat around here
Even, they tell me, our pronunciation.
That's why we use these big words
Our betters and the redskins left behind*

I mean, like "nigra," "pickaninny," "Tennessee"

*

Just then, it happens.
The boss (who never liked this dude)
Begins to wonder
"Say Jim, you think
You might could handle
Nashville?"

Unseemly pride of Equal Opportunity
The presidency of the local NAACP
Fades into visions of the local Klan
Clumsily setting up a sputtering rood
On your front lawn in Nashville, Tennessee:
*That's what you get for your mouth
Saying you love her more than life itself*

III

The there it is,
I swear to God

That's when it happens:
Dimly, he wavers
Like tv sets of those too cheap to subscribe to the cable
Who can't afford it because their lives are sad
Because there is some tragedy way back
That kept them pure and poor in quarantines of sense

Quite educational.

That's when he wakes metabolized in sleep
Without her cool, soft hand to soothe his sweat
After the dream that shows in twenty years
His broken body managing the shop in South Dakota

Or, worse than that, consulting in New York
Dodging muggers, while she sits watching *Kojak* in Tulsa
As he frets sitting, lonely in an Oyster Bar
Of some dull town's insipid Marriott
Watching ugly blond waitresses bore him
Finally to the disgraceful confession:

"I've made a complete omelette of my life!"

Or else
She sits complacent in her negligee
Watching soap operas
Chewing and snapping gum to old time movies
Dinah Shore
The $100,000 waste of time
While he swinks on at luncheons, demonstrations,
Conferences, sales meetings, briefings, and arguments,
She sits

Becoming sunlight flatters her awhile
While simple sense tells him that women age
Longer than men, since men have heart attacks
From overwork. And, dammit, he can see it all now!
A sense of time or timing counsels him,

434

Beware. Women have tricks up their sleeves
Even naked

So, sensible women always understand,
A young man's pride goes on the punctual shelf
Of duty after the first date
Until the crucial moment when he dreams
Again of flirting with himself in his disguises:
Always clean and cool
Single, and, for that reason,
Free to act a fool.

IV

Helen dramatized the smallest incidents . . .
—Anais Nin

Only a foolish child falls to despair.

At this point, woman reaps
The fruit of sisterhood.
People will talk. It does her good to listen
Even if they heap badmouth on her man,
It's good advice, experience, instructions.
You want an apple or a wedding ring?

Paris my foot. The thought! That stuck-up
Sucker

One man, three women
Who he think he is?

One who thinks she's got him
    Even if he strays
One who yearns to keep him
    If he stays
One who feels she's lost him
Still dreams of other days
My dear, it's worth your time to learn
At least those three graces,
And not be caught confused
Between a man's natural two-facedness
Lord, yes! A woman's strength

That leaves
Him, who fears another's feeling,
Defeated finally in merely choosing
Defeated formally in memory's anticipations
Like the last time you thought you saw
Just what you thought you saw
A kind of fleeting shame and frozen sorrow;
Control of nothing left but needless options

But now, the deal was closing in her eyes

Carolyn Rodgers
(1945—   )

HOW I GOT OVAH

i can tell you
about them
i have shaken rivers
out of my eyes
i have waded eyelash deep
have crossed rivers
have shaken the water weed out
of my lungs
have swam for strength
pulled by strength
through waterfalls with electric beats
i have bore the shocks
of water deep deep
waterlogs arc my bones
i have shaken the water free of my hair
have kneeled on the banks
and kissed my ancestors of the dirt
whose rich dark root fingers rose up reached out
grabbed and pulled me rocked me cupped me
gentle strong and firm
carried me
made me swim for strength
cross rivers
though i shivered
was wet was cold
and wanted to sink down
and float as water, yea—
i can tell you.
i have shaken rivers
out of my eyes.

IT IS DEEP
(don't never forget the bridge
that you crossed over on)

Having tried to use the
witch cord
that erases the stretch of
thirty-three blocks
and tuning in the voice which
   woodenly stated that the
   talk box was "disconnected"

My mother, religiously girdled in
her god, slipped on some love, and
laid on my bell like a truck,
blew through my door warm wind from the south
concern making her gruff and tight-lipped
      and scared
that her "baby" was starving.
she, having learned, that disconnection results from
               non-payment of bill (s).

She did not
recognize the poster of the
grand le-roi (al) cat on the wall
had never even seen the books of
Black poems that I have written
thinks that I am under the influence of
         communists
when I talk about Black as anything
other than something ugly to kill it befo it grows
   in any impression she would not be
considered "relevant" or "Black"
                  but
there she was, standing in my room
not loudly condemning that day and
not remembering that I grew hearing her
curse the factory where she "cut uh slave"
and the cheap j-boss wouldn't allow a union,
not remembering that I heard the tears when
they told her a high school diploma was not enough,
and here now, not able to understand, what she had
been forced to deny, still—

she pushed into my kitchen so
she could open my refrigerator to see
what I had to eat, and pressed fifty
bills in my hand saying "pay the talk bill and buy
some food; you got folks who care about you. . . ."

My mother, religious-negro, proud of
having waded through a storm, is very obviously,
a sturdy Black bridge that I
crossed over, on.

AND WHEN THE REVOLUTION CAME

(for Rayfield and Lillie and the whole rest)

and when the revolution came
the militants said
niggers wake up
you got to comb yo hair
the natural way
          and the church folks say oh yeah? sho 'nuff . . .
and they just kept on going to church
gittin on they knees and praying
and tithing and building and buying

and when the revolution came
the militants said
niggers you got to change
the way you dress
and the church folks say oh yeah?
          and they just kept on going to church
with they knit suits and flowery bonnets
and gittin on they knees and praying
and tithing and building and buying

and when the revolution came
the militants said
you got to give up
white folks and the
          church folk say oh yeah? well?
never missed what we never had
and they jest kept on going to church

with they nice dresses and suits and
praying and building and buying
and when the revolution came
the militants say you got to give up
pork and eat only brown rice and
health food and the
church folks said uh hummmm
and they just kept on eating they chitterlings and
going to church and praying and tithing and
building and buying

and when the revolution came
the militants said
all you church going niggers
got to give up easter and christmas
and the bible
cause that's the white man's religion
and the church folks said well well well well well

and then the militants said we got to
build black institutions where our children
call each other sister and brother
and can grow beautiful, black and strong and grow in
    black grace
and the church folks said yes, lord Jesus we been calling
    each other
sister and brother a long time

and the militants looked around
after a while and said hey, look at all
these fine buildings we got scattered throughout
the black communities some of em built wid schools and
    nurseries
who do they belong to?

and the church folks said, yeah.
we been waiting fo you militants
to realize that the church is an eternal rock
now why don't you militants jest come on in
we been waiting for you
we can show you how to build
    anything that needs building
and while we're on our knees, at that.

A BRIEF SYNOPSIS

at fifteen
pain
called me.
i went to one of the
accounting departments,
the hospital
tallied up
came home
with an appendix in a jar
all swollen, pickled and pinkened

each year after that
i reported in
for some kind of
duty.

by 18,
i had grown something else
with a lot of adjectives
like a notebook,
i was a running account
of cuts and bruises
a writer
you might say . . .

every three years
after 21
i helped somebody
doctors, lawyers and various other kinds of chiefs . . .
the last hospital
sent me home
in a cab
well pilled and still
very much preserved.

i can list so many
scars and abrasions
they make a fine cross
word puzzle
in my consciousness
i tell all my admirers

i'm a different kind of
poet.

i
told Jesus
be allright
if he
changed
my
name.

FEMINISM

our mothers,
when asked
may speak of us
in terms of our accomplishments.
my daughter is a flower
shedding buds of brown babies.
she holds two diplomas in
her fists as she shows her
obliqueness to a world that
only cares for credentials.
what is your claim to fame?
what is your claim to life—
when there are no diplomas
to be lauded,
no husband to be pillared upon,
no buds to be babied.
when does the wind blow on your face
and in what direction do you turn
when it rains?

Kalamu ya Salaam
(1947–)

IRON FLOWERS

sluggish, semi-stagnant
the water in Haitian gutters,
small gullets, trickles green,
sewerage green, here even
the dirt is poor and
there is a cloying dullness
camouflaging even strongly
persistent colors

in squared, white walled
cemeteries
funeral flowers are made of
painted iron/i see no roses
rising through this Port
Au Prince poverty

i hesitate to take pictures
it is like thievery
almost like
i am stealing precious light
that these, my brothers and sisters,
need to live

STILL LIFE, STEALING LIFE
CAUGHT RED-HANDED

—when you dine with sharks
be careful less you become
the meal

how it hurts
a whole country arrested
by progress,
the gleaming manacles
of modern transnational management
mangling and mutilating the wrists
of a youthful labor force

in the airport
a sign, a slogan
the words "economic
revolution" originally
writ large in red,
now nigh invisible,
are fading away

c'est la vie,
revolutions are never easy
never negotiated nor agreed
with handshake and signature

more often
it is a bullet
which reorders the wealth
and the severed hands
of traitorous thieves
cut off
that seals
the success of struggle

WE HAVE BEEN SEEN

we have been seen
flying graciously through the air
a foot here

444

the left hard titty of some brother's
            chest there
slowing arching away
across far eastern smoke strewn skies
chunks of charred well done
black meat winging high
like black crows crossing the sun

we have been seen
flaming in the night
the juices of our manhood frying,
popping like sausage in our
dangling veins
strung out from trees
for flies to play on and
race circling around the remnants of our
burnt heads

we have been seen
crippled crazy bowlegged
and lame
hopping and pushing our
bodies across this jagged land
scape like brokeleg jackrabbits
in frightened flight trying to escape a
swift falling eagle's claws

we have been seen
our bodies scarred by war
mutilated by men who were but
            murdering machines
twisted by certain christian cogs of an alleged
            perfect system gone awry in overdrive

we have been seen
and not seen
observed and yet un
recognized all our lives
in africa scars on a man's body are
tribal tattooes, tribute
to his manliness
in america they are but signs
that he has somehow survived
this war

445

BUSH MAMA

*

i want to bust out

oh, my nerves, battered
vacant eyes torn
like tenement windows
looking out into emptiness
and onto so much unprettiness

some changes
same changes
clothes get dirty
pile up, get washed
get dirty, pile up, nothing
much changes, cynicism

i am locked into
these cycles of
life, non-living

i am locked in and don't
fully understand what for,
what did or didn't i do?

i know i am
not innocent
but nor am i guilty
of this

i must bust out

* *

initially i was
unaware, unconscious, unthinking
full of noncritical acceptance
of victim fate

but i am life
and like fertile earth
am rising full of
importance and auspiciously
augur something else

like accountant auditing,
rectifying ledger
amid erasures and clarifications
i am coming to balance
my entries

and while there is still much
i don't know, there is also much
i do understand

i understand drinking
  sloe gin into a quick stupor
  warm wine the morning after

i understand smoking
  two packs a day and weed
  when we could

i understand fucking
  and scratching and screaming
  and shaking like shit

i understand pills
  and iud's, getting pregnant
  and who the babies will belong to

i understand crazy niggers
  with razor hands
  and stone hearts
  dirt in they eyes
  wasting my womaness
  pissing it, like used beer,
  casually onto walls into alleys

i understand dope in the afternoon
  a pusher for a brother
  headaches, aspirin and tranquilizers
  coffee and coke all day long

i understand sweet baby jesus
  and lord do i understand the cross
  and crazy chicken eating cadillac driving
  pimp dressed pretty nigger preachers
  with shiney lips and sugar teeth

i understand lay-a-way
wanting what i don't need
buying with what i ain't got
stuff i see on t v

i understand working below wage
welfare and food stamps thrown at me
like i'm trash and social workers sniffing,
looking between my legs for a man

and because i understand this much
i am beginning to search beyond
illusionary lights seeking
to identify the actual sources
of physical and psychological shock

* * *

i grow more confident now and
although this is serious,
at last i can laugh and really smile
now that i fight without fear

fighting is what frees us
frees us not just from external enemies
but frees us also from our own
weaknesses

a jet whooshes cross the sky going somewheres
i shoot it out the air with my eyes
and a thousand rich people die
their made in the usa napalm luggage
falling inconsequential into the sea

tomorrow i will be called
a nappy headed terror
because of my growth
and social transformation
they won't want to recognize me
and will claim that i am crazy

and will claim that i am crazy

they don't understand
but i will,

448

i will
and do understand

i know that
birthing beauty means breaking blockages
blood must flow, blood must flow

virgins and innocents
never have babies
my children cover the earth
registering ten on richter
social seismometers

we must get down

i feel a war
growing inside of me

do you understand?

DANNY BARKER/DANNY BANJO
Can't you hear me
talkin' ta ya, talkin' ta ya

Danny Banjo
wry great griot elegance
tight as taut
strings stretched cross
tough goat hide
yr strong, still fertile
mind whips past sambo
songster into venerable sageness

Danny man
yr forceful songs shake
south louisiana
canebreak and cotton
dock, yr airs move like
awe filling, rippling
muscles in a crescent city
stevedore's straightening

449

black back casually tossing
heavy burlap sack,
are captivating and cunning
as a seventh ward woman's walk
strutting with sassy
central african sway

Danny Danny Banjo
coffee colored
tabacco tinted
juice of juke joint
and dusky brothel
tarnished coins in
yr vast memory bank, oh
how them dirty rich
mamajammers thought
you was dumb and didn't
know, didn't look,
didn't listen while
yr nimble fingers was
picking and yr thin
mustached full lips
was laughing
secular ditties

Danny Banjo Banjo
you are sacred, you
and all you know and
all you done and seen
and sung, and clean,
clean like the creases
of yr blue suits
you wear, the poise in
yr bemused defiant stance,
the beautiful way
you wear life, like
a natural straw panama,
spotless; a little cocky
with a small feather
or flower

Danny Barker/Danny Banjo
way down, way down, way

down upon the Niger river
where they still celebrate
the fast breaks
of old men who
shout stories of struggle
and whisper slave state
secrets in lyrics
of colored songs

Kora, kora, kora
Banjo Danny Barker, kora
calling in nouvelle
orleans, in old
new o., searching
for new life
long after you are
gone we will still dance
wild in the streets
in serious memory
of you, so hard
have you slammed
singing up the
narrow banquets of
twentieth century
African–American life
leaving a syncopated
legacy of something
as strong as a
loving man's arms,
or basic as yr
burnished thumb
hitting them hidden
chords, or important
as the vast water distance
between ear and home that
yr vital songs
regularly cross
like a sweet man
making it on home
like a sweet man
making a home,
yes sir, I do
hear ya talkin'

man, do I hear
Banjo barking
Danny talkin'
Banjo Barker
Danny Barker
we hear you
talkin', we
hear you

George Barlow
(1948–   )

GABRIEL

*From what he said to me, he seemed to have
made up his mind to die, and to have
resolved to say but little on the subject of the
conspiracy.*

—James Monroe

I

The Trumpeter

He is Gabriel;
black man & slave;
blacksmith/rebel leader;
Thom Prosser's nigger;
black man, armed & thinking,
blending with the landscape,
plotting in the swamp.

He is Gabriel;
big black preacher man;
conspirator & warrior;
Samson in Virginia,
who won't apologize
in the end,
who'll be mute
like Miles
in the end—
black & beautiful
in the end.

He is Gabriel,
who blows walls down;

fighter of thunder & lightning;
Shango in Virginia,
betrayed by monkeys & rain;
black man & slave,
who carries a big stick.

He is Gabriel;
history & myth;
blood & guts & change;
legend & husband;
brother & black man.
                    Gabriel.
Gabriel is a black man.

II

The Will & The Swan

In the slave quarters
& the tobacco fields,
under pine branches

& hardwood leaves,
in the marsh grass
of the swamp,

the kitchens,
stables & smokehouses
of the plantations,

the rebels
dream of the blow
on Richmond,

Monroe, Jefferson
& the country.
Silently,

through the seasons,
they burrow into
the fertile underground

& ready themselves.
In the perfect light
of their own darkness,

the private gleam
of their own
golden will,

they watch their leader
become
a great black swan,

& under his wing
they patiently, soulfully
let the plot ferment.

III

Spirit in the Dark

*They that walked in darkness sang songs in the olden
days—Sorrow Songs—for they were weary at heart.*
— *W.E.B. DuBois*

Here is the spirit in the dark
Here is the spirit in the dark
Here is the spirit in the dark

One heart, one voice,
one purpose: Black angels
singing in a shack
near Richmond; blowing
the Sorrow Songs
that are hope & renewal.

Hear it in the dark
Here is the spirit in the dark

One people, one dream,
one collective beauty
gathered in secret to feel
the spirit in the dark:
rhythm, harmony, melody:
the seeds of soul:
Aretha, Mahalia, Nina.

See it in the dark
Touch it, hear it, feel it in the dark

Under an old roof that leaks
& an old system
that won't let them breathe,
they blow their urgency,
rebirth & survival, sweetly
like wind through reeds & treetops.

Get it in the dark
Gotta get the spirit in the dark

In the guts of slavery,
in the horror of the times,
they sing the songs
loudly & softly,
feeling the spirit in the dark;
planting the seeds:
B.B., Otis, Sam.

Hear it in the dark
I know you hear the spirit in the dark

They're ready in the dark
'cause they've got the feeling;
Africans in the dark; strong
in the spirit in the dark;
Trane in the dark;
Billie, Diz, & Bird in the dark;
feel them in the spirit,
feel them in the dark.

Seed, ancestors, angels in the dark;
all feeling, all spirit in the dark;
all powerful in the spirit;
heart, soul & love in the dark;
freedom in the spirit;
Gabriel in the dark;
the Trumpeter in the spirit in the dark.

Here is the spirit
Here is the dark
Here is the spirit in the dark

Coming & Going:
Gabriel's Song

Fixing my eyes downward,
moving slow & easy
to go unnoticed,
I enter Richmond
for the twentieth time.

I squint kindly
at the masters' & mistresses'
Sunday dress
as it brightens up the storefronts—
every porch, every door, every window
has a place in my mind.
Smiling at these folks,
bowing my head
as they pass,
I note the sidewalk;
how it's gotten
hard & rough & dusty
under their evil feet.

Gotta get so I
can call up
every board, every nail,
every footprint
in my mind; gotta be ready
to call every splinter.

Come next Saturday evening,
Lord willing,
we're coming in to open up
all these doors & windows
& all these big white bellies.
We're gonna stand up tall
& sing up to heaven
when we take this town.

V

The Rainbow

Here
is America's killing;
death by knife & fire;
& in the rainbow
are the Methodists,
the Quakers,
some poor whites,
some Frenchmen,
the Catawba Indians,
& the Blacks
in brown, tan,
jet, high yeller—
the various colors
of a conspiracy
to survive.

Blending
perfectly & desperately,
they know
that in this last blaze
only monsters will die.

Here
is America's killing:
survivors will be
radiant, guiltless,
human.

VI

*White Blues:
the Master's Song*

Dawn again
& no sleep;
jumping & sweating
where sweet dreams
should be.
Red-eyed & trembling,
he sits on the back porch,
watches the sun

sneak up
over the tobacco rows
& thinks about
the easy, lazy world
that suckled him—
the plump black Mammy
whose lap & songs
sent him off each night,
the white pony
his daddy bought,
& old Josh
who'd dance,
tell him stories
& tickle him.

He sits
digging his nails
into the arm
of an ancient white rocker
wondering where
that world went,
wondering what happened
to the blacks—
"No good niggahs,
ungrateful black devils,
what the hell happened to 'em?
Ain't like they used to be!"

Lately he's felt
something brewing
right here
in Henrico County—
insurrection maybe—
but that's silly,
he thinks,
just silly fretting.

In the dawn shadows
he can barely make out
the figure
of his blacksmith, Gabriel,
scratching a strange rhythm
on the whetstone:

putting a fine edge
on the cook's butcher knife.
Silly fretting.
This will be
a good day;
a hog up for slaughter;
plenty for all,
like always.

VII

History Is Thunder & Rain

Wind, rain,
cracks in the sky:
a strange storm
has come to stop
the march;

high water
splashing from hell;
the Brook Swamp bridge
washed out—

Gabriel
& one thousand armed blacks
can't cross
into Richmond.

Shocked, hunched
& glazed,
they stand soaked
in the impotence
of this strange rain.

Those months
of building, whetting,
oiling the secret arsenal
have turned to mud
under their feet.

Across the flood
the militia waits;
howling

in the freak Virginia night;
signalled by Mosby Sheppard

whose two black sheep,
Tom & Pharoah,
lost their way
into history, thunder & rain,
a plot to insurrect.

VIII

The Ferrets

 The ferrets are out!
 The ferrets are out!

  Run away, run away

The ferrets are out
covering the county
  Hide & keep quiet
white phantoms of inquisition

  Run away, run away

covering the countryside

  Damn 'em, Damn 'em

howling & hunting
  Quiet, keep quiet

through mud & woods
through kitchens & fields
tracking blacks
howling & hunting

 The ferrets are out!
 The ferrets are out!

to purge & ferret

  Run, Gabe, run

shoot & kill

> *Steal away, brother, steal away*

question & question

> *Run away, run away*

kill & kill

> *Sail away, Gabriel, sail away*

The ferrets are out!
The ferrets are out!

"Where is Gabriel?"

> *Run, run*

"His bitch? His brother?"

> *Sail, Gabe, sail*

"Get the blacksmith!"

> *Can't sail, can't sail*

"Find him!"

> *Can't hide*

"Dig the coon out!"

> *Can't run anymore*

"Get him! Get him!"

> *They'll get me but I'm a man*

"Take him alive. He must talk!"

> *Ain't saying a mumblin' word*

462

"Get the nigger, make him talk!"

I can die

"He's got to tell us how he did it!"

I'm Gabriel
I'm a black man
I ain't afraid

IX

Life and Death:
The Bitch's Brew
The Readiness is ALL

He is death
in life
& life in death
in the dim pregnancy

of these eleven days
in the hold
of the schooner *Mary*
in Norfolk harbor;

waiting for posse,
trial & rope;
waiting to be born
into martyrdom;

waiting for white Justice—
a blind bitch—
to deliver him, stillborn,
into her bleeding history;

a tapestry of
swollen middle passage blacks
drowned in a net
& gelded bucks in poplar trees.

Having tossed bayonet & bludgeon—
his only arms—

463

overboard,
he contemplates providence,
revisits that stormy night,
& worries about his wife, Nanny,
his lieutenant, Jack Bowler,
his two brothers, Solomon & Martin.

Secretly he tightens his resolve
to say nothing of them
in the end;
to be mute in the end.

Hearing no sounds
but the music
of his own heartbeat
& breathing,

he privately,
fearlessly prepares
for the stages of his stillbirth:
mock trial, mob, scaffold.

How many times
can the bitch kill him,
swing the trap open
& break his neck?

She will hear
no confession, see no fear,
& scream out,
unsatisfied.

X

October, 1800:
A Son in the Continuum

Behold, a son!

The product of our love:
a worker
born into the slavery
of Southampton,

464

born sturdy & black
on this 2nd day of the month.

Behold, a cosmic birth!

We welcome this newborn
& note his timing;
Gabriel's conviction
is tomorrow—on the 7th
he will hang.

Behold, a manchild!

A newborn worker
of the soil; a black boy
in the tidewater landscape:
a son in the continuum:
Africa in Virginia,
manchild in Southampton,
Gabriel in the manchild.

Behold, a gift!

Our own substance:
black flesh, black bone,
black fiber & liquids—
a newborn warrior—
our son,
Nat! Nat Turner!

Ntozake Shange
(1948–)

INQUIRY

my questions concern the subject poetry
is whatever runs out/ whatever digs my guts
til there's no space in myself
cryin wont help/ callin mama wont help
lovers are detours/ no way to assuage this
poem/ but in the words & they are deceitful/
images beat me confuse me/ make me want
all of you to share me/
& i hide under my bed/

poetry is unavoidable connection/
some people get married/ others join the Church
i carry notebooks/ so i can tell us what happened/
midnight snacks in bed with whoever/
are no compensation/ when
i'm listening to multitudes of voices/ i consume
yr every word & move/

durin the day you are initiated into *the holy order
of prospective poems*/ i dream in yr voice/ sometimes
act yr fantasies/ i've made them my own/
whatever is here/ is what you've given me/
if it's not enough for you/
give me some more

ON BECOMIN SUCCESSFUL

'she don't seem afrikan enuf to know bt . . .'
'seeems she's dabblin in ghetto-life . . .'

why dont you go on & integrate a
german-american school in st. louis mo. / 1955/
better yet why dont ya go on & be a red niggah in a
blk school in 1954/ i got it/ try & make one friend at
camp in the ozarks in 1957/ crawl thru one a jesse
james' caves wit a class of white kids waitin outside to
see the whites of yr eyes/ why dontcha invade a clique
of working-class italians tryin to be protestant in a
jewish community/ & come up a spade/ be a lil too
dark/ lips a lil too full/ hair entirely too nappy/ to be
beautiful/ be a smart child tryin to be dumb/ you go
meet somebody who wants/ always/ a lil less/ be cool
when yr body says hot & more/ be a mistake in racial
integrity/ an error in white folks' most absurd
fantasies/ be a blk girl in 1954/ who's not blk enuf to
lovingly ignore/ not beautiful enuf to leave alone/ not
smart enuf to move outta the way/ not bitter enuf to
die at a early age/ why dontcha c'mon & live my life for
me/ since the poems aint enuf/ go on & live my life for
me/ i didn't want certain moments at all/ i'd giv em to
anybody/

ELEGANCE IN THE EXTREME

(for cecil taylor)

elegance in the extreme
gives style to the hours
of coaxing warmth outta
no where

elegant hoodlums
elegant intellectuals
elegant ornithologists
elegant botanists

but elegance in the extreme helps most
the stranger who hesitates

to give what there is
for fear of unleashing madness
which   is sometimes
uninvolved in contemporary mores
archetypal realities or graciousness

in the absence of extreme elegance
madness can set right in like
a burnin gauloise on japanese silk
though highly cultured
even the silk must ask
how to burn up discreetly

Kenneth A. McClane
(1951–)

JAZZ

Deify the room/space/drive . . . mass control
into love . . .
get medium/brake into high/find mellow/
perch there/drift . . . find her/move/
stop . . .
Impress the air cool with love turning over
every tremor to find new note/new time to
woo bass and feet tap.
Drift sky/sea/earth motion on without you/
within you/ . . . you . . .
Follow up/expand/chill/blow to extinction
then find second breath and leave/new life
yelling deep . . .
Vibrate/rap your sad tale blue plus black/
don't dwell . . . too long . . . sing of your dreams
different . . .
Burn hell with new freakish devil/new man wants
new world to love him/new 7th brakes peace
and upsets what is, or isn't
Sounds ruptured realize brother's tale/tale of
millions waiting/some lost/direction
smacks home/news news/
what's happening . . .
Coltrane did it,
tamed for a second
broke prison
free . . .

TO HEAR THE RIVER

for Langston Hughes

To hear
to hear
to hear the
to hear the strong
black song
to hear it—to hear the river
is to know

its ways: to know
the gaunt-thin
source which somehow
like Hughes
becomes long black water, becomes
(so that much might come after it)
a handhold, a griot:

And so long black song
comes dark, provident, absolute:

And finally coming to the river, facing
the dogs and white men, facing what is lost
and possible, *we hear the river, we hear
the river, we hear the river*

SONG: A MOTION OF HISTORY

for Cecil

Once more I've begun the treatise; once more
I shall place my thoughts at the foci of wisdom
moving in that inner wheel, hoping like Ezekiel
that the patterns of nature—the laws
shall let my orbit stand:

I'm speaking about time and continents.
I'm speaking about what it exacted, borne, and somehow
carried. I'm speaking about
the world of our fathers: the song and the past song:

And much has been asked of song. Don't
doubt it. Like love, like jazz, like the endless

visions which give us a life, song
is an awesome thing.
We must not betray it.
There is grief; there is grief enough.

So I think of Tanner's boy, kneeling
at his grandfather's knee, kneeling at the wide
mouth of guitar, the strongest source:

Free, intimate with time, burdened and lightened,
finally carried in a sea, a motion, a music: nothing
may turn him around. Listen:
the music is ours; it will not abandon us.

THE BLACK INTELLECTUAL

for W.E.B. DuBois

We have shored up so much
to keep from rioting. To keep it down
we move in and out of our skins
in some grotesque obeisance, some wretching of our forms
as if we were addled neon signs.

Indeed we are afraid of ourselves.
Riding in the least seat, in the last car, in the longest
train is still riding; it is safe.
Powers still mightily discipline the universe: and gods
(be they august or sweet) provide a cadence.

Yet when I walk near their big clovered houses,
see their doom-eyed children, watch
their ornamental boats flounder in the river, I
want to save them.

And when they press
me in class, when they want
to know how soil is gathered, how earth
shares so little, I find myself answering:

But sometimes the other voice in me
heaves from the gut.
Cold, defiant, persuasive

471

it seems to hold everything: Attica
Soweto, Chile, Little Rock, Mozambique:

And now I see nothing in their stunted lives
but death; I see nothing in their hopeless
celebration but blood; I see nothing but the ceaseless waste
of dark bodies, piling up as they ask:

the questions always coming, always coming
as if questions might stop it. Today I have given up
answering: today I no longer look upon or care about the easy
offerings to insatiable gods: today
should a wind swell on the river and wrack their foundering
boat
I might only wish that all were present.

VI

VOICES FOR A
NEW AGE—
1980s/1990s

Colleen McElroy
(1935–)

WHILE POETS ARE WATCHING

(for Quincy Troupe)

Harlem is on parade
recalling St. Louis
as if like us
the whole scene
has been transplanted here
Stanford White's window offers
remnants of James Van Der Zee's world
it is filled with urgent gospels
infecting us both with memories
of our common birthplace
I see you take notes
always the poet
but in the dry space
where I have stored words
pictures from this Harlem window
kaleidoscope faster
than any pen will move

you have to come back you say
this is rich and heavy
like good food
you say here
are our poems
smiling as your next words
are drowned in tambourines
and harsh songs of salvation
blasting from loudspeakers
lampposted below the window
for a moment the hymns
from the corner tabernacle

outdrum the cadence
of the parade

this is the third Sunday
in August and thirty-second-
degree Masons
strutting like crested pigeons
swell the black heart of this town
we watch from the window
matching faces with memories
the skinny old woman next door
praises the past
like any other church lady
she is powdered like a turn-
of-the-century matron
her sunken black cheeks
dusted with pale blue, ivory or rose
to match pastel dress, stockings, shoes
you take note chanting
come back, come back
this is home and love

we are poets watching
tight-hipped black girls
swing their batons
to the high-step
rhythms of vaseline-smoothed legs
while the oompahs of school bands
count march time for drill teams
we watch until dusk
until the bands
grouped like gaudy flowers
have played their last notes
until the old men have
placed their callused feet
on the nearest footstools
and the girls have gum-chewed
their mothers into silence

these faces are familiar
as Van Der Zee's photos
as my mother's snapshots
of cookouts in Uncle Brother's
backyard or your own scrapbook
of our high-school homecoming

it is all predictable
from the street smells
of old whiskey and urine
to the sun fading
against Columbia's canker-
green roof
we are home, coming back
always coming back

CUTTING A ROAD FROM MANAUS TO BELÉM

the Amazon peeled back to gold and rubber
the clink of coins more definite than the purulent
yellow of common colds and aboriginal hunger

Xingu bankers thumbing gilded bills
mouthing numbers like thick throat
mints peppering mud-fevered palates

the green everybody wants, eyeball
blade-edged, cucumber-new green

land robbers shimmering cobalt on camera
faces bloating like seafoam backwash
of graph-green images

movietone civilizados wallowing
in wealth, their wives long in the tooth
and up to the neck in emeralds and bad luck

potent jealousy of have and have-not, of defoliating
for the sake of money in air too thick to breathe
voice-overs spitting Mato Grosso credit card power

the earth's heart-belt of mold, madness and business
names of lost tribes full of x's, j's, and double l's
surrounding a one-lane road named progress

the bait of big bucks, the white man's duty, the one good
turn of being in the *Black*—yeah

the challenge, my little chickadee,
the go-for-it of greenhorns of slick
palms and mossy dollar bills

WHY TU FU DOES NOT SPEAK
OF THE NUBIAN

she draws fat birds
in strokes tight as geography
their plump bodies
arch above bent twigs and flowers
in a splash of boneless color
remember the leaves and veins she says
Chinese painting captures the spirit
the character of space
the observer looks down
stresses only foreground
the use of line gives substance
to the motion
these contours fall into simple patterns
like Tu Fu's poems
easy she says watching my brush
tremble toward the paper
but it is difficult
these fat birds and simple bamboo stalks

they have no urban counterparts
I want to fill the space
with fat black babies
with the veined hands of wretched old men
and big mamas in flowered dresses
shying away from welfare lines
the slender fingers of these thin twigs
should bend to the sweet pain
of old love songs played on
clear water and clean rocks
should ease the sullen jokes
of schools gone bad
while colors blend like Ashanti rhythms
played on Osebo's drum
draw them many many times she says
they grow from the mind without roots
so I bend over porcelain-white paper
remember to pull all lines toward the center
and always the dark into light

Sybil Kein
(1939–   )

FRAGMENTS FROM THE
DIARY OF AMELIE PATINÉ
QUADROON MISTRESS OF
MONSIEUR JACQUES R-------.

New Orleans, 14 Novembre, 1825

Morn.
Coeur cassé. My life is settling in a cup of
silk shadows, blue and brown Madras on the divan.
Will he return? Not a fortnight but he was here in my
arms, weeping in delicious agony. Has my body withered
suddenly?
For three years, we wore the tastes of love's wild
oranges; his flesh mine, my soul his. He was my saint;
I wore his smile. My mouth twitches at the memory. Now,
this chilled day rends at my bodice. I fear my bosom will
explode. I have seen her! She is wife. But to leave me?
I would that we were spirits flying together between hell
and heaven.

Noontide.
Am I abandoned in this latticed cottage on Rue Esplanade?
Coffined between stiff red velvet drapes and mirrored
plafond?* Should I wrap my hair around the bed posts to
cover those carved Cupids and their forever taut bows? He
could have warned me. We would have fled or died sweetly
imprisoned here. My fingers pinch and swell at this quill.

Eventide.
And how she flung the words. *Fongasse!* Whore! Some I dare
not say. Heaven's worst lost gift to white men. O lady,
were you in my stead. Could you live bought, adored,

*Ceiling.

despised paramour, blight made flesh; hidden, held in
dire esteem, yet sought for bare beauty, fate begging?
Privileged sister, you know me not!
Who but I have planted the blush that he transfers to your
pale cheeks? How heavy would beat your heart if it were
not for his lambent ecstasy that is constantly renewed at my
lips, my loins. Your peasant crudeness flares for what I am.
What shallow passion, frivolous morality do you wear as mask
for this worthless vengeance? He must not leave me! Love is
not fabricated nor tarnished but by the petty decrees of a
society wrought with fraud, deceit, and barbarous wickedness.

Candle-light.
Jacques. I am no longer afraid to write your name.
We have met. She is sworn to revenge.
Where can I hide now, as this taper burns in quiet
pools of thick secretion? What will become of us?
Beguin. My shadow lies withdrawn upon the bed.
Shall I continue to sip this darkened Spanish wine
at your hour of eventide? Who will feel the vapors
rising under my skin? Who will muff my little cries,
unruff these violet sheets that stare coldly at my
spine? Must this night slip with me into eternity?
Oh blaze the heavens with this memory: my lover,
fallen on his knees, his tender mouth closed in
my bosom repeating endlessly my name!

Such sorrowful murmurs I scrape across these pages.
The doleful moon breaks against my window. Or did
my shadow move?

LETTER TO MADAME LINDÉ
FROM JUSTINE, HER CREOLE SERVANT

New Orleans, 1832

Chère Madame:

     You no doubt will be surprised at finding
This letter writ by my own hand, in the language which
We both hold dear. As you see, Madame, I am not ignorant
Of the rules of grammar, nor am I illiterate as you have
So many times referred to me to your friends on various
Social encounters. I chose to pretend indifference to

Your ignorance of this particular facility of my character,
In order to preserve your integrity in the manner dictated
By the social creed of our times.

However, your recent assault on my dignity, on the
Occasion of my daughter's impending plaçage, forces me to
Drop any hint of dishonesty. In truth, Madame, the fact that
My daughter was fathered by your husband was not altogether
The fault of your servant, as you have alleged. Men, being
The formidable creatures they are, are more likely to seek
The sweets of their liberty where it is easier and more
Pleasant to acquire them.

Further, Madame, as your faithful servant of twenty
Years, I hold many secrets which, if made known, would
Surely bring disgrace to you in the eyes both of your
People and of the Church. I am thinking in particular of
The many visits of one Madame Celeste whom you have taken
To Your Bosom as more than friend. Indeed, Madame, one
Occurrence of your peculiar love-making with your dear
Celeste piqued my curiosity by the nature of the sounds
Coming from the attic room. I was just outside the door,
And saw with mine own eyes the dresses and underthings in
A heap upon the floor, and witnessed, though briefly, the
Fierce eagerness with which you both spent your passion.

Madame, I am not condemning your particular capacity
For such love, nor am I judging the sincerity of your lover
Madame Celeste. I am, however, writing this to demand that
You see to it that my place as your free servant is secured
For as long as I live, and that the honor of my daughter is
Preserved as fitting a young woman of her beauty and station.
I am sure that you will therefore reconsider the foolish
Threats to my daughter and myself that you made on yestereve,
And consequently take whatever action necessary to rectify
This affaire.

If you need to forward your courage after reading this
Letter, you have only to ring the bell for kitchen. I will
Be happy to send up a toddy of brandy, and if you please,
Some tea-cakes.

I remain,

                    Your servant,
                    Justine, f.w.c.

COFAIRE?*

Ma cousine Tee-Ta, she say she Cajun;
et me, I'm Creole, name Tee-Teen.
She still live up on de Bayou, you know;
but me, I move to New Orleen.

Now something is wrong in dem words,
what you say? Creole, Cajun? No balance!
Something is wrong bout de way dey is tole;
mais, you tell me la difference!

Mon Papa was Boudreaux, from Bayou Moustique;
she Papa, he was de same.
So how come den, we both be two kind of folk,
when mais yeah, we got him same name!

Oh long time ago, ain't nobody write
in de book when dey bebe she come out;
so maybe dat why dis confusion, comme ça,
"qui c'est qui," who is who, come about!

Ma cousine, she jolie, she petit, full of conte;
and she love to dance de day!
And me, you can see, I'm de vary same too:
Bon-temp! Chanté ess ma way!

We cook de same food, jambalaya, crawfish bisque,
but I make de gumbo, mais yes!
With file, big blue crab, and oysters and shrimp—
ma cuisine "ou-la-la" smell de best!

Eh, tings not so bad up by de Bayou;
we parlé, when somebody die;
but in New Orleen, she pretend she don know me
if one of her friend sashay by.

So one day I tole her, "You make me so mad,
'gros cochon!' your nose in de air!"
She explain, it because she is French (white, you know)
which means "passé blanc" to me, chere!

*How come?

Well, *dit pas rien*, she do what she please;
and me, I just laugh all de time.
"Cajun" and "Créole," we cousine, that's for true;
cause her "French" folks is "French"—same as mine!

JELLY ROLL MORTON

Winin' boy,
if you were mine,
I'd rock you in my
cradle of careless love—
true blue love,
and let you jass me
with your sporting house,
red gravy, diamond-studded,
gambling, hot Creole
rambling, down-town
ragtime blues.

Lord Jelly, Oh Mister Jazz King,
You salty dog.

Virgia Brocks-Shedd
(1943—1992)

SOUTHERN ROADS/CITY PAVEMENT

Southern Roads
>Held me virgin and
>barefoot in the dust
>that circled up to cover my face,
>my hair, and engaged my nostrils
>to inhale the dust of life
>for me to become when I am dead.

My Southern Dusty Roads
>Led me from the deep piney woods
>of my shacky home to the
>pavement of Highway number 49
>to see cars going to or coming
>from the city 30 miles away;
>waving my blackberry buckets,
>hoping the riders would stop
>and leave fifty cents for
>my three hours of picking, and dodging snakes,
>and getting untangled, while
>envisioning money to leave
>at the white folks' store
>for nickel bars of delightful
>but seldom had candy bars,
>and then go home and say to
>my daddy's widow,
>"Mama, I made some money today."

My Southern Roads
>In the little world of my life;
>didn't know our folks could not afford
>to take us to see the city streets;

I wonder now if I knew they existed;
and we thought everyone was like us,
except the folks in cars;
and me and my sisters and brothers
were jumping up and shouting everytime
we saw Black folks in cars as we
exclaimed which car was our own;
the cars, passing us, and now I recall,
some riders, glancing with pity
at those poor, poor children,
and stopping to buy our
fifty cents syrup bucket of blackberries.

The only other world we knew was
in the cowboy movies that we saw
in a tent during one season on unused,
unplowed dusty or grassy grounds,
because it was early 60s before we saw
television regularly to reject
our own lives, to imagine ourselves
dancing to Welk's champagne music
and wearing fine clothes.

Southern Roads

That held and carried us barefoot
and occasionally with new cheap shoes
to school and our country church,
where we tried to look and be
without sin and important, too,
among those who were; and,
trying to get to heaven in one day
from the preaching and shouting and the
baptizing in our white sheets of goodness;
and going back home just before night
to play, fight, court and whisper
and glance and touch the boyfriends
and girlfriends we paired with unnoticed,
we thought, by our parents, and grandparents,
and aunts and uncles and senior cousins
who told us ghost tales and
superstitions and family histories,
as we listened to fox sounds and panther wails
and saw community, not homebox, entertainment

in pennies disappearing from and reappearing to
my daddy's hands while he lived to 1951

To wake and kill home raised chickens,
and cook them on the fires we stoked
in our wood stoves; pick greens, pull corn,
pick plums; stomp on clothes in a big tin tub,
stir them up in a big black pot,
and wait for hog killing time when we knew
we would eat homemade skins and the pig's feet;
and when with no meat, have homemade
buttermilk and cornbread

Southern Roads

In the grassy, dusty paths that led
to Mrs. Eleases's house, Mrs. Clara's
and Mr. J.P.'s, Mr. Horse's,
Lynette's and Nooky's, Herman's and Billy's
on rutted walkways, or little craggy clay hills,
leading to springs of water for drinking,
branches of water for washing the clothes
from the bodies, the lives of sawmill, paperwood
workers; men touching women and children in the
new corners of our everyday life,
after our mommies came home from cleaning
the white folks' homes and our daddies bringing
very tired bodies home in their overalls
on

Southern Roads

A peaceful haven for
floating southern spirits,
rejuvenating their times when they
physically touched the soil,
protecting living lives in the
meekness of us as we moaned together
in blackness of nationwide black care and
love for the Emmett Tills and the
Mack Charles Parkers; and, saying
deeply inside of us,
"Lord, have mercy; please have mercy."
And cry and shout at Mahalia's throaty notes
singing, "Precious Lord," and to later

486

feel the fleeting joy when we would
wind and grind to the lightning music of
Brother Hopkins or scream in pleasure
to know that B.B. was singing about women
who could love and cause or leave misery.

Southern Roads
Leading to death in the lynch sites of
forest of trees; to burial grounds in rivers,
in the soil of dams; in carports and living
rooms of modern homes; in unpillowed beds
on railroad cars; on lawns adjacent to
dormitories; in the paved streets of cities,
at Parchman, Whitfield, and even the whiskey stills

Southern Roads
Tapping and rooting and growing to and with
the lives that left for Chicago, LA, New York,
the army, Oakland, Detroit, Milwaukee,
the street corners, bars, heroin, coke—
the best of life, we thought, in escape from

Southern Roads
I miss you since all I now touch
is asphalt or concrete or carpet;
gritty dust, not the fine kind
that blew with the clean winds through trees,
or kicked up with dusty barefoot feet
in the rows of fields we chopped to
make food for ourselves or money for the others
who hired us for $3.00 a day,
and then to shop at their stores for processed
foods we thought better than our natural
homemade brands or the fish we caught and ate
from creeks and natural lakes.

Southern Roads
I now seldom walk anywhere,
but I do drive back to visit
the roads of my youth;
touching the soil, bringing some of its rocks,
its dirt to my city street;
and bringing the memories and the caresses

of the senior ones and the younger ones
who never left whom I see
still shaped and living in the
southern dust, home with me.

Southern Roads

From the dust of you I have risen,
and have come and produced from me
two other lives to replenish you, too,
along with all the juniors from my sisters
of every race;
children to teach us loving and how to care
as those who were taught before
to care for the present us.
And, I wish to leave you naturally made
by bare or animal skinned feet;
to leave you laying paths to a world of peace
in unpaved, unpolluted by concrete and asphalt,
and gasoline and machine air;
and that airplanes will always pass by you
and not land too near;
that the blues and spirituals you give
will be orchestrated by southern homing birds
which won't ever have to fly away;
all creature; including me, who need you
to remain dusty or muddy when wet,
just dusty or muddy, good southern roads.

Southern Roads

Foundation of my life,
holding all that made me,
my expired families and friends,
my ancestral anchors, so far
from where I am now.
But, what sorrows at each birth
these ancestors must have given in hopes
and prayers that the children
of black lives and black spirits
would have lives better than their own . . .
to try and not ever miss the early lives
of their scrotums and wombs which had died
from disease or natural miscarriages;
yet,

Southern Roads,
>You've paved a permanence in my life,
>for I am bounded by gentle southern spirits
>that travel you, too, and still,

Southern Roads,
>You will lead those to me
>when I lie still, covered in death,
>under southern love,
>returning myself to you,
>O precious southern soil.

Houston A. Baker, Jr.
(1943–)

No matter where you travel,
You still be Black,
You carry all your history
On your own damn back.

Your momma raised you proper
Your daddy caused you pain
You understand Beethoven,
But you still love Trane.

LATE-WINTER BLUES AND PROMISES OF LOVE

The promise of a thousand suns,
Printless ground, swirling flakes against the sky.
Morning in the heart of this surprised city,
Laid seige by a March storm,
Found me listening to out-of-tune guitars;
Slack strumming of black boys
With trains and big-legged women in their voice.
My mind caught in sound and light of winter,
Turned gymnist,
Vaulted somber years to youth.

Closed doors and "WHITE ONLY" signs of Louisville
Changed the sun's birth to sounds of loss.
A loving absence,
Lyrical savior who took the midnight special and left us.
Highballed it home to heaven.

In the heart of this city, I await
A second coming.

The light of bursting suns,
Baked atoms coming to a new birth:
Black boy strumming a surrealist guitar,
A vision wholly modern . . .

Got no time for the preacher,
Honey, all I want is you,
If yo' lovin' gets the best of me,
Then my travellin' days is through.

Sounds sweet as forsythia
Beneath spring snow.

THIS IS NOT A POEM

This is not a poem, nor
Aesthetic experience.
This is the story of my grandmother's
Hands chapped from white folks' wash,
An account of her back spasmed
From scrubbing floors.
This is not a poem, nor
Icey "art emotion."
This is a narrative of my father's father
Scraping pennies from a rocky economy.
Depression devouring everything in sight.
This is no poem, nor
Subtle tingle down your spine while shaving:
This is a tale of my mother
Rebuked for calling a black man "gentleman":

("Lizzie, tell your daughter, **niggers** are not gentlemen!")

This is no poem, nor
Am I blessed to be impersonal.
I will make no attempt to distance you.
Had you been there while I was growing up, or
Even in the thin/worn time of their decline,
I would have introduced you.
Allowed you to share the fine goodness of ancestral
Caring.

Wanda Coleman
(1946–)

DOING BATTLE WITH THE WOLF

1.

i drip blood
on my way to and from work
i drip blood
down the aisles while shopping at the supermarket
i drip blood
standing in line at the bank
filling my tank at the gas station
visiting my man in prison
buying money orders at the post office
driving the kids to school
walking to bed at night
i drip blood

an occasional transfusion arrives in the mail
or i find plasma in the streets
an occasional vampire flashes my way
but they don't take much
my enemy is the wolf
who eats even the mind

the wolf will come for me sooner or later
i know this
the wolf makes no sexual distinctions
i am the right color
he has a fetish for black meat and
frequently hunts with his mate along side him

he follows my trail of blood

i drip blood for hours
go to the bathroom and apply bandages

i've bled enough
it's my monthly bleeding of poison
getting it out of my system
watching it as it flows from the
open sore of my body into the toilet stool
making a red ring
so pretty
flushing it away—red swirls
a precious painful price i pay

my man cannot protect me
the wolf has devoured most of my friends
i watched them die horribly
saw the
raw hunks of meat skin bone
swallowed
watched as full, the wolf crept away
to sleep

2.

the wolf has a beautiful coat
it is white and shimmers in moonlight/a coat of diamonds
his jaws are power
teeth sharp as guns glisten against his red tongue
down around his feet the fur is dirty with the caked blood
    of my friends

i smile
i never thought it would come to this

scratching
scratching at my door
scratching to get in

howls howls howls
my children are afraid
i send them to hide in the bedroom

scratch scratch scratch
the door strains
howl howl howl
cries of my children "mama! mama! who is it?"

i am ready
—armed with my spear inherited from my father as he
    from his mother
(who was a psychic) as she from her father (who was a
    runaway slave) as he
from his mother (who married the tribal witch doctor)—
    me—african warrior
imprisoned inside my barely adequate female form
determined
i open the door
a snarl
he lunges
the spear
against his head
he falls back
to prepare for second siege
i wait
the door will not close
i do not see the wolf
my children scream
i wait
look down
am wounded
drip blood
cannot move
or apply bandages
must wait
wolf howls and the roar of police sirens

WORD GAME

once upon a time, i a poet, transformed myself into a poem
i was very happy
my line was intriguing and audacious
it could take many forms—a gun, a sword, a heart that
    throbbed
a hand gentle as a kiss
it could express any emotion i sought to convey, as well as
i could master it

then one day i was published

now i do not know whether i am a poet writing a poem
or a poem writing a poet

LAS TURISTAS NEGRAS GRANDE

my feet kiss the pavement on castillo
a vendor tosses tripe and chicken parts over the fire
azteca gold eye winks sweat beads
la joya la joya (this joy in the streets of la raza)
we are natives of tunisia
we are hunters of obsidian
we are incan gods mad for the blood of our oppressors
pain in abalone butterflies
wide-eyed indian girls in hip length earth brown braids
today there was a minor revolution being conducted

wind against the rocks
sea sucking the shore

·

Julius E. Thompson
(1946–)

SONG OF INNOCENCE

O Africa, know thou not my call?
Know thy rivers not my love?
Claim thy mountains not my heart?
O Africa! Homeland of my own!
I come with my heart afire;
I come with a soul in search of light!
O Africa! Hear a voice in search of hope,
Welcome home a brother lost;
Receive a heart of melody;
O Africa! Knows thou not my plight?
For all sight, I seek a light in thee!
O Africa! My Africa! Know thou not my flight?
Will thou not take me back,
Reclaim my heart and soul on sight!

IN MY MIND'S EYE

In my mind's eye,
I see Black people
In the cotton fields
And up north
Crying in the cities.

In my mind's eye,
I see no solutions—
Only a million
And a half
Unanswered questions.

In my mind's eye,
I see jesus

496

On my people's mind
Every hour of
Every day.

In my mind's eye
I see booker t. washington
Laughing with uncle tom;
They both were given special medals
For going beyond the call of duty.

In my mind's eye,
I see jordan river.
It won't let no
Negroes enter for fear of
Upsetting the water table.

In my mind's eye,
I can't roll over
Or under Egypt;
And Ethiopia is below *that*.
How's i gonna get home?

In my mind's eye
Comes the spirit
Of my ancestors,
Telling me not to worry if I don't
Come up with an answer, they will.

In my mind's eye
Is the image of a dying man.
His only crime was
Trying to live
And let others do the same.

In my mind's eye
Is a memory of a journey
Across a sea.
I saw my mother jump in
And my father go after her.

In my mind's eye
Is a story about how we landed
On these shores.

The only greeting we got
Was, "you are now niggers!"

In my mind's eye
Is a second of that first whip.
It went across all our backs
And reached Africa to tell
My brothers left that they were next.

In my mind's eye
Moves a part of me
That can never forget
Where it has been.
Home, home in a dream.

In my mind's eye—
Cover up her body,
Cover up her remains.
Don't let those white folks see her.
Her spirit got to be free!

In my mind's eye
Love knows I understand.
She was tied up too,
And under the prison walls
Her tears could not reach our gods.

In my mind's eye
Is a movement I cannot figure out.
It wants to tell me something,
But fearful I won't answer,
It moves away.

In my mind's eye
Are all those brothers and sisters
Who through the long years
Made a way that
We might one day yet understand.

In my mind's eye
Moves a part of me
That the gray ghost tried
To destroy.   his gods were
Not powerful enough!

In my mind's eye
Moves a part of me
That knew I never was a slave,
Though I had no freedom
And no land.

In my mind's eye,
Lord, the spirit
Moves me
Back and forth between
Two worlds.

In my mind's eye
Something is saying
"Awake from your
Walking sleep
And follow me."

In my mind's eye
I see 500 million
Walking home free!
Spirit, Spirit moves over me.
In my mind's eye!   home!   free!

THE DEVIL'S MUSIC IN HELL

(For Billie Holiday, 1915–1959)

Ethel Waters sleeps in the stable
Looking up at the moon and the stars;—
It's a bright night in Lexington, Kentucky,—
But the Colored Folks in town will not
Rent a room to a girl who's in
A carnival for entertainment tonight.
—And so Ethel is looking way-up again,
There by the side of the Milky Way,
She sings the St. Louis Blues for Jim.

Yusef Komunyakaa
(1947–)

LOST WAX

I can't help but think
of bodies spoon-fashion
in the belly of a ship.

Gods pour us into the molds
they dream; Legba mends
hope, the breath-cup, footsteps

in plaster of Paris. A bird
so perfect, the wind
steals it from my hand.

Inscription on a vase—
I am whatever it holds,
songs that fit into my mouth.

I am without mercy
because I am what
night poured her lament into,

here on the edge of Kilimanjaro.
All the raw work gone
into each carved ghost

of an antelope, loved
no less than the gods
who spring from our loins.

Woman-mold, man-mold:
whatever shape we think
will save us, what's left

in us preserved by joy.
We won't trade our gods
for money. The hot wax

bubbles up like tar,
& the dream's scaled down
to a gazelle, a figure

with *Benin* printed
on the forehead.
How about a lamp to see by?

Two hands folded together
as a drinking cup,
something that simple.

VILLON/LEADBELLY

Two bad actors canonized by ballads
flowering into dusk, crowned with hoarfrost.
But the final blows weren't dealt in Meung-
sur-Loire or the Angola pen. "Irene,
Irene, I'll see you in my dreams."

Unmoved by the hangman's leer,
these two roughhouse bards ignored
his finger traveling down the list.
They followed every season's penniless
last will & testament. Their songs

bleed together years. A bridge,
more than a ledger of bones.
Ghosts under the skin in bedlam,
Princes of Fools, they prowled
syncopated nights of wolfbane

& gin mills of starlight
at The Golden Mortar & The Bucket
of Blood, double-daring men across
thresholds, living down the list,
strung out on immortality's rag.

Crawling down headfirst into the hole,
he kicks the air & disappears.
I feel like I'm down there
with him, moving ahead, pushed
by a river of darkness, feeling
blessed for each inch of the unknown.
Our tunnel rat is the smallest man
in the platoon, in an echo chamber
that makes his ears bleed
when he pulls the trigger.
He moves as if trying to outdo
blind fish easing toward imagined blue,
pulled by something greater than life's
ambitions. He can't think about
spiders & scorpions mending the air,
or care about bats upside down
like gods in the mole's blackness.
The damp smell goes deeper
than the stench of honey buckets.
A web of booby traps waits, ready
to spring into broken stars.
Forced onward by some need,
some urge, he knows the pulse
of mysteries & diversions
like thoughts trapped in the ground.
He questions each root.
Every cornered shadow has a life
to bargain with. Like an angel
pushed up against what hurts,
his globe-shaped helmet
follows the gold ring his flashlight
casts into the void. Through silver
lice, shit, maggots, & vapor of pestilence,
he goes, the good soldier,
on hands & knees, tunneling past
death sacked into a blind corner,
loving the weight of the shotgun
that will someday dig his grave.

TU DO STREET

Music divides the evening.
I close my eyes & can see
men drawing lines in the dust.
America pushes through the membrane
of mist & smoke, & I'm a small boy
again in Bogalusa. *White Only*
signs & Hank Snow. But tonight
I walk into a place where bar girls
fade like tropical birds. When
I order a beer, the mama-san
behind the counter acts as if she
can't understand, while her eyes
skirt each white face, as Hank Williams
calls from the psychedelic jukebox.
We have played Judas where
only machine-gun fire brings us
together. Down the street
black GIs hold to their turf also.
An off-limits sign pulls me
deeper into alleys, as I look
for a softness behind these voices
wounded by their beauty & war.
Back in the bush at Dak To
& Khe Sanh, we fought
the brothers of these women
we now run to hold in our arms.
There's more than a nation
inside us, as black & white
soldiers touch the same lovers
minutes apart, tasting
each other's breath,
without knowing these rooms
run into each other like tunnels
leading to the underworld.

Kiarri T-H. Cheatwood

VISIONS OF THE SEA

I

From him came the Sea
                                    and
                                            from her came the Ocean.

A time far away . . . so far away . . . and deeper than our
    mother's

                        womb

the waters met and all that was sacred glistened on the
    wingspan
of a velvet airwave.   Velvet airwaves . . . lyrical and
    earthly currents
uncracked by lesions of despair. To these waters came
    the shores

came the shores   came the shores to nourish their
    sands   and
know the healing salts of hungry and tired souls.

All the voices of time were born and blessed here
aretha's, trane's, tosh's, mahalia's, duke's, Sisters of emotions,
                                    Brothers
of ojays, tremaine's, marley's, pharoah's, sarah's, masakela's,
                                    smokey's,
zenzi's and on and on
until the skies gave way and begged for the waters' beauty

blue world of roar and chant   of sweet harmony cool with
tone color and content   this is where peace once knew to
    refresh
itself.

II

So came the anointer to join the shores   to look across
    the horizon
into the recesses of time.

So came the anointer   before the waters choked with
    bones and

                              blood

before young mothers died on high seas   died full with new
                              generations
unaccounted for
but vomited overboard   making the waters nauseous as
    unwilling

                              accomplice

So he came to bathe and be renewed in the waters' cool
    fragrances
to reach within himself to find the high tide of his
    timeless energy
to rest without, possessed of the ocean's sweet and
    perfect fruit.

III

In this time of the first waters,
the sun knew, and shared, great gentleness   it gave color
    without

                              burning

So came the anointer . . . possessed in flowing beige
    garments . . . to

                              sit with

the shores on laps of centuries . . . to sit in coolness and
    lyrical

                              peace . . .

to rest and look inwards.
Ringlets of hair,

                    perfect in the breezes, beard spreading
across a chest, breathing the purity of grace . . . a psalm
    for life . . .

                              come
be rested . . . a psalm for life . . . come be rested . . .

505

IV

In this time, words were not dead things
useless and without resonance of meaning   they too
  knew the
purity of the waters   and lived . . . and lived

these were times when nonsense was inconceivable
when the waters and their human presences would have
  curled up
at the thought of having a cake that could not be eaten, too . . .
of immaculate conception . . . of original sin . . . of beasts
  holding
                             sway
over the destiny of the earth

In this time, the rains came and brought with them
cleansed realities . . . and waves and waves and waves,
  rushing into
                            eternity.

V

In their running together, the Ocean and Sea
procreated the Anointer and with him visions beyond

the transient realm of peace. Listen, O people of this earth,
listen to the son of the waters:
                        My parents have given
forth the visions of what must be—this time. But even now
there are poisonous shifts that will take us from this
  moment
into the caves of many cacophonies. Many seasons will
  pass, so many
as to defy all the fingers and toes that have ever existed
  . . . And
their passing will be engorged with much venom and
  misdirection.
                    Even the
waters will cry.
          But this you must remember: it is the time of the
                    original waters
we must return to . . . return to with the lessons of the
  seasons passed
             and full

of poison . . . Only then will peace guide us forever, only
  then.
                    Only when we discover and enter into the
  sacredness
of the voices and listen carefully to—then heed—the prophets
will peace guide us forever, only then.

                    Only when the long travail of prophets ends
and inner peace predominates through the fulfillment of
  destined
acts, Only then will peace guide us.

And my wisdom, gathered with the shores
from precious waters, teaches that life will always be
but not that the waters will always wait for us . . .

These waters—his Sea, her Ocean—look out and caress
  the universe

It is so peaceful here. Curses to the bearers of poison,
  stiff-legged
beyond the horizon. *It is so peaceful here.* Curses to the
  cowards
who wait too long to crack the shanks of the ill-begotten
  bearers.

It is so peaceful here.

And the Anointer arises . . . airwaves dancing in beige
  garments . . .
ringlets perfect, spreading . . . turning around, heads
west . . . The shore recedes, engulfed in roars, engulfed in cool
                    moments
and tiny ripples.

BLOODSTORM

(For Ngugi wa Thiong'o)

They were moving gracefully
huge as they were
and then they began to fall fall fall
displacing the earth into the heavens

                    And my soul froze

507

Their bodies beautiful and streamline, their ears the
    wings of gods
huge as they were
and then the ugly *cracking* tearing air and flesh
changing blue earth to red flood

                    And my guts somersaulted in pain

Have you seen Brother Hannibal recently?
huge as they were
they carried him to victory and African honor
but, now, a new beast scours the earth, leaving only deformed
carcasses
tusks gone and life raped
                    a new beast, a new beast, a new beast
displacing earth and beauty
                    and driving my heart into a frenzy.

II

How many times have we watched our people
step and run   steal into the night   step and run   build and
fall
pickup and move   push and persevere   step step over
    sand and
stone gravel and
deathly white
            how many times?

            And so, too, we have watched gentle people
caught in the rotting armpit of survival—and tricked into
    selling
each other.

        Sell your brother, Brother, and you will see tomorrow

Demands demands *more slaves, you bastard you, or I'll
    sell* you
And a gentle people retched forth the best of themselves
in sour graves . . .

III

Do you know the old man?
A mighty warrior with the poisoned tipped arrow of
slow-death   and in tokyo
and london/

on wall street and rue de le mort

beasts pull their hanging ropes and african dignity flushes into
vomit and memory
                    (and neocolonial enterprise)

Do you remember him?
notorious leader of a band who tortures gods' wings to death
for a pittance and a few piano keys

An old man, a gentle people, committing suicide
for the ugly music of capitalism   for the stenchfilled
    cacophony
of our own demise.

IV

In this place
there are always new sounds. But our horizon has
    become too
full of them
and they run together   run together.

My memory of the *crack* and the huge animal falling
is now replaced by the living screams that ascend from
    burning
grasses
what refuge is left when those that carry gods' wings
are burned to death because they will not die fast enough

> The old man, he is so gentle, so gentle
> stalking the animal and its young to the grasses their last
> refuge
> screams from caves his mother his father
> gold coast ivory coast shorelines bleeding
> disfigured smoke chasing slaves into chains

iron nee the perverse cycle into chains
into chains into screams of smoke beasts
and generations aborted past raped line
torn torment vomit transformation the devil
cast from hell

What refuge does an old man know
who must kill himself to survive   who must kill what he loves
for its
most insignificant/
parts   who must swim in the bloodstream of his own future

V

Paralysis
is a mean thing
And its chill damn near killed me in an instance. But, then,
    African
poets
do not die/
so easily. They remember and call. And I will never forget the
agony of
the fallen/
not merely because they are our own   But also because
    my soul
aches like
grandmama's knee/

Bloodstorm
Bloodstorm
Bloodstorm

And like grandmama I wrap it, prepare it, in anticipation.
    No more
screams
from burning grasses/

Bloodstorm

No more gentle people turned against themselves

Bloodstorm
510

No more love tolerance or whatever the hell it is for
capitalists/beasts

Bloodstorm

Break forth and swim break forth and be yourselves
    again break
forth and
douse the flames/
with our blood break forth   bloodstorm bloodstorm
bloodstorm   and fly home
                        on the wings of gods.

SWAMP RAT

Dedicated To: Sister Mari & Ken McClane

Water bubbles with night larvae
green blades rock and sway in thick breezes
Dogs lead the rising of hell

Fire on his steps   Swamp rat trod trods

Mosquitos whistle painful litanies
trees whisper the secret
Change coming in heavenly heat

Fire on his steps   Swamp rat trod trods

Snakes dance with a sense of soon come
explosions bide their time
Hours coagulate into stones

Fire on his steps   Swamp rat trod trods the meantrod

And he charms the dogs
into refined cane
Inverts their spirits' direction

Fire on his steps   Swamp rat trod trods the meantrod

Yelpings cease as dark silences
swallow the heat of night
Zero flash time of retribution drawing nigh

And with Fire on his steps   Swamp rat trod trods the
  meantrod

Zero flash time of retribution draws nigh
Zero flash time of retribution draws nigh
Zero flash time of retribution draws nigh-de-nigh

Fires on his step   Swamp rat trod trods the meantrod

And bleached brick and wood and cloth and columns
crackle toward explosion
Flames gulping in whole liters of sky

Fires on his step   Swamp rat trod trods the meantrod

As from a nordic cavern, Marse rumbles
into the blossoming front yard full of released oils

Only to face bared teeth snarling sweetness gone sour

Fire on his step   Swamp rat trod trods the meantrod

Family, including houseniggers, sear Marse with their
  screams
while secret servants dive toward curses
Only to meet the barking flames of retribution

Fire on his step   Swamp rat trod trods the meantrod

And Marse, his family, including houseniggers, weakly
curse the night
As Zero flash time of retribution draws nigh
nigh-de-nigh   draws nigh

And the Swamp rat trod trods the meantrod   With
  Fire on his
step.

9/28/85

E. Ethelbert Miller
(1950–)

MOSES

her body was on fire beneath his.

her hands on his back scratched words
into his flesh. his shoulders were like
tablets. broad and strong.

they loved
until morning
until daylight forced him from her bed.
out the room and door.

hair uncombed.
it stood like horns upon his head.

an old woman passing
was shocked by his presence

frightened by the fire in his eyes.

SPANISH CONVERSATION

in cuba
a dark skin woman asks me
if i'm from angola
i try to explain in the no spanish i know
that i am american

she finds this difficult to believe
at times i do too

SWEET HONEY IN THE ROCK

(for b. reagon)

on the nights when the sky comes down
winged demons feast on my flesh
the taste of blackness drips from their beaks
drops of my blood take root beneath my feet
my blood a river in this land of deserts
      a river carving itself through the sands of time
      a river forever running

on the nights when the sky comes down
justice is a barren tree in search of moonlight
freedom is a falling star
illuminating the people of the dark
the dark swelling with life
my life a shadow in the dark

on the nights when the sky comes down
the vultures hand me prayers
they hide the unknown under their wings
they flock together like pilgrims ready to steal the land
the birds barter with my bones
the bones of my people

on the nights when the sky comes down
my spirit lifts its head and shines like a sun
a sun blinding the heads of demons
      until i hear the spirituals sung
      until i hear the voice of jubilation
      until i taste the taste of honey
      until i see the mountains move before my eyes

on the nights when the sky comes down
we give it back its light
we make this world holy once again

2/18/78

GRENADA

near the beach
grenada enjoyed taking long baths
instead of quick showers
she would mix her oils & select
her soaps depending on her mood

grenada would comb the sunlight
from her hair every morning before
she dressed

the clothes she wore were colorful
oranges & greens/yellows & blues
around her neck grenada wore her
precious jewels

jewels her neighbors
found room for in their gossip

"where grenada get dem things
she poor as we
& she think she something
she think she big u know"

& grenada would laugh
wonder to herself why people were so jealous
& quick to judge

so grenada went looking for someone
she could share her time with
someone who could understand
what she already knew—the joy of being free

outside her village
grenada found her friend
an old woman who lived in the mountains
where spanish hung from the branches of trees
where the rivers were named after jose marti

the old woman called herself cuba
her mother's name was angola
her grandmother's egypt

so when grenada went for long walks
she headed for the mountains
she would walk barefoot along the narrow roads
her feet barely kissing the untouched earth

grenada would always find cuba
planting something in the small garden
behind her house

there

the two women
would sit for hours
surrounded by trees/birds/plants/flowers

"once I almost lost this"
cuba whispered to grenada

her voice
so soft
the wind stopped to listen . . .

& once
when grenada left cuba
it was dark
the way back to the village
seemed too far to walk

she knew
someone was following her
she ran
her jewels falling to the ground
as she stumbled

then the night engulfed her like a hand on her throat

&
cuba could be heard crying
in the mountains

A WALK IN THE DAYTIME
IS JUST AS DANGEROUS AS
A WALK IN THE NIGHT

a simple dirt road
surrounded by all these mountains
trees and lakes
does not offer calmness
to my soul or mind
even here in upstate new york
the stillness drives a fear
through my heart like mississippi
or history and i cannot walk
without hearing the barking of dogs
or the yell from some redneck
screaming "there he goes"
i try to accept all these things
as irrational fears that
i should enjoy this time in the
country to relax and be at peace
with myself and i am happy
to be out walking in the morning
on this road which runs into
route 28 near eagle lake
not far from the small town
where i plan to purchase stamps
and postcards and while
i'm walking along the highway
feeling good about the weather
and thinking about nothing in particular
two vans filled with people
speed by and disturb the quiet and call me
        "nigger"
and the peaceful walk is no more
and in the midst of all this
beautiful scenery i become a woman
on a dark city street vulnerable
to any man's attack
it is not yet mid-afternoon
but the virginity of my blackness
has been raped
and this is no longer

a simple walk into town
this is like every walk i have taken
in my life wherever and whenever
i have been alone and my fears are
as real as this dirt beneath
my feet

Quo Vadis Gex-Breaux
(1950–   )

WILLIE NOTE 9/28/91

We cross the vast divide
joined by loving souls
so why not write a love poem
i can only agree

in my soul of souls
i respond to your intangible sensibilities
that grab my inner stretches
where flesh and blood abandon
the core of being

in my current meditation
that leaves so little space
for creative thought
i pray for peace
of a lasting, intimate yet universal variety
a space where fewer of our choices
are dictated by lack and limit
and there is more time
for caring exchange like that we imagine
if there were freedom for all
our minds were clear
our debts paid or payable
our parents still here to share the living
unconditional love that we eternally yearn

let's bask for this brief moment
in this bit of sunshine
aided by soft breezes
making this day
yet another to be remembered
put away in our storehouse
where we share outrage at our trappings

peoples' notions of their right to bind and control
and a sense of our undying connectedness

i will forever be grateful
for sharing in the splendor of your sight,
your graphically clear vision of our world
and what is most important in it

and thank you too
for reminding me of the importance of
an occasional love poem.

BLUE DEEP

She thought herself inspired
watching blue light from the green lamp shade
and gnats making rounds in the glare

Shadows hung low and loud
in the silent house
doors were left open
but stayed closed
she had a mind to leave it
but there never seemed anyplace to go
inside was too cluttered
to take the time to clean
too much ragged, broken baggage
the weight of old hard times
losses and rejection
the empty spaces filled with scar tissue

No shrink of a plastic surgeon
could repair and make beautiful again
the guts permanently stained
red wined inside out
where not even the sun
would dry the wound

Blow wind on these heavy bags
that should move like will-o'-the-wisps
or weeds tumbling
and would
if the mind could again
conjure up the spell for motion

Angela Jackson
(1951–)

A BEGINNING FOR NEW BEGINNINGS

and some where distantly
there is an answer
      as surely as this breath
      half hangs befo my face
and some where
there is a move meant.
      as certain as the wind
      arrives and departs
      from me.
and always.

there is the struggling to be
and constantly
our voices rise. in silent straining
               to be free . . .

and some where
there is an answer. a How.
that i can feel and be felt in.   and live
within a Reason
and a Way.
and some time

there is a Morning.
the rise of an Other Day.
(but the Fight
  is in the wading. waiting
  out this night.
  the Fight is in the living thru
  til mornings rise
  close/d and secure in u.)

but this time.
our eyes cannot see.
and the night lends no helping hand.
the waters of this land
are freezing.
still.
i. and we. struggle.
and we float.

children. together (u. me. she. and us. and him.
together. children.
we learn How
to swim.

WHY I MUST MAKE LANGUAGE

For
A Voice
  like a star.
  Shining.
  With points to pierce
  space,
  and be
  simple, superb
  clarity.
Incandescent.
Some thing
a child might carry
down the black hall,
and make peace with Mystery.
Or woman
into a wooded place
where she may see
the shapes and
names of trees.
Anonymous awe be called
Glory.
Or man
might seek
in the cave
of a woman
and see the writing

on the wall,
and find some
Luminosity.
Ancestors may descend
on streams of light.
Or
all look up
and listen
deep
into the night.
The wild
and civilized
Sky.

Rita Dove
(1952–)

GEOMETRY

I prove a theorem and the house expands:
the windows jerk free to hover near the ceiling,
the ceiling floats away with a sigh.

As the walls clear themselves of everything
but transparency, the scent of carnations
leaves with them. I am out in the open

and above the windows have hinged into butterflies,
sunlight glinting where they've intersected.
They are going to some point true and unproven.

PARSLEY

1. The Cane Fields

There is a parrot imitating spring
in the palace, its feathers parsley green.
Out of the swamp the cane appears

to haunt us, and we cut it down. El General
searches for a word; he is all the world
there is. Like a parrot imitating spring,

we lie down screaming as rain punches through
and we come up green. We cannot speak an R—
out of the swamp, the cane appears

and then the mountain we call in whispers *Katalina.*
The children gnaw their teeth to arrowheads.
There is a parrot imitating spring.

El General has found his word: *perejil*.
Who says it, lives. He laughs, teeth shining
out of the swamp. The cane appears

in our dreams, lashed by wind and streaming.
And we lie down. For every drop of blood
there is a parrot imitating spring.
Out of the swamp the cane appears.

2. *The Palace*

The word the general's chosen is parsley.
It is fall, when thoughts turn
to love and death; the general thinks
of his mother, how she died in the fall
and he planted her walking cane at the grave
and it flowered, each spring stolidly forming
four-star blossoms. The general
pulls on his boots, he stomps to
her room in the palace, the one without
curtains, the one with a parrot
in a brass ring. As he paces he wonders
Who can I kill today. And for a moment
the little knot of screams
is still. The parrot, who has traveled

all the way from Australia in an ivory
cage, is, coy as a widow, practising
spring. Ever since the morning
his mother collapsed in the kitchen
while baking skull-shaped candies
for the Day of the Dead, the general
has hated sweets. He orders pastries
brought up for the bird; they arrive

dusted with sugar on a bed of lace.
The knot in his throat starts to twitch;
he sees his boots the first day in battle
splashed with mud and urine
as a soldier falls at his feet amazed—
how stupid he looked!—at the sound
of artillery. *I never thought it would sing*
the soldier said, and died. Now

525

the general sees the fields of sugar
cane, lashed by rain and streaming.
He sees his mother's smile, the teeth
gnawed to arrowheads. He hears
the Haitians sing without R's
as they swing the great machetes:
Katalina, they sing, *Katalina,*

mi madle, mi amol en muelte. God knows
his mother was no stupid woman; she
could roll an R like a queen. Even
a parrot can roll an R! In the bare room
the bright feathers arch in a parody
of greenery, as the last pale crumbs
disappear under the blackened tongue. Someone
calls out his name in a voice
so like his mother's, a startled tear
splashes the tip of his right boot.
My mother, my love in death.
The general remembers the tiny green sprigs
men of his village wore in their capes
to honor the birth of a son. He will
order many, this time, to be killed

for a single, beautiful word.

DAYSTAR

She wanted a little room for thinking:
but she saw diapers steaming on the line,
a doll slumped behind the door.

So she lugged a chair behind the garage
to sit out the children's naps.

Sometimes there were things to watch—
the pinched armor of a vanished cricket,
a floating maple leaf. Other days
she stared until she was assured
when she closed her eyes
she'd see only her own vivid blood.

She had an hour, at best, before Liza appeared
pouting from the top of the stairs.
And just *what* was mother doing
out back with the field mice? Why,

building a palace. Later
that night when Thomas rolled over and
lurched into her, she would open her eyes
and think of the place that was hers
for an hour—where
she was nothing,
pure nothing, in the middle of the day.

Lenard D. Moore
(1958–)

A POEM FOR LANGSTON HUGHES

You Langston,
you black man who is waiting
for our tomorrows
not to be underground
and lost to oblivion,
whose afrikan eyes have sealed
like a vault,
whose metaphors live on,
whose poems tremble the world
like a great earthquake,
whose spirit lifts heads, young and old,
whose books will always be read . . .
you who were not afraid to seek revolution/
a revolution of liberation—
you were not afraid to retrace the Nile,
to show how stable your memory,
how untimid your voice
for your people,
how brilliant you were.

You Langston,
you black man who is waiting
for our tomorrows
not to be underground
and lost to oblivion,
whose sentient words have brought salvation,
have led brothers and sisters
to cast words upon page after page . . .
create piercing poems/
and treasure their heritage.
Oh, you black man insisted on electrifying

the world when others sought
to cage you like a bird.
Always it is the rhythm of your words,
jazz rhythm,
stroking freedom in ears,
burning in minds
so deep
so deep

MESSAGE TO ETHERIDGE KNIGHT

Don't stop rummaging, through sacred silence,
Inside the head. Yes, it does matter
that you've found the being, the speaker.
How brilliantly you sustain your voice,
capture the rhythms of jazz.
You are the one, the soulful one,
making music, lifting spirits.
It is so magical. We are waiting
In the earthlight, ears attuned:
listening, listening to whatever comes into existence.

There is a sense of belonging, a perpetual aesthetic
like rhythm and blues, kept transforming.
Our ancestors who knew about secret cadences,
who held fast to dreams,
sang so jubilantly, so naturally,
while working cultivated ground
against the sun's glare.
Jazzman, we know your art will survive.
Soon enough your fiery words will help people
define their being; oh sing, Etheridge, ease the spirit.

HAIKU

Sipping the new tea
his wrinkled face absorbs steam . . .
the smell of roses

Summer evening sun;
a row of tombs—their shadows
reaching the ditchbank

529

a black woman
breastfeeding her infant—
the autumn moon

Winter stillness—
old barn's splintered remnants caught
in a crescent moon

Harryette Mullen
(1960–   )

MOMMA SAYINGS

Momma had words for us:
We were "crumb crushers,"
"eating machines,"
"bottomless pits."
Still, she made us charter members
of the bonepickers' club,
saying, "Just don't let your eyes
get bigger than your stomachs."
Saying, "Take all you want,
but eat all you take."
Saying, "I'm not made of money, you know,
and the man at the Safeway
don't give away groceries for free."

She trained us not to leave lights on
"all over the house,"
because "electricity costs money—
so please turn the light off when you leave a room
and take the white man's hand out of my pocket."

When we were small
she called our feet "ant mashers,"
but when we'd outgrow our shoes,
our feet became "platforms."
She told us we must be growing big feet
to support some big heavyset women
(like our grandma Tiddly).

When she had to buy us new underwear
to replace the old ones full of holes,
she'd swear we were growing razor blades in our behinds,
"you tear these drawers up so fast."

Momma had words for us, alright:
She called us "the wrecking crew."
She said our untidy bedroom
looked like "a cyclone struck it."

Our dirty fingernails she called "victory gardens."
And when we'd come in from playing outside
she'd tell us, "You smell like iron rust."
She'd say, "Go take a bath
and get some of that funk off you."
But when the water ran too long in the tub
she'd yell, "That's enough water to wash an elephant."
And after the bath she'd say,
"Be sure and grease those ashy legs."
She'd lemon-cream our elbows
and pull the hot comb
through "these tough kinks on your heads."

Momma had lots of words for us,
her never quite perfect daughters,
the two brown pennies
she wanted to polish
so we'd shine like dimes.

FLOORWAX MOTHER

My mother warned me I'd perish in dirt:
Girl, how you going to take care of a filthy man
when you got so many nasty habits yourself?
Ambition don't make you immune to the facts of life.
Ask me, you do too much dreaming and scheming and
not nearly enough cleaning.

Let me tell you, honey, even career women have to
wipe their man's pee off the toilet seat before
they sit down.

You got to get realistic one of these days,
or do you think you going to

      paint finger pictures in grimy window panes,

grow gardens under gritty fingernails,

practice broadjumping the length of the unswept hall
with a pile of dirty laundry to cushion your landing,

and raise bacteria cultures for research on greasy
kitchen plates?

Girl, don't you know men's mamas tell them stuff like:
Look under a woman's bed to see if there's dust
so you'll know if she'd make a bad wife.

Mama, don't let me get ugly now,
but if I let a man into my bedroom
it aint going to be so he can check for dust.
And any man I catch looking *under* the bed,
I'll send him right back to his floorwax mother.

BÊTE NOIRE

Life aint all beer and skittles
for the white minstrel man
who hums ragtime tunes
and whistles the buckdancer's choice
while he darkens his face
with boneblack
made of human charcoal.

Sometimes, just as he goes onstage,
the holy jimjams grabs him,
shakes him loose
from his professional jollification,
and with a giant thumb and forefinger,
holds him dangling
over the dark mouth of the bête noire.

PINEAPPLE

pineapple is armored flower

with panache of green & ruthless headgear
it parries your bare-handed grasp
in the marketplace

its swollen flower body
covered over with scabs of thick brown
pineapple petals

tough skin of eye spines
hard coat of nails

but a sweetness you can smell
budding lazy in the buzz of summer

sun's shimmering heat
knife-flash through firm fruit flesh
& cool juice sweet-stings
the corner of your mouth
stickydripped liquid
l
o
w
t
r
i
c
k
l
e
s

down your arm
a sweet itch
you lick with the salt off your skin

& you're hoping that your tongue
can reach your elbow

Charlie R. Braxton
(1961–)

JAZZY ST. WALK

hip hitting riffs
split my brain on past
the sullen refrains
of trane' free jazz movement

going on & on & on & on & on

and now even though
i don't know exactly
where it all begins
or ends
i do know that i've
spent decades untold
doing an old blues walk/dance
down these old mean & empty streets
sweating between the sheets
of satin dolls & many moochers
singing goodnight irene
'cause papa's got a brand new bag
of rhythm (& blues)
rocking and rolling all the way live
down main street harlem
by the way of muddy springs mississippi
you see
contrary to the all popular belief
jazz ain't no kind of music
it's an artful way of life
spiced like a pickled pig tail
steaming on a peppermint twist stick
                    dig what i mean
yeah

i walk alone along
these rough rugged robust roads
of jazz
the same damn way i walked
the dirty dusty rows of cotton way back
                          down in the
                                    deep
                                        deep south

nobody knows the troubles i've seen
glory glory
hallelujah
lord have mercy mercy mercy
hallelujah
see you don't know
what it's like to live
the lyricless life of
a poet in exile
lost without vision
with only the bittersweet ruta baga memories
of life back home

HOME

                          where the heart beats
                          tom tom voodoo chants

HOME

                          where a small pin in
                          the bottom of a home-
                          made rag doll is a sudden
                          sharp pain in the ass
                          of massa jack

HOME

                          where shango's hammer
                          swings like basie's
                          big band on a one
                          night stand in a funky
                          joint north of gutbucket
                          U.S.A.
i say yeah
i do walk alone
along these pitch black back streets
crying and bleeding blue jazzy sounds

536

from the raw pockets of my fatal wounds
desperately pleading for ancestral elders
holy wisdom to close
the gaping holes
in my soul before
i expose too much
        too quick
        too soon
for these old mean & angry streets are just
too too mean to be seen without
an axe to grind behind
if you dig my meaning

SAY HEY HOMEBOY

(For Sterling Plumpp)

say hey homeboy
what's happening
up there in the big ole windy city
where the cold hawk blows
and the music flows mellow steady
like cool sweet muscadine wine in the summertime
from down home blues to modern jazz
i heard you hear it all. . . . live
at least one hour a day
five days a week
working laborously on a bluesy feeling
taking notes & trapping them into rhythmic beats
of iambic & trochaic pentameter
your words wailing from between the pages
of history
bring the world a little closer
to the pain
the anguish & beauty of a native son
just a few generations removed
from the chains that bind the flesh
but not the spirit
for your spirit moves through
the timeless magic of the mojo hand
as it writes your message
under your name
in the burning sands of time

this is to say
go on homeboy
take it on further
and bring us all on back home
to the red clay hills
of mississippi

CONTRIBUTORS' NOTES

Allen, Samuel (1917–)
Allen, who spent many years abroad, published some of his early poetry in *Presence Africaine,* and his collection *Elfenbein Zähne* (1956) was published in Germany. He has served as an associate professor of law at Texas Southern University, writer-in-residence at Tuskegee, and professor of English and Afro-American Literature at Boston University. Allen's books include *Ivory Tusks and Other Poems* (1968), *Paul Vesey's Ledger* (1975), and *Every Round and Other Poems* (1987).

Angelou, Maya (1928–)
The first Reynolds Professor of American Studies at Wake Forest University, Angelou gained national attention with the publication of *I Know Why the Caged Bird Sings* (1970). Her substantial body of work in poetry and prose includes *Just Give Me a Cool Drink of Water 'fore I Diiie* (1971), *And Still I Rise* (1978), *The Heart of a Woman* (1981), *I Shall Not Be Moved* (1990), *The Complete Collected Poems of Maya Angelou* (1994), and *Phenomenal Woman: Four Poems Celebrating Women* (1995).

Aubert, Alvin (1930–)
Founder of the magazine *OBSIDIAN*, Aubert served for many years as Professor of English at Wayne State University. His first collection, *Against the Blues,* was published by Broadside Press in 1972. His most recent collections of poems are *If Winter Comes: Collected Poems, 1967–1992* (1994) and *Harlem Wrestler & Other Poems* (1995).

Baker, Houston A., Jr. (1943–)
Professor of English and Albert M. Greenfield Professor of Human Relations at the University of Pennsylvania, Baker is a leading theorist of African-American literature and culture. Among his many publications are *Blues, Ideology, and Afro-American Literature* (1984), *Afro-American Poetics*

(1988), and *Rap and the Academy* (1993), and three volumes of poetry: *No Matter Where You Travel, You Still Be Black* (1979), *Spirit Run* (1982), and *Blues Journey Home* (1985).

Baraka, Amiri [Leroi Jones] (1934–)

One of the chief proponents of the Black Arts Movement in the 1960s, Baraka is a poet, essayist, playwright, music and social critic, and fiction writer whose work continues to influence the production of African-American literature. In 1968 he co-edited the groundbreaking anthology *Black Fire* with Larry Neal. He has written seven nonfiction books and fifteen volumes of poetry, the most recent being *Transbluesency: The Selected Poems of Amiri Baraka/Leroi Jones (1961–1995)*.

Barlow, George (1948–)

A professor of English and American Studies at Grinnell, Barlow is the author of *Gumbo* (1981), a volume chosen for publication in the National Poetry Series. His first collection, *Gabriel,* was published by Broadside Press in 1974.

Barrax, Gerald (1933–)

A professor of English at North Carolina State University and editor of *OBSIDIAN II: Black Literature in Review,* Barrax is the recipient of a Callaloo Creative Writing Award in Nonfiction Prose. He has written *Another Kind of Rain* (1970), *An Audience of One* (1980), *The Death of Animals and Lesser Gods* (1984), and *Leaning Against the Sun* (1992).

Bennett, Gwendolyn (1902–1981)

Though she never published a collection of her own work, Bennett's poems have appeared in several prominent anthologies: *Caroling Dusk* (1927), *Singers in the Dawn* (1934), *The Poetry of the Negro, 1946–1970: An Anthology* (1970), and *The Poetry of Black America: Anthology of the Twentieth Century* (1973).

Bontemps, Arna (1902–1973)

Poet, biographer, novelist, editor, and librarian, Bontemps, like Langston Hughes, devoted much of his time to shaping how African-American poetry would be discussed in the future. Bontemps's early poems appeared in *Crisis* and *Opportunity.* "Golgotha Is a Mountain" won the Alexander Pushkin Award for Poetry in 1926. The following year, "Nocturne at Bethesda" won first prize in the *Crisis* poetry competition. Bontemps did not publish his book of poems, *Personals,* until 1963.

Braithwaite, William Stanley (1878–1962)

The founder of the B. J. Brimmer Publishing Co., Braithwaite is better known as an editor than as a poet. He edited the *Anthology of Magazine Verse and Yearbook of American Poetry* from 1913 to 1929. Braithwaite's books include *The House of Falling Leaves* (1902), *Sandy Star* (1926), *Selected Poems* (1948), and *The Bewitched Parsonage: The Story of the Brontës* (1950). *The William Stanley Braithwaite Reader* was published in 1972.

Braxton, Charlie R. (1961–)

A poet, playwright, and freelance journalist who lives in Hattiesburg, Mississippi, Braxton's first poetry collection is *Ascension from the Ashes* (1990). His work appears in numerous magazines and in the anthologies *In the Tradition* (1992) and *Soulfires* (1996).

Brocks-Shedd, Virgia (1943–1992)

A librarian, Brocks-Shedd was strongly influenced by Margaret Walker, her teacher at Jackson State College, and later by Alice Walker and Audre Lorde. Her poetry appeared in the chapbooks *Mississippi Woods* (1980) and *Mississippi Earthworks* (1982), and in *Mississippi Writers,* Vol. III (1988).

Brooks, Gwendolyn (1917–)

A Street in Bronzeville (1945), her first book of poems, brought Brooks's works to national attention. She won a Pulitzer Prize for *Annie Allen* (1949). Brooks is respected for her precise language, technical facility, and special perspectives on everyday life. In 1968, she was named Poet Laureate of Illinois. She received an award for outstanding achievement in literature from the Black Academy of Arts and Letters in 1976, and was named Poetry Consultant to the Library of Congress (1985–86). Among her many books of poetry are *The Bean Eaters* (1960), *Selected Poems* (1963), *In the Mecca* (1968), *Riot* (1969), *Family Pictures* (1970), *To Disembark* (1981), *Blacks* (1987), *The Near Johannesburg Boy, and Other Poems* (1987), *Children Coming Home* (1991), and *Winnie* (1991).

Brooks, Jonathan Henderson (1904–1945)

Born near Lexington, Mississippi, Brooks was a 1930 graduate of Tougaloo College and a minister. Some of his poems were anthologized in *Caroling Dusk* (1927) edited by Countee Cullen, and in *The Negro Caravan* (1941). During his college years and in the three years he served as assistant to Tougaloo's president, Brooks encouraged students to engage in dramatic activities and writing. His collection *The Resurrection and Other Poems* was published posthumously in 1948.

Brown, Sterling Allen (1901–1989)

A native of Washington, D.C., Brown taught for many years at Howard University. His first book of poems, *Southern Road,* was published in 1932, and his poems were featured in many anthologies. As a poet, Brown gave careful attention to the nuances of speech and reproduced them superbly in his poems. His second collection, *The Last Ride of Wild Bill,* was published in 1975. He won the Lenore Marshall Poetry Prize for *The Collected Poems of Sterling A. Brown* (1980). Brown's other works include *The Negro in American Fiction* (1937) and *Negro Poetry and Drama* (1937). He was also co-editor of the landmark anthology *The Negro Caravan* (1941).

Campbell, James Edwin (1867–1896)

The first principal of the West Virginia Colored Institute (now West Virginia State University), Campbell served on the staff of the *Pioneer* (1887), a black newspaper. A contributor to *The Book of American Negro Poetry* (1922) and *The Negro Caravan* (1941), Campbell's own books include *Driftings and Gleanings* (1887) and *Echoes from the Cabin and Elsewhere* (1895).

Cheatwood, Kiarria T-H.

A poet, novelist, and critic, Cheatwood lives in Richmond, Virginia. He is the author of the poetry collections *Valley of the Anointers* (1979), *Psalms of Redemption* (1983), *Elegies for Patrice* (1984), and *Bloodstorm* (1986), and the novels *Seeds of Consistency, Fruits of Life* (1990) and *A Life on an April Canvas* (1992).

Christian, Marcus B. (1900–1976)

A native of Louisiana, Christian served as supervisor of the Dillard University Negro History Unit of the Federal Writers' Project, worked for a time in the Dillard Library, and as poetry editor for the *Louisiana Weekly.* Christian's most important books are *The Common People's Manifesto of World War II* (1948) and *Negro Iron Workers of Louisiana* (1972).

Clifton, Lucille (1936–)

Clifton is the recipient of several NEA grants and the Juniper Prize, as well as honorary degrees from the University of Maryland and Towson State University. Her books include *Good Times* (1969), *An Ordinary Woman* (1974), *Generations*

(1976), *Good Woman: Poems and Memoir, 1969–1980* (1987), *Quilting: Poems, 1987–1990* (1991), and *Book of Light* (1993). Clifton has written many books for young readers.

Coleman, Wanda (1946–)

The recipient of fellowships from the National Endowment of the Arts and the Guggenheim Foundation, Coleman is the author of *Mad Dog Black Lady* (1979), *A War of Eyes and Other Stories* (1988), *African Sleeping Sickness: Stories and Poems* (1990), *American Sonnets* (1994), and other works. In the late 1960s, she was writer-in-residence at Studio Watts; she has also written for television and hosted interview programs for Pacific Radio.

Corrothers, James David (1869–1917)

Corrothers worked at a lumber mill, factories, a steamboat, and a hotel before he began publishing poetry, articles, and fiction in the mid-1880s. In 1898, he became a Methodist minister and then a Baptist minister. Corrothers published one book of verse, *The Black Cat Club* (1902), and the autobiography, *In Spite of the Handicap* (1926).

Cortez, Jayne (1936–)

The recipient of an NEA fellowship in creative writing and a New York Foundation for the Arts Award, Cortez has lectured and read her work throughout the United States, Africa, Europe, Latin America, and the Caribbean. Her published works include *Festivals and Funerals* (1971), *Scarifications* (1973), *Firespitter* (1982), *Coagulations: New and Selected Poems* (1984), and *Poetic Magnetic* (1991).

Cotter, Joseph Seaman, Sr. (1861–1949)

The founder and principal of the Paul L. Dunbar School, and later the principal of the Samuel Coleridge-Taylor School, Cotter published several books such as *A Rhyming* (1895), *A White Song and a Black One* (1909), *Collected Poems of Joseph S. Cotter, Sr.* (1938), and *Negroes and Others at Work and Play* (1947).

Cotter, Joseph Seaman, Jr. (1895–1919)

Cotter's one book of poems, *The Band of Gideon and Other Lyrics* (1918), identified him as a writer of great promise in the New Negro period. His one-act play *On the Fields of France* appeared in the *Crisis* (June 1920) and two series of poems were published in 1920 and 1921 issues of *A.M.E. Zion Quarterly Review.*

Cullen, Countee (1903–1946)

One of the most gifted of the Harlem Renaissance poets, Cullen taught French, English, and creative writing in New York until 1945. His first collection, *Color,* was published in 1925. Two years later, he published *Copper Sun* and edited the anthology *Caroling Dusk.* Among his other books of poetry are *The Ballad of the Brown Girl: An Old Ballad Retold* (1927), *The Black Christ, and Other Poems* (1929), *The Medea and Some Poems* (1935), *The Lost Zoo* (1940), and a selection of his best poems in *On These I Stand* (1947).

Danner, Margaret Esse (1915–1984)

The recipient of many awards for her poetry, Danner was an assistant editor of *Poetry* magazine (1951–57). During her tenure as writer-in-residence at Wayne State University, Danner founded Boone House, a center for writers and artists. Her books include *To Flower: Poems* (1963), *Poem Counterpoem* (1966), *Iron Lace* (1968), and *The Down of a Thistle: Selected Poems, Prose Poems, and Songs* (1976).

Davis, Frank Marshall (1905–1987)

A former editor of the *Atlanta Daily World,* Davis also served as the executive editor for the Associated Negro Press. In 1937, he was awarded a Julius Rosenwald Foundation grant. Davis's books include *Black Man's Verse* (1935), *I Am the American Negro* (1937), *Through Sepia Eyes* (1938), *47th Street: Poems* (1948), and *Awakening, and Other Poems* (1978). *Livin' the Blues: Memoirs of a Black Journalist and Poet,* his autobiography, was published in 1993.

Delany, Clarissa Scott (1901–1927)

Delany, daughter of Emmett J. Scott, the noted secretary to Booker T. Washington, spent her early years at Tuskegee Institute and attended Wellesley College. She taught for three years at Dunbar High School in Washington, D.C., before her death. Some of her poems were anthologized in *The Poetry of the Negro, 1746–1949.*

Dent, Thomas C. (1932–)

A member of the legendary Umbra Workshop in the early 1960s, Dent served as assistant and executive director of the Free Southern Theater and later as executive director of the New Orleans Jazz and Heritage Foundation. He is a poet, essayist, playwright, and oral historian. His writing has appeared in such magazines as *Southern Exposure, Callaloo, OBSIDIAN, Freedomways,* and *African American Review.* He was one of the editors of *Free Southern Theater by the Free*

Southern Theater (1969). His two poetry collections are *Magnolia Street* (1976) and *Blue Lights and River Songs* (1982). His most recent book is the historical study *Southern Journey: My Return to the Civil Rights Movement* (1996).

Dodson, Owen (1914–1983)

Best known for his work as Professor of Drama and department chair at Howard University, Dodson also served as the drama director at Spelman College and a consultant to community theater at the Harlem School of Arts. The recipient of Rosenwald, Guggenheim, and Rockefeller Foundation fellowships, Dodson was the author of the plays *Divine Comedy* (1938) and *New World A-Coming: An Original Pageant of Hope* (1944); the novels *Boy at the Window* (1951) and *Come Home Early, Child* (1977); and the poetry collection *Powerful Long Ladder* (1946).

Dove, Rita (1952–   )

Professor of English at the University of Virginia, Dove was awarded a Pulitzer Prize for the volume *Thomas and Beulah* (1986). Among her many books of poetry are *Museum* (1983), *Grace Notes* (1989), and *Mother Love: Poems* (1995). Her novel *Through the Ivory Gates* (1992) is a fine example of how poetic sensibility might inform fiction. In 1993, Dove was named Poet Laureate of the United States, a post she held for two years.

Dumas, Henry L. (1934–1968)

The former teacher and director of language workshops for Southern Illinois University's Experiment in Higher Education, Dumas was a poet and fiction writer of extraordinary imagination. His books have been published posthumously. He was the author of *Poetry for My People* (1970; reprinted in 1974 as *Play Ebony, Play Ivory*), *Ark of Bones, and Other Stories* (1970), *Jonoah and the Green Stone* (1976), *Ropes of Wind* (1979), *Goodbye, Sweetwater* (1988), and *Knees of a Natural Man* (1989).

Dunbar, Paul Lawrence (1872–1906)

Dunbar was the most popular African-American poet of the late nineteenth century, lauded for the "humor and pathos" of his dialect poems and underappreciated for the quality of his work in Standard English. James Weldon Johnson gave special attention to Dunbar's dilemma in *The Book of American Negro Poetry* (1921). Among Dunbar's numerous collections of poems are *Oak and Ivy* (1893), *Majors and*

Minors (1896), *Lyrics of Lowly Life* (1896), and *Lyrics of Sunshine and Shadow* (1905).

Evans, Mari (1923–)
Evans, who lives in Indianapolis, has taught at Cornell University, Spelman College, and other schools. She won a Black Academy of Arts and Letters award for *I Am a Black Woman* (1970). Evans has written a number of books for children and edited *Black Women Writers (1950–1980): A Critical Evaluation* (1985). Among her poetry collections are *Night Star: Poems 1973–1978* and *A Dark & Splendid Mass* (1992).

Fabio, Sarah Webster (1928–1979)
A pioneer in efforts to institutionalize Black Studies in higher education, Fabio was the author of the poetry volumes *A Mirror: A Soul* (1969) and *Black Is a Panther Caged* (1972). In 1974, she collected all of her poems in seven volumes under the general title *Rainbow Signs.* Her work appeared in such anthologies as *The Black Aesthetic* (1971) and *Understanding the New Black Poetry* (1972).

Fields, Julia (1938–)
The recipient of the seventh Conrad Kent Rivers Memorial Fund Award, Fields has contributed her work to such magazines as *Massachusetts Review, Callaloo,* and *First World.* Her books include *I Heard A Young Man Saying* (1967), *A Summoning* (1976), *Slow Coins* (1981), and *The Green Lion of Zion Street* (1988). Fields has served as poet-in-residence, lecturer, or instructor at several universities and colleges, including St. Augustine College, Howard University, and the University of the District of Columbia.

Gex-Breaux, Quo Vadis (1950–)
A poet and essayist who lives and writes in New Orleans, Gex-Breaux works in development at Dillard University. Her work has appeared in local and national journals and in the anthology *Life Notes* (1994).

Giovanni, Nikki (1943–)
A professor of English at the Virginia Polytechnic Institute, Giovanni has published several books of poetry and essays, such as *Black Feeling, Black Talk/Black Judgment* (1968), *Ego Tripping and Other Poems for Young People* (1973), *Those Who Ride the Night Wind* (1983), and *Racism 101* (1994). National Book Award nominee for the autobiography *Gemini* (1971) and Ohioana Book Award recipient for *Sacred Cows . . . and Other Edibles* (1988), she has conducted poetry read-

ings throughout the United States and abroad. Her important conversations with other writers are *A Dialogue: James Baldwin and Nikki Giovanni* (1973) and *A Poetic Equation: Conversations between Nikki Giovanni and Margaret Walker* (1974).

Grimké, Angelina Weld (1880–1958)

Grimké was an active participant in the Harlem Renaissance. Though she published no collection of poems in her lifetime, Grimké did contribute her work to several anthologies, including *Caroling Dusk* (1927), *The Negro Caravan* (1941), and *The Poetry of the Negro, 1746–1949* (1949).

Hammon, Jupiter (1711–1806)

A deeply religious slave, Hammon is better known for his suggestion that slavery was endurable in "An Address to the Negroes in the State of New York" (1786) than for his Christian verse. His poem "An Evening Thought: Salvation by Christ with Penetential Cries" (1761) was the first poem published by a black man in North America.

Harper, Frances Ellen Watkins (1825–1911)

A tireless worker for the Underground Railroad and lecturer for the cause of abolition, Harper used her talents to write poetry and fiction that reveal much about how literacy functions to achieve social and aesthetic ends. Her books of poetry include *Poems on Miscellaneous Subjects* (1854), *Poems* (1871), and *Sketches of Southern Life* (1872).

Harper, Michael S. (1938–)

The director of the writing program and the I. J. Kapstein Professor of English at Brown University, Harper is the recipient of the Black Academy of Arts and Letters award for *History Is Your Own Heartbeat* (1971) and a Guggenheim fellowship. He has published a large body of work in magazines and anthologies and many books of poetry. Among them are *Song: I Want a Witness* (1972), *Images of Kin: New and Selected Poems* (1977), *Healing Song for the Inner Ear* (1985), and *Honorable Amendments: Poems* (1995).

Hayden, Robert E. (1913–1980)

One of the most accomplished poets of the twentieth century, Hayden taught at Fisk University for more than twenty years and served as Consultant in Poetry for the Library of Congress (1976–78). He received the World Festival of Negro Artists grand prize in 1966 for *A Ballad of Remembrance* (1962). Hayden's collections include *Heart Shape in the Dust* (1940), *Figure of Time* (1955), *Selected Poems* (1966), *Words in the Mourning Time* (1970), *The Night-blooming Cereus* (1972), *Angle of Ascent* (1975), and *American Journal* (1978). *Robert Hayden: Collected Poems* was published in 1985.

Henderson, David (1942–)

The author of such books as *Felix of the Silent Forest* (1967), *The Low East Side* (1980), and *'Scuse Me While I Kiss the Sky: Life of Jimi Hendrix* (1983), Henderson was a member of the Umbra Group. He has conducted poetry readings and workshops at various colleges and universities, and his work has appeared in the *Paris Review, Evergreen Review,* and *Journal of Black Poetry.*

Hernton, Calvin (1932–)

A professor of Black Studies and Creative Writing at Oberlin College, Hernton was the cofounder of *Umbra* magazine. Hernton's books include *Sex and Racism in America* (1965), *Coming Together: Black Power, White Hatred, and Sexual Hang-ups* (1971), *Medicine Man* (1976), and *The Sexual Mountain and Black Women Writers: Adventures in Sex, Literature, and Real Life* (1987).

Horton, George Moses (c. 1797– c. 1883)

To call Horton the first black professional man of letters is indeed to signify. A slave in North Carolina, Horton was a gifted poet who wrote on demand for undergraduates at the University of North Carolina-Chapel Hill. Two of Horton's volumes, *The Hope of Liberty* (1829) and *The Poetical Works of George M. Horton, The Colored Bard of North Carolina* (1845), enabled him to publicize his antislavery sentiments in a small degree. *Naked Genius* (1865), published by the newly freed Horton, contains the largest body of his work; it represents the range of his experiments with poetic techniques and his outrage regarding the "peculiar institution."

Hughes, Langston (1902–1967)

From the Harlem Renaissance until the early stages of the Black Arts Movement, Hughes was one of the most prolific African-American writers, and one of the most popular. He wrote fifteen collections of poetry, two novels, two autobiographies, and seven collections of short stories, as well as several juvenile books and translations. Among the many anthologies he edited or co-edited is *The Poetry of the Negro, 1746–1949.* Among Hughes's best-known works are *The Weary Blues* (1926), *Fine Clothes to the Jew* (1927), *The*

Dream Keeper and Other Poems (1932), *Montage of a Dream Deferred* (1951), *Ask Your Mama: 12 Moods for Jazz* (1961), and *The Panther and the Lash* (1967).

Jackson, Angela (1951–)

The winner of the Hoyt W. Fuller award for Literary Excellence and the American Book Award for *Solo in the Boxcar Third Floor E.*, Jackson lives in Chicago. In addition to writing several plays, she is the author of *VooDoo/Love Magic* (1974), *The Man with the White Liver* (1987), and *Dark Legs and Silk Kisses: The Beatitudes of the Spinners* (1993).

Jeffers, Lance (1919–1985)

An assistant professor of English at North Carolina State University at the time of his death, Jeffers was widely regarded as the Negritude poet of his generation. Jeffers was the author of the volumes *My Blackness Is the Beauty of This Land* (1970), *When I Know the Power of My Black Hand* (1974), *O Africa, Where I Baked My Bread* (1977), *Grandsire* (1979), and the novel *Witherspoon* (1983).

Joans, Ted (1928–)

A painter, travel writer, jazz musician, and poet, Joans was one of the leading figures in the Beat Movement. His books include *Black Pow Wow* (1969), *A Black Manifesto in Jazz Poetry and Prose* (1971), *Afrodisia* (1976), *The Aardvark-Watcher: Der Erdferkelforscher* (1980), and *Sure, Really I Is* (1982).

Johnson, Fenton (1888–1958)

The founder of *Favorite* magazine and the founder of the Reconciliation Movement (to promote cooperation between the races), Johnson served as a writer for the Chicago W.P.A. in the 1930s, and for the Eastern Press Association in New York City. A former English teacher at the State University in Louisville, Kentucky, Johnson was the author of *A Little Dreaming* (1914), *Visions of the Dusk* (1915), *Songs of the Soil* (1916), and *Tales of the Darkest America* (1920), a book of short fiction.

Johnson, Georgia Douglas (1886–1966)

Johnson taught school in the South before she moved to Washington, D.C. She worked in government agencies and served as the Commissioner of Conciliation in the Department of Labor (1925–34). Johnson's books include *The Heart of a Woman, and Other Poems* (1918), *Bronze* (1922),

An Autumn Love Cycle (1928), and *Share My World: A Book of Poems* (1962).

Johnson, James Weldon (1871–1938)

A professor of creative literature and writing at Fisk University at the time of his death, Johnson received a Rosenwald, the W.E.B. DuBois Prize for Negro Literature, and the Harmon Gold Award for *God's Trombones* (1927). Johnson was the author of the novel *The Autobiography of an Ex-Coloured Man* (1912) and *Sainted Peter Relates an Incident: Selected Poems* (1935). Johnson also edited *The Book of American Negro Poetry* (1921).

Jordan, June (1936–)

A poet and essayist whose work is informed by a sense that poetry should give voice to the deepest personal and political concerns, Jordan teaches at the University of California (Berkeley). She has received many awards, among them the Nancy Bloch Award for *The Voice of the Children* (1971). Her books of poetry include *New Days: Poems of Exile and Return* (1973), *Things That I Do in the Dark* (1977), *Passion* (1980), *Living Room* (1985), *Naming Our Destiny: New & Selected Poems* (1989), and *Harukol Love Poems* (1994).

Kaufman, Bob (1925–1986)

A nominee for the Guinness Poetry Award and the recipient of an NEA grant, Kaufman was the founder and co-editor, along with Allen Ginsberg, William Margolis, and John Kelley, of the poetry magazine *Beatitude,* and a legendary figure in the San Francisco poetry scene. His books include *Does the Secret Mind Whisper* (1959), *Solitude Crowded with Loneliness* (1965), *Golden Sardine* (1966), and *The Ancient Rain, 1956–1978* (1981). *Cranial Guitar: Selected Poems of Bob Kaufman* was published in 1996.

Kein, Sybil (1939–)

Kein, the author of *Gombo People* (1981) and *Delta Dancer* (1984), is a poet, dramatist, and scholar who was born in New Orleans and who seeks through her work to preserve the Creole language and culture.

Knight, Etheridge (1931–1991)

Knight was noted for excellence in blending oral and literary poetic traditions. His works include *Black Voices from Prison* (1968), *Belly Song and Other Poems* (1973), *Born of a Woman: New and Selected Poems* (1980), and *The Essential Etheridge Knight* (1986).

Komunyakaa, Yusef (1947–)
A professor of English at Indiana University-Bloomington, Komunyakaa won both the Pulitzer Prize and the Kingsley Tufts Poetry Award for *Neon Vernacular: New and Selected Poems* (1993). His poetry collections include *Lost in the Bonewheel Factory* (1979), *I Apologize for the Eyes in My Head* (1986), *Dien Cai Dau* (1988), and *Magic City* (1992).

Lane, Pinkie Gordon (1923–)
Professor Emeritus of English at Southern University (Baton Rouge) and Poet Laureate of Louisiana from 1989 to 1992, Lane has won widespread recognition for her lyric forms. Her collections of poetry include *Wind Thoughts* (1972), *The Mystic Female* (1978), *I Never Scream: New and Selected Poems* (1985), and *Girl at the Window* (1991).

Les Cenelles (New Orleans, 1845)
Publicized as "the first published anthology of Negro verse in America," *Les Cenelles* is seldom mentioned in discussions of African-American poetry. Nevertheless, what this volume might suggest about a tradition that is continued in the work of Sybil Kein and other poets from New Orleans is of critical importance.

Lorde, Audre (1934–1992)
The founder of the Kitchen Table: Women of Color Press, Lorde served as both a professor of English at John Jay College of Criminal Justice and the Thomas Hunter Professor of English at Hunter College. She was a National Book Award nominee for poetry for *From a Land Where Other People Live* (1973), and the American Book Award recipient for *A Burst of Light* (1988). Lorde published numerous books of poetry and prose, including *The First Cities* (1968), *Coal* (1976), *The Black Unicorn* (1978), *The Cancer Journals* (1980), *Zami, A New Spelling of My Name: A Biomythography* (1982), *Sister Outsider* (1984), *Our Dead Behind Us* (1986), *Hell Under God's Orders* (1990), and *The Marvelous Arithmetics of Distance* (1993).

Madgett, Naomi Long (1923–)
Professor Emeritus at Eastern Michigan University, Madgett is the founder of the Lotus Press. The recipient of the Ester R. Bear Poetry Award and the National Coalition of Black Women citation, Madgett was awarded the Creative

Achievement Award from the College Language Association for *Octavia and Other Poems* (1988). Her books include *Pink Ladies in the Afternoon* (1972), *Exits and Entrances* (1978), *A Student's Guide to Creative Writing* (1980), and *Remembrances of Spring: Collected Early Poems* (1993).

Madhubuti, Haki R. (Don L. Lee) (1942–)

The publisher of Third World Press and the founder of *Black Books Bulletin,* Madhubuti has served as writer-in-residence at such universities as Cornell, Northeastern Illinois State, and Howard; he now teaches at Chicago State University. His books include *Earthquakes and Sunrise Missions: Poetry and Essays of Black Renewal, 1973–1983* (1984), *Killing Memory, Seeking Ancestors* (1987), and *Claiming the Earth: Race, Rape, Ritual, Richness in America & the Search for Enlightened Empowerment* (1994). Books published under the name Don L. Lee include *Don't Cry, Scream* (1969), *We Walk the Way of the New World* (1970), and *Directionscore: Selected and New Poems* (1971).

Major, Clarence (1936–)

Poet, novelist, editor, and winner of the National Council of the Arts Award and the Western States Book Award for his novel *My Amputations* (1986), Major is well known for his work with the Fiction Collective. His books include *Symptoms and Madness* (1971), *The Syncopated Cakewalk* (1974), *Inside Diameter: The France Poems* (1985), *Painted Turtle: Woman with Guitar* (1988), and *Surfaces and Masks* (1989). Major's most recent anthologies are *Calling the Wind: Twentieth-Century African-American Short Stories* (1993) and *The Garden Thrives: Twentieth-Century African-American Poetry* (1996).

McClane, Kenneth A. (1951–)

An associate professor of English and the director of the creative writing center at Cornell University, McClane was awarded the Clark Distinguished Teaching Award in 1983. His books include *Moons and Low Times* (1978), *A Tree Beyond Telling: Poems, Selected and New* (1983), *These Halves Are Whole* (1983), and *Walls: Essays, 1985–1990* (1991).

McElroy, Colleen (1935–)

The winner of the American Book Award for *Queen of the Ebony Isles* (1985), McElroy is currently a professor of English at the University of Washington in Seattle. She is the author of such books as *Music from Home* (1976), *Winters Without Snow* (1980), *Driving Under the Cardboard Pines:*

And Other Stories (1989), and *What Madness Brought Me Here: New & Selected Poems, 1968–88* (1990).

McKay, Claude (1889–1948)
Jamaican by birth, McKay established himself as an important participant in the Harlem Renaissance with his famous poem "If We Must Die" (*Liberator,* 1919) and such books as *Spring in New Hampshire* (1920), *Harlem Shadows* (1922), and *Home to Harlem* (1928). McKay's autobiography, *A Long Way From Home* (1937) and his social study, *Harlem: Negro Metropolis* (1940) are important sources for understanding early twentieth-century African-American literary and intellectual concerns.

Miller, E. Ethelbert (1950–)
The director of the African-American Resource Center at Howard University, Miller is the founder and organizer of the Ascension Poetry Reading Series, Washington, D.C. The recipient of the Columbia Merit Award, Miller has written and edited several books, including *Season of Hunger/Cry of Rain: Poems 1975–1980* (1982), *Where Are the Love Poems for Dictators?* (1986), *First Light: New and Selected Poems* (1993), and the anthology *In Search of Color Everywhere* (1994).

Miller, May (1899–1995)
The former chair of the Literature Division of the Commission on the Arts of D.C., Miller also served as a reader, lecturer, or writer-in-residence for such institutions as Monmouth College and the University of Wisconsin. Miller published nine volumes of poetry, including *Into the Clearing* (1959), *The Clearing and Beyond* (1973), *Dust of an Uncertain Journey* (1975), *The Ransomed Wait* (1983), and *Collected Poems* (1989).

Moore, Lenard D. (1958–)
Internationally recognized for his haiku, Moore has published three volumes of poetry, the most recent being *Desert Storm: A Brief History* (1993). His poetry has appeared in several anthologies, including *Soulfires* (1996) and *The Garden Thrives* (1996).

Mullen, Harryette (1960–)
A professor of English at UCLA, Mullen is the author of four books of poetry: *Tree Tall Woman* (1981), *Trimmings* (1991), *S*PeRM**K*T* (1992), and *Muse & Drudge* (1995). Her poetry has been included in *Washing the Cow's Skull*

(1982), *The Jazz Poetry Anthology* (1991), and *O Two* (1991). Her short stories have been anthologized in *Her Work* (1982), *South by Southwest* (1986), and *Common Bonds* (1990).

Neal, Larry (Lawrence P.) (1937–1981)

The recipient of a Guggenheim fellowship in 1971, Neal co-edited the groundbreaking anthology *Black Fire* (1968) with Leroi Jones. Within his lifetime, Neal published *Black Booga-loo* (1969), *Trippin': A Need for Change* (with Imamu Amiri Baraka and A. B. Spellman) (1969), and *Hoodoo Hollerin' Bebop Ghosts* (1974). His selected works were published in *Visions of a Liberated Future: Black Arts Movement Writings* (1989).

Patterson, R. Raymond (1929–)

Patterson, a former professor of English at the City College of the City University of New York, is the author of *Twenty-Six Ways of Looking at a Black Man* (1969) and *Elemental Blues* (1983).

Payne, Daniel A. (1811–1893)

Born in South Carolina, Payne moved north in the 1830s, became an ordained African Methodist Episcopal minister, and later served as president of Wilberforce University. His collection *Pleasures and Other Miscellaneous Poems* (1850) is strongly marked by his religious sensibility. Among his other writings are *The History of the A.M.E. Church* (1866) and *Recollections of Seventy Years* (1888).

Plato, Ann (c. 1820–?)

Little is known of Plato's life aside from her teaching in Hartford, Connecticut, and her publication in 1841 of *Essays: Including Biographies and Miscellaneous Pieces in Prose and Poetry.*

Plumpp, Sterling D. (1940–)

Professor in Black Studies at the University of Illinois at Chicago Circle, Plumpp received the Carl Sandburg Literary Award for Poetry for *The Mojo Hands Call, I Must Go* (1982). He has written many books of poetry, including *Half Black, Half Blacker* (1970), *Steps to Break the Circle* (1974), *Clinton* (1976), *Blues: The Story Always Untold* (1989), *Johannesburg & Other Poems* (1993), and *Hornman* (1995). Plumpp is the major blues poet of his generation.

Prince, Lucy Terry (1730–1821)

Prince's account of an Indian raid in Deerfield, Massachusetts, on August 25, 1746 ("Bars Fight") is the single extant example of her work. Although it was written in 1746, the poem was transmitted orally until it was printed in Holland's *History of Western Massachusetts* in 1855.

Randall, Dudley (1914–)

The founder of and presently the consultant to Broadside Press, Randall has been the recipient of the Kuumba Liberation Award, NEA fellowships, and the Tompkins Award from Wayne State University. Randall played a major role in providing a forum for African-American poetry in the 1960s and 1970s. His books include *More to Remember: Poems of Four Decades* (1971), *After the Killing* (1973), *A Litany of Friends: New and Selected Poems* (1983), and *Homage to Hoyt Fuller* (1984).

Ray, Henrietta Cordelia (1849–1916)

Earning a Masters in Pedagogy from New York University (1891), Ray taught in the New York public school system for thirty years. Ray published four books in her lifetime: *Sketch of the Life of the Rev. Charles B. Ray* (1887), *Lincoln; Written for the Occasion of the Unveiling of the Freedmen's Monument in Memory of Abraham Lincoln* (1893), *Sonnets* (1893), and *Poems* (1910).

Redmond, Eugene (1937–)

Poet, editor, historian, essayist, and playwright, Redmond has dedicated much of his work to preserving and enhancing oral poetic traditions. His *Drumvoices: The Mission of Afro-American Poetry* (1976) is the most comprehensive literary history of the genre to date. Redmond is founder and publisher of *Drumvoices Revue*. His many books include *River of Bones and Flesh and Blood* (1971), *Consider Loneliness as These Things* (1973), *A Confluence of Colors* (1984), and *The Eye in the Ceiling* (1991).

Reed, Ishmael (1938–)

A novelist, poet, essayist, dramatist, and social critic, Reed teaches at the University of California (Berkeley) and continues his project to reshape the multicultural sensibilities of his audiences. Reed is the co-founder of The Before Columbus Foundation and of the magazines *Yardbird, Y'Bird,* and *Quilt.* He is a proponent of multiculturalism. His books of poetry include *catechism of d neoamerican hoodoo church* (1970), *Conjure: Selected Poems, 1963–1970* (1972), *Chattanooga* (1973), *A Secretary to the Spirits* (1977), and *New and Collected Poems* (1988).

Rodgers, Carolyn (1945–)

The recipient of an NEA grant, the Carnegie Award, PEN Awards, and the National Book Award nomination for *how i got ovah: New and Selected Poems* (1975), Rodgers is the author of *Now Ain't That Love* (1970), *The Heart As Ever Green: Poems* (1978), *A Little Lower Than Angels* (1984), and *Finite Forms: Poems* (1985).

Salaam, Kalamu ya (1947–)

Poet, playwright, essayist, music critic, and former editor of *The Black Collegian,* ya Salaam lives in New Orleans. His plays have been anthologized in *Black Theatre, USA* (1974), *New Plays for the Black Theater* (1989), and *Black Southern Voices* (1992). His collections of poetry include *Ibura* (1976), *Revolutionary Love* (1978), *Iron Flowers* (1979), and *A Nation of Poets* (1990). His most recent collection of essays and poetry is *What Is Life?* (1994).

Sanchez, Sonia (1934–)

The Laura H. Carnell Professor of English at Temple University, Sanchez received the American Book Award for *Homegirls & Handgrenades* (1984). The recipient of a PEN Writing Award, NEA Awards, the Lucretia Mott Award, and the Oni Award from the International Black Women's Congress, Sanchez continues to define the womanist dimensions of culturally informed poetry. Among her more than twenty books are *Homecoming* (1969), *I've Been a Woman: New and Selected Poems* (1980), *Under a Soprano Sky* (1987), and *Wounded in the House of a Friend* (1995).

Shange, Ntozake (1948–)

Shange won national acclaim for her choreopoem *For Colored Girls Who Have Considered Suicide/When the Rainbow Is Enuf* (1975). Among her many works are the novels *Sassafras, Cypress, and Indigo* (1982), *Betsy Brown* (1985), and *Liliane* (1994); the poetry collections *Nappy Edges* (1978), *A Daughter's Geography* (1983), and *From Okra to Greens: Poems* (1984); and the prose volumes *See No Evil* (1984) and *Riding the Moon in Texas: Word Paintings* (1988).

Spencer, Anne (1882–1975)

A former public school teacher at Bramwell, West Virginia, Spencer later taught at the Virginia Seminary, Lynchburg, Virginia, and worked toward the establishment of an NAACP chapter in that city. Though Spencer published no collections of her own poetry, she did contribute to such anthologies as *The Book of American Negro Poetry* (1922), *Caroling Dusk* (1927), and *The Poetry of the Negro, 1746–1949* (1949).

Stuckey, Elma (1907–1988)

Born in Memphis, Tennessee, Stuckey moved to Chicago in 1945 and worked for the Department of Labor of the State of Illinois. She later became a full-time writer and lecturer, publishing two books in her lifetime, *The Big Gate* (1976) and *The Collected Poems of Elma Stuckey* (1987), both of which are strongly marked by the black oral tradition and historical memory. She gave readings for high schools and community organizations as well as at such universities as Harvard, Cornell, and Stanford, reaffirming the importance of oral presentation.

Thomas, Lorenzo (1944–)

Thomas, who teaches at the University of Houston, Downtown, was a member of the legendary Umbra Group. His books include *Fit Music* (1972), *Framing the Sunrise* (1975), *The Bathers: Selected Poems* (1978), and *Chances Are Few* (1979).

Thompson, Julius E. (1946–)

Director of the Black Studies Program at the University of Missouri-Columbia, Thompson is a historian and poet. He has published two volumes of poetry, *Hopes Tied Up in Promises* (1970) and *Blues Said: Walk On* (1977), and four historical studies, including *The Black Press in Mississippi, 1865–1985* (1993). His major study, *Dudley Randall, Broadside Press, and the Black Arts Movement in Detroit, 1960–1995*, is scheduled for publication in 1997.

Tolson, Melvin B. (1898–1966)

A former Avalon Professor of the Humanities at Tuskegee Institute, Tolson before that was a professor of creative literature and the director of the Dust Bowl Theatre at Langston University. The Poet Laureate of Liberia, Tolson published the poetry collections *Rendezvous With America* (1944) and *Libretto for the Republic of Liberia* (1953). *A Gallery of Harlem Portraits* (1979) and *Caviar and Cabbage* (1982), a collection of prose, were published posthumously. Tolson was a leading American Modernist poet.

Toomer, Jean (1894–1967)

Toomer's reputation, until recently, was based mainly on *Cane* (1923), an avant-garde work of the Harlem Renaissance.

After the appearance of *Essentials* (1931), he found it difficult to get his works published. Toomer was given slight notice until more of his writing was made available in *The Wayward and the Seeking: A Miscellany of Writings* (1980) and *The Collected Poems of Jean Toomer* (1988).

Touré, Askia Muhammad (1938–)

One of the earliest and forceful voices in the Black Arts/Black Aesthetic Movement, Touré has also been a member of the legendary Umbra Group. Touré's books include *Earth* (1968), *JuJu: Magic Songs for the Black Nation* (with Ben Caldwell) (1970), *Songhai!* (1972), and *From the Pyramids to the Projects* (1990), which won an American Book Award.

Troupe, Quincy (1943–)

Troupe is the author of ten books, including five volumes of poetry, the latest of which is *Avalanche* (1996). He edited *James Baldwin: The Legacy* and co-authored *Miles: The Autobiography*, both published in 1989. He is the recipient of two American Book Awards and a Peabody Award for the Miles Davis Radio Project which he wrote and co-produced. Troupe is Professor of Creative Writing and American and Caribbean Literature at the University of California, San Diego.

Walker, Alice (1944–)

The recipient of the Pulitzer Prize and the American Book Award for *The Color Purple* (1982), Walker also received a Lillian Smith Award for *Revolutionary Petunias and Other Poems* (1973). Her other books of poetry are *Once* (1968), *Good Night, Willie Lee, I'll See You in the Morning* (1979), *Horses Make a Landscape Look More Beautiful* (1984), and *Her Blue Body Everything We Know: Earthling Poems, 1965–1990* (1991).

Walker, Margaret (1915–)

Walker's first book, *For My People,* was published in 1942 as a result of her winning the Yale Younger Poets contest, and the title poem has acquired a very special status within African-American culture. She received a Houghton Mifflin Fellowship for her acclaimed novel *Jubilee* (1966). Critical interest in the full body of her poetry has been revitalized since the publication of *This Is My Century: New and Collected Poems* (1989), which includes her earlier volumes *Prophets for a New Day* (1970) and *October Journey* (1973).

Watkins, Nayo Barbara Malcolm (1940–)

Watkins, a poet, playwright, and essayist, published her first book of poems, *I Want Me a Home,* in 1969 as part of the

BLKARTSOUTH workshop in New Orleans. Her work has appeared in numerous magazines and anthologies, including *New Black Voices* (1972) and *Black Southern Voices* (1992).

Wheatley, Phillis (c. 1753–1784)

Despite the fact that her single volume, *Poems on Various Subjects Religious and Moral* (1773), was first issued in London, Wheatley has the honor of being the first African writer in North America to publish a collection of poems. Sold into slavery from her native West Africa, Wheatley was brought to Boston in 1761. She mastered English and its poetic forms rapidly, publishing her first poem in 1770. Among the Colonial poets who were influenced by English neoclassical verse, Wheatley must be judged one of the best.

Whitfield, James M. (1822–1871)

Whitfield became involved in the American Colonization Society in 1858, five years after the publication of his only book of verse, *America and Other Poems*. Whitfield's poetry is at once romantic and militant.

Whitman, Albery A. (1851–1901)

The pastor of several A.M.E. churches in Ohio, Kansas, Texas, and Georgia, Whitman served as general financial agent at Wilberforce University. The protégé of Daniel A. Payne, Whitman published several books, including *Essay on the Ten Plagues and Miscellaneous Poems* (c. 1871), *Not a Man and Yet a Man, Miscellaneous Poems* (1877), and *An Idyll of the South, An Epic Poem in Two Parts* (1901).

Wright, Richard (1908–1960)

In addition to writing such powerful works of fiction as *Uncle Tom's Children* (1938), *Native Son* (1940), and *The Long Dream* (1958), Wright published poetry in left-wing journals during the 1930s; toward the end of his life, Wright became very interested in haiku poems and wrote approximately 4,000 of them.

Young, Al (1939–)

Young, who lives in California, is a poet, novelist, and musician. He has published many books of poetry, fiction, and nonfiction. His works include *Ask Me Now* (1980), *Heaven: Collected Poems* (1988), *Straight No Chaser* (1994), and *Drowning in the Sea of Love: Essays on Music* (1995).

Zu-Bolton II, Ahmos (1935–)

Born in Poplarville, Mississippi, Zu-Bolton was the founder and editor of *HooDoo* magazine and coeditor of *Synergy: D.C.*

Anthology. His work has appeared in numerous magazines and in the anthologies *Giant Talk* (1975), *Mississippi Writers,* Vol. III (1988), and *Black Southern Voices* (1992). Zu-Bolton, who currently lives in New Orleans, is the author of *A Niggered Amen* (1975).

ACKNOWLEDGMENTS

"At the Carnival" and "Letter to My Sister" copyright by Anne Spencer. Permission to reprint granted by Chauncey E. Spencer.

"Song of the Son," "Georgia Dusk," and "Imprint for Rio Grande" copyright © 1962 by Jean Toomer. Permission to reprint granted by Marjorie Toomer Latimer.

"The Band of Gideon," "Is it Because I Am Black?" and "Rain Music" copyright Joseph Seaman Cotter, Jr. From *Joseph Seaman Cotter, Jr.: Complete Poems* by James Robert Payne. Permission to reprint granted by the University of Georgia Press.

"Harlem," "Uncle Rufus," and "Madame Alpha Devine" copyright © 1979 by the Curators of the University of Missouri. First appeared in *A Gallery of Harlem Portraits* by Melvin B. Tolson; edited, with an afterword by Robert M. Farnsworth. Reprinted by permission of the University of Missouri Press.

"Calvary Way," "The Wrong Side of the Morning," "The Scream," and "Where Is the Guilt" copyright © 1975 by May Miller. Permission to reprint granted by Lotus Press, Inc.

"Selassie at Geneva," "Go Down, Moses!" and "The Craftsman" copyright © 1948 and 1988 by Marcus B. Christian. First appeared in *Ebony Rhythm* (Exposition Press, 1948). Permission to reprint granted by the University of New Orleans.

"Southern Road" copyright © 1932 by Harcourt, Brace & Co.; renewed 1960 by Sterling Brown. First appeared in *Southern Road*. Permission to reprint granted by HarperCollins Publishers, Inc. "Ma Rainey" copyright © 1932 by Harcourt Brace & Co.; renewed 1960 by Sterling A. Brown. Permission to reprint granted by HarperCollins Publishers, Inc. "Strong Men" copyright © 1932 by Harcourt Brace & Co.; renewed 1960 by Sterling Brown. Permission to reprint granted by HarperCollins, Inc. "Transfer" copyright © 1980 by Sterling A. Brown. From *The Collected Poems of Sterling A. Brown*, edited by Michael S. Harper. Reprinted by permission of HarperCollins Publisher, Inc. "Crossing" copyright © 1932 by Harcourt Brace & Co.; renewed 1960 by Sterling Brown. Reprinted by permission of HarperCollins Publisher, Inc.

"The Negro Speaks of Rivers" copyright © 1926 by Alfred A. Knopf, Inc., and renewed in 1954 by Langston Hughes. Permission to reprint granted by the publisher. "Mother to Son" copyright © 1926 by Alfred A. Knopf, Inc. and renewed 1954 by Langston Hughes. Permission to reprint granted by the publisher.

"A Black Man Talks of Reaping," "Nocturne at Bethesda," and "Golgotha Is a Mountain" copyright © 1963 by Arna Bontemps. Permission to reprint granted by Harold Ober Associates, Inc.

"Sonnets" by Gwendolyn Bennett copyright © 1963, 1974 by Gwendolyn Bennett. Permission to reprint granted by the estate of the author.

"Heritage" copyright © 1925 by Harper & Brothers; copyright renewed 1953 by Ida M. Cullen. First appeared in *Color* by Countee Cullen. Reprinted by permission of GRM Associates, Inc., Agents for the Estate of Ida M. Cullen. "From

564

565

566